Motivating Primary-Grade Students

Motivating Primary-Grade Students

MICHAEL PRESSLEY
SARA E. DOLEZAL
LISA M. RAPHAEL
LINDSEY MOHAN
ALYSIA D. ROEHRIG
KRISTEN BOGNER

THE GUILFORD PRESS
New York   London

© 2003 The Guilford Press
A Division of Guilford Publications, Inc.
72 Spring Street, New York, NY 10012
www.guilford.com

Printed in the United States of America

This book is printed on acid-free paper.

Last digit is print number: 9   8   7   6   5   4   3   2   1

Library of Congress Cataloging-in-Publication Data

Motivating primary-grade students / Michael Pressley ... [et al.].
    p. cm.
  Includes bibliographical references.
    ISBN 1-57230-915-6 (alk. paper) — ISBN 1-57230-914-8 (pbk. : alk. paper)
    1. Education, Primary. 2. Motivation in education. 3. Teacher–student
relationships. I. Pressley, Michael.
  LB1513.M68 2003
  370.15′4—dc21
                             2003008097

About the Authors

Michael Pressley, PhD, is a Professor in the Department of Teacher Education and the Department of Counseling, Educational Psychology, and Special Education at Michigan State University. He is the author of more than 300 articles, chapters, and books; the recipient of many awards for his research in reading and educational psychology; and the immediate past editor of the *Journal of Educational Psychology.*

Sara E. Dolezal, Lisa M. Raphael, and **Lindsey Mohan** are graduate students in the College of Education at Michigan State University.

Alysia D. Roehrig recently completed her PhD in Psychology at the University of Notre Dame, specializing in developmental and educational psychology. Her contributions to this volume were in the context of her larger program of research on effective elementary teaching. She is the coauthor of *Stories of Beginning Teachers: First-Year Challenges and Beyond.*

Kristen Bogner is a graduate student in School Psychology at the University of Minnesota.

Preface

One of the most dramatic accomplishments in educational psychology during the last three decades has been the increased understanding of academic motivation, with many studies evaluating specific potential motivational mechanisms—from letter grades to praise to student images of themselves in the future. Despite increased understanding of what teachers can do to increase motivation, until the work summarized in this volume, there has been no attempt to understand all that teachers do every day to affect their students' motivation. The authors of this volume decided to do the research summarized here following observations of very engaging primary-grade teachers, who obviously did much to motivate their students (Pressley, Allington, Wharton-McDonald, Block, & Morrow, 2001). That is, we decided to study such teachers' motivation in much greater detail than in the previous work. We wanted to understand it as scientists, but to do so in such a way that we could communicate to classroom professionals what can be done to improve the motivation of students in the primary elementary grades.

This volume includes chapters summarizing our work, complemented by reports of three case studies of very effective, very motivating primary-grade teachers. The teachers in these case studies prove that primary-grade classrooms can be motivationally flooded, and when the classrooms are so flooded, there is high student engagement as part of productive academic work. We hope that this volume inspires many more teachers to be so motivating.

Acknowledgments

The research reported in this book was completed while all of the authors were at the University of Notre Dame. Michael Pressley was the Notre Dame Professor of Catholic Education, with funds from that endowed chair supporting both the research and writing of this book. Sara E. Dolezal, Lisa M. Raphael, and Alysia D. Roehrig were supported by fellowships from the Graduate School while this work was carried out. Lindsey Mohan and Kristen Bogner participated as undergraduate honors students, and both were involved in the design, execution, analysis, and write-up of the studies contributing to this volume. The final writing of the book was supported by funds from Michigan State University.

We are indebted to all of the teachers from the South Bend area who permitted the study of their classrooms. A huge thanks in particular to Nancy Masters, Angel Shell, and Chris Nemeth, who are featured in Chapters 3–5. You inspired us at every step of the journey, just as you inspire your students every moment of every school day.

Contents

CHAPTER 1

Introduction to the Many Motivational Mechanisms in Education

Teachers want to know much, much more about how to motivate students (e.g., O'Flahavan et al., 1992). Why? The evidence that many students are not academically motivated is apparent in many schools: Spend a day in a school, and there are inevitable encounters with students who are inattentive in class, with some daydreaming and others actually dreaming as they snooze during lessons. Talk with the students, and there will be plenty who report being bored or turned off by what they are doing and learning (or failing to learn) in school.

There are several interwoven motivations for this book. The most important is to provide information about how primary-level (K–3) teachers motivate their students, with a focus on those who do it very, very well. Thus, much more attention will be paid to classrooms where students are attentive, consistently working hard at worthwhile academic tasks, and definitely not bored. Even so, there also will be examination of what goes on in classrooms in which student motivation is lower. What is unique about the classes that are most engaging for students will be more obvious by contrast with classrooms where student motivation is not so high. In addition, there are important lessons that can be learned from the classrooms where the academic engagement of students is lower. In particular, much can be learned about what primary teachers should avoid doing if they are to succeed in motivating their students. Providing such cautionary information is a second purpose of this book

Because we believe that teachers will be better able to act on the ideas presented here if they understand why motivating teaching has its beneficial effects, we spend considerable time providing background in-

1

formation about academic motivation in this chapter. This is consistent with the third purpose of the book, which is to increase teachers' understanding about why some teaching behaviors are more motivating than others.

Although the primary target audience for this volume is teachers—both those now teaching and those preparing to teach—there are a number of other audiences with a need to know about the perspectives developed here. School-based administrators and curriculum and instruction specialists, including reading specialists, will experience a different vision of excellent primary-grade teaching than is offered in any other source. Similarly, policymakers whose background in reading instruction is largely restricted to documents such as the National Reading Panel (2000) report will find a broader perspective in this book. So, too, will researchers interested in academic motivation. Most researchers focus on single motivational mechanisms in their work. In contrast, we report here that engaging teachers use many motivational mechanisms simultaneously, suggesting that the focus on individual mechanisms in basic research may be somewhat misguided. Among academics, however, we are especially determined to reach teacher educators, for, if we can persuade them that better primary-grade teaching is possible, we may be able to affect their teaching of the next generation of teachers. In short, there is a very big and different message in this book for anyone interested in elementary education, including parents. What many parents will discover is that what goes on in the most engaging primary-grade classrooms is not much like what goes on in their own child's classroom. We hope this book stimulates some concerned parents to ask the teachers of their children to do more to motivate children to do things literate. Thus, our fourth purpose in writing this book was to change the way primary-grade students are taught, that is, change primary-grade classrooms in the direction of being much more motivating.

What the discerning reader will note in going through this chapter is that there was a great deal of research on classroom motivation in the last quarter of the 20th century. In fact, many of the findings reported herein are considered classical by educational psychologists, that is, they are findings that have been around long enough to be replicated. That psychologists now understand how to motivate students in classrooms, however, has not broadly translated into classroom practice, as subsequent chapters of this book make clear.

Readers may be surprised that there are numerous individual instructional mechanisms that can affect motivation. Some might even feel that reading about so many mechanisms in this chapter is tedious. The reason we present them all is that by the end of the volume it will be clear that engaging primary-grade teachers, in fact, do use many varied mechanisms as they teach, and that to fully appreciate their teaching it is important to understand the range of mechanisms they draw upon. Therefore, this first chapter is meant to be studied; it is not intended as a quick read. We suspect that readers who get the most out of this book, those who decide they are going to understand motivation well enough to make their own classrooms more motivating, will be returning to this introductory chapter often to construct as complete an understanding as possible about the many ways that motivation can be primed in kindergarten through third-grade classrooms.

THE DEVELOPMENT OF ACADEMIC MOTIVATION

We observed students at the neighborhood school on the second day of the new school year. Although there were tears from some of the kindergarten children when they departed from their parents on the first day of school, there were no such tears on the second day. Indeed, what was striking was the enthusiasm of the 5-year-olds and their certainty that this was going to be a good year for them at school. When their teacher read aloud the book *Madeline*, she asked the kids, "Are we going to learn to read this year?" Every one of the children responded with an enthusiastic "Yes!"

In fact, whenever researchers have looked for academic enthusiasm and confidence among children in the early primary grades, they have found it (Clifford, 1975, 1978; Entwisle & Hayduk, 1978; Flavell, Friedrichs, & Hoyt, 1970; Goss, 1968; Lepola, Vaurus, & Maeki, 2000; Levin, Yussen, DeRose, & Pressley, 1977; Parsons & Ruble, 1977; Stipek & Hoffman, 1980). Ask first graders if they are going to do well on an upcoming test, and they are certain of it. First graders are confident and excited to get on with learning. Their beliefs that they can do well go far in affecting their attitudes toward learning and their motivations to read (McKenna, 2001).

In the part of the local school building housing the grade 5 and grade 6 students, a different scene was apparent on the second day of the academic year. They were not as excited about being in school as the primary-level students. Moreover, they were not nearly as optimistic about whether they would do well. In schools across the country, many students in the upper elementary grades perceive they are doing poorly academically (Juvonen, 1988; Kloosterman, 1988). The ones who have done poorly are really pessimistic about the upcoming year (Renick & Harter, 1989), with such pessimism undermining any motivation to try hard (Fincham, Hokoda, & Sanders, 1989). By the end of the grade-school years, students are much less interested in school and what goes on there than they were at younger ages (Harter, 1981; Wigfield, Eccles, MacIver, Reuman, & Midgley, 1991; see Wigfield, 2000, for a review of the literature). Some may be at the point of believing that there is nothing they can do that will result in achieving at levels acceptable to their teachers. They have failed so often that they believe any effort they would make would result in failure; hence, they display what is termed "learned helplessness," characterized by an unwillingness even to try anymore (e.g., Dweck & Licht, 1980).

One response to the relative lack of motivation in middle-elementary-grade students compared to primary students is that there is no need to study motivation in the primary grades, for those students are motivated. However, although they are more motivated, the sad fact is that academic motivation and motivation to read, in particular, begin to decline in the primary grades, which becomes apparent when there is careful measurement of motivation within the primary-grade years (Gambrell, Mazzoni, & Korkeamaki, 1996; Lepola, Salonen, & Vauras, 2000; Mazzoni, Gambrell, & Korkeamaki, 1999; Sperling & Head, 2002).

Students who are struggling with reading during the primary years have proven especially vulnerable to declines in motivation to read. There is more to the decline with increasing grades than student failure, however. Educators also behave in ways that aggravate the situation. In this chapter, we cover briefly some of the most egregious educational practices that seem to exacerbate declining motivation.

On a more positive note, much has been learned about how to increase academic motivation during the elementary years, that is, how to keep students charged up about learning in school and confident that they can do well. In part this work was stimulated by the recognition that academic motivation drops during the elementary school years and that by fourth, fifth, and sixth grades, there are many students who have given up on school and on themselves as students. The work was also stimulated, however, by theoretical and empirical analyses identifying an important determinant of declining student motivation during the elementary years—the way that schools do business. Schools might actually be structured so as to undermine motivation. Before taking up how academic motivation can be increased, we examine in the next two sections the way education can and does undermine it.

HOW CLASSROOM COMPETITION UNDERMINES STUDENT MOTIVATION

A central tenet of capitalist economic philosophy is that competition is good. When different providers of service compete for customers, prices tend to be lower. Thus, airfares are typically lower in cities serviced by several airlines than when one airline has a monopoly.

Quality also improves when there is competition. For example, the quality of American automobiles improved in the last quarter of the 20th century, with much of this improvement attributed to foreign competition.

Given American commitment to competition in the marketplace, competition in American schools makes sense, a commitment that goes back to the beginnings of the republic. For example, Thomas Jefferson felt that an important function of schooling was to serve as a testing ground to permit society to rake "a few geniuses from the rubbish" (Mondale & Patton, 2001, p. 23). Bell-curve thinking is deeply steeped in American thought, translating into a system of schooling where a few students earn A's, more students receive B's, and still get more C's. Those who consistently win the K–12 race for A's are rewarded with acceptance into the best universities and colleges, with graduation from such institutions further rewarded by the capitalist economy in the form of preferred jobs and roles in life.

What does it mean to a child to receive A's? The message is "You're smart!" Conversely, for the child getting C's, the message often is "You're not so smart, and certainly not as smart as the A students (Nicholls, 1989). Years of such messages make a difference. Thus, by the end of the grade-school years, students who have struggled in school are convinced they have low ability (Jacobsen, Lowery, & DuCette, 1986; Pearl, 1982). Often these kids have tried hard. Failing has been devastating for them, an experience full of negative affect, one leading them to believe that there is nothing they can do to achieve now or in the future either (Covington & Omelich, 1979a, 1979b). It does not help that there are other kids in the class doing much better, with those classmates being rewarded saliently with high grades (Covington, 1987). Struggling learners come to believe there is nothing they can do to achieve; when they come to believe that, there is no motivation to try (Carr, Borkowski, & Maxwell, 1991; Dweck & Bempechat, 1983). The really horrible part of classroom competition is not that some children fail badly and come to believe they cannot do well but, rather, that the system is designed so that more children feel they are failures than feel they are successes. In any class, there are only a few A students. Relative to these A students, all the rest are failures! Competitive grading provides many more students with reason to feel bad rather than good, reducing the motivation of many students (Ames, 1984; Ames & Ames, 1981). A real irony is that competitive grading even undermines the motivation of the students getting the A's. Some of these students probably could achieve at an even higher level than they are achieving, but why bother? After all, they are already getting the top grade in the class. All that really counts is doing better than the other students, not doing the task really well (Ames & Felker, 1979; Barnett & Andrews, 1977; Johnson & Johnson, 1974; Levine, 1983). Thus, just as the A's received by A students undermine the motivation of other students in the class, they also undermine the academic motivation of the students receiving them!

Schools do a really thorough job of sending the message to most students that they are not as able as their peers (Nicholls, 1989). First, there is a lot of grading on the bell curve, described earlier. Moreover, rather than such grading being done quietly and discreetly, it is often done so all know who are the A, B, and C students. When students exchange papers for grading, students know how others in the class did. "Calling" the grades into the grade book definitely shouts to the entire class who is on top and who is not! Such calling in was so embarrassing to one student in Oklahoma that the family took the issue all the way to the U. S. Supreme Court. Although the court ruled that exchanging papers and calling in of grades did not violate federally guaranteed rights to privacy, the case made obvious that such grading is very painful for many, many children. In addition, sometimes the A papers will be posted, so that the non-A students have additional opportunity to reflect on how well they did not do! It can be very tough to be a non-A student in a school in the United States.

Teachers and parents also make it clear when students do not do as well as others. Thus, when Johnny, whom the teacher just praised for beginning the third-grade basal reader, overhears the teacher tell Mary that she is reading fifth-grade books, Johnny knows he is not doing as well as

Mary. There also are parents who respond to their student's report card by talking about how well the child across the street is doing, which only increases the sting of less than A grades. It can hurt even more if the local paper publishes the names of kids on the honor roll, again reminding those who did not make it that they did not do very well relative to classmates.

In addition to the teacher-constructed assessments which are assigned conventional grades from A to F (or U), there are also standardized tests, presumably scientifically constructed, which adds to their authority as benchmarks of excellent and not-so-excellent studentship. If every child in Lake Wobegon is above average, that definitely is not the case on standardized tests in most classrooms where low standardized test performances are a regular part of life for many children today. The message is loud and clear to these children that they did not do as well as others, their status formalized as a percentile that provides a precise estimate of the percentage of students who scored better than they did on the test.

For children who cannot possibly get the A, one option is simply to stop trying to do well. Not trying can reduce the pain in several ways. First of all, not trying means that all the frustrations associated with trying and doing poorly evaporate. Beyond that, however, when you fail after not trying, you can honestly say, "I didn't try," which is better than facing the reality that if you failed after trying, it was probably because of low ability! Thus, you can actually feel better about yourself by not trying than by trying and failing (Covington & Omelich, 1981, 1984; Nicholls, 1989). We recall our teachers saying "I'd rather you try and fail than not try at all." When the teacher oversees a competitive grading situation, however, many students can feel a lot better by not trying. The competitive classroom actually provides incentives for not trying. Although competition is a good model for the American economic marketplace much of the time, it is not so for the academic marketplace. Competition does harm rather than good in school.

TEACHER EXPECTATIONS
AND STUDENT MOTIVATION

In the 1960s, Harvard psychologist Robert Rosenthal and his colleagues (e.g., Rosenthal & Jacobson, 1968) carried out a famous set of analyses. They tested the idea that teachers' expectancies about academic performance were a powerful determinant of actual student achievement. That is, if the teacher expected a student would do well, in fact, the student did well.

In the most famous study conducted by Rosenthal's group, all children in a school were administered a standardized test that was represented as predicting which children would excel in the upcoming school year. The researchers presented the outcomes of the test to the teachers in the school, with 20% of the children identified as likely to blossom during the school year ahead. In fact, at the end of the school year, the 20% of children cited as likely to blossom did, in fact, bloom. They had a lot of improvement on the standardized test over their fall performance. Did this demonstrate the power of the fall test to predict who could achieve? Hardly, for the 20% of students that the researchers told the teachers were likely to improve during the upcoming school year actually were selected at random. There was no objective basis for expecting them to improve any more than any of the other children in the school. Rosenthal and Jacobson (1968) argued that the teachers' expectations propelled these children to achieve highly during the year. Just as Eliza had been transformed by Henry Higgins' expectations in *Pygmalion,* so it was in Rosenthal and Jacobson's (1968) study, which became known as *Pygmalion in the Classroom.*

Rosenthal and Jacobson's work inspired a number of follow-up studies. However, in general, other researchers failed to obtain the dramatic outcomes of the initial study (Goldenberg, 1992). The effects of teacher expectations alone on student achievement tend to be small on average (Jussim, Smith, Madon, & Palumbo, 1998; Rosenthal, 1985). A student does not do dramatically better or worse over the course of a school year just because a teacher is told the child is going to do well or poorly, as was the case in Rosenthal and Jacobson's (1968) original research. Nevertheless, teachers' expectations do matter very much in how teachers respond to children, and teacher expectations that affect their teaching are formed early.

Consider another classic analysis of teacher expectations and their effects. Rist (1970) studied a group of disadvantaged urban children when they were in kindergarten, grade 1, and grade 2. On the 8th day of kindergarten, the teacher placed the students in reading groups. How did the teacher do it? Entirely on information pertaining to social class! She had information from the school registration forms, input from a social worker about children living in homes receiving welfare assistance, a brief interview with each mother, and information about her own and other teachers' experiences with other family members who attended the school. The more economically advantaged children were placed in the highest reading group, with signs of poverty much more apparent in the other two reading groups (e.g., the children in the lower reading groups did not dress as well as the children in the top reading group).

Did placement in the reading groups affect the students for the rest of the kindergarten year? It certainly did. Rist (1970) summarized: "The fundamental division of the class into those expected to learn and those expected not to permeated the teacher's orientation to the class" (p. 277). For example, the students in the top group were called on more often, with more positive experiences, during these interactions with both the teacher and their peers. Over the course of the year, the students in the lower reading groups became more withdrawn, although they also misbehaved more than the students in the top reading group. As Rist (1970) followed the children through first and second grade, the stratification established on day 8 of kindergarten generally held. The top reading group remained intact and the students in the lower two reading groups remained in the lower reading groups.

Brophy and Good (1970, 1974; Brophy, 1985) did a very systematic study of how teachers behave toward first graders whom they perceived to have higher versus lower ability. Their basic finding was that teachers treated students very differently depending on their perceptions of the children's abilities:

- Teachers do not wait as long for low-ability students to answer questions as they do for high-ability students.
- When low-ability students hesitate to answer a question, teachers are more like to give them the answer or call on someone else.
- Low-ability students receive more teacher criticism, less praise, and less helpful feedback than high-ability students.
- Teachers pay less attention to and call less frequently on low- than high-ability students.
- Low-ability students are seated farther from the teacher than high-ability students.
- Teachers attempt to control the behaviors of low-ability students more than high-ability students.
- Teachers demand less academically from low-ability than high-ability students.
- With respect to grading, teachers are less likely to give the benefit of the doubt to low-ability compared to high-ability students.

- Teachers are less friendly with low-ability compared to high-ability students.
- Teachers do not respond as completely to questions posed by low- compared to high-ability students.

In short, simply telling a teacher that a child is low or high ability does not make much difference with respect to achievement. Nonetheless, teachers are sensitive to differences in student abilities and behave differently toward low- versus high-ability students. Usually, teachers size up students on the basis of past accomplishments, but sadly, as Rist (1970) observed, sometimes decisions are made on the basis of social and socioeconomic factors, a phenomenon subsequently documented by a number of other researchers (see Jussim et al., 1998, for a review). Teachers often interact with students in ways that might be expected to undermine student motivation. What motivation is there to participate in class if the teacher cuts you off when you have to think about an answer? What motivation is there to try hard when criticism is common, praise seldom, and helpful feedback rare? Why try hard when the teacher does not pay attention to you or is not friendly to you in comparison to other kids? Why try hard when breaks in grading go to the other students and not to you? Why ask questions if there is not much of a response from the teacher? In fact, before this book is through, much more will be said about how teachers can and often do undermine academic motivation.

More positively, there are many approaches that teachers can take to increase students' motivation to learn. The competitive classrooms filled with negative expectations can be replaced by classrooms brimming with teaching that really cooks! That is what most of this book is about, beginning with the next section.

MANY MEANS OF INCREASING ACADEMIC MOTIVATION

Individual researchers interested in educational motivation typically have focused on one or a very few mechanisms that might promote student motivation and achievement. By analyzing numerous research programs, however, educational researchers have produced a great deal of information about a variety of ways that academic motivation can be increased. The perspective in this book is not that some of these mechanisms are better than others, but that well-informed teachers have a repertoire of various mechanisms that they match to curriculum, instructional situations, and student needs. A primary message of this book is that motivating classrooms are flooded with motivational mechanisms. This process can be understood better by examining some of the techniques used by excellent teachers.

High Expectations

Although, on average, teacher expectancy effects on achievement are small, sometimes they are not—as in the original *Pygmalion* study. Even though large effects are the exception rather than the norm, in this case the exception justifies teachers taking care to avoid the possibility of their low expectancies undermining their students. Thus, all who think about educational motivation agree that teachers should have realistically high expectations of their students—that they should expect them to be able to achieve. With appropriate effort, teachers should be confident that their students can do a little better than they currently do (Au, 2001; Flippo, 1998; Good & Brophy, 2002, Chapter 7; Jussim et al., 1998).

Reinforcement

Anyone who has ever taken a psychology course recalls that positive consequences for a behavior increase the likelihood of the behavior. Such positive consequences are referred to as reinforcers, or reinforcement, by psychologists. This was the central idea in the theories of B. F. Skinner (1953) which were appealing because they made horse sense: If you do something and are rewarded for it, you are more likely to do it again. As sensible as reinforcement is as a concept, it is not an idea that has gone unchallenged. Indeed, sometimes providing reinforcement actually undermines motivation.

Specifically, if a student is given a reward for doing something he or she would do in the absence of reward (i.e., the behavior is intrinsically motivating to the student), the likelihood of doing the behavior in the future is reduced when no reward is available. That is, the behavior that was once intrinsically motivating now only occurs if there is an extrinsic reward in the form of a reinforcer. Thus, consider the child who is an avid reader in September. The teacher announces that pizza certificates now will be given as rewards for reading books. The child continues to read and collects handfuls of pizza certificates in October, November, and through the end of the program in March. In April, the child reads very little, announcing to her parents that there's no point in reading now, since there are no longer pizzas as rewards for reading. In fact, this is exactly how the child of one of the authors of this book reacted at the end of the pizza certificate program in his classroom.

What is going on here? The pizza certificates are a very salient reward. All the kids in the class talk about them, all are excited to get them. Some of the kids who are not reading before the program begins even think of the certificates as a bribe of sort. The kids in the class, including the initially avid readers, begin to explain their reading of books as due to the certificates. "I'm reading all these books to get lots of pizza certificates!" Thus, when the certificates end, there seems to be no reason to read, even for the youngster who used to do so much reading on her own. Subsequently, previously intrinsically motivated students do not read in the absence of the pizza certificates as rewards (Lepper, Greene, & Nisbett, 1973; Lepper & Hoddell, 1989).

Does it happen every time that a child who is rewarded for doing a bahavior that is intrinsically motivating loses intrinsic motivation? The answer is clearly no (Cameron & Pierce, 1994, 1996; Tang & Hall, 1995), with considerable debate about just how general an effect this is (Cameron, 2001; Deci, Koestner, & Ryan, 2001a, 2001b; Lepper & Henderlong, 2000). Think about kids in punt, place, and kick contests. The winners leave the competition still very much intrinsically motivated to perfect their football skills. None of us have ever known a winner in these competitions who did not continue to play a lot of sandlot football with playmates! And, of course, even after the pizza certificates stop, many of the avid readers remain avid readers.

That rewards do not always undermine intrinsic motivation does not diminish the fact that rewards do undermine intrinsic motivation at least for some children some of the time. When McQuillan (1997) evaluated the available evidence on incentive programs for reading, he found very mixed results: For every study that found a positive effect of incentives, there was one that did not. When Fawson and Moore (1999) examined incentive programs used in schools, they found that such programs were anything but engineered carefully, and were indeed likely to undermine the motivation of many students.

Extrinsic rewards should be used with care, with the teacher alert to the possibility of negative consequences of rewarding children who are already intrinsically motivated. Thus, a suggestion that we make to classroom teachers who are considering pizza incentive programs is that participation be limited to students who are not reading enough already. Our experience has been that, if the teacher explains that the pizza incentive program is to encourage people who are not already avid readers, students who do not participate in the program are fine with it. If the teacher is concerned with equity, perhaps other reward programs can be developed in which avid readers can participate (e.g., rewards for reading books to younger children in the school).

Although we acknowledge the need for caution by teachers in using rewards when behavior is intrinsically motivated, there are lots of occasions when educators should use rewards. Specifically, they should use them when students are not intrinsically motivated for doing an important academic behavior (Bandura & Schunk, 1981; Lepper & Hoddell, 1989; Loveland & Olley, 1979; McLoyd, 1979). Thus, providing pizza certificates to readers who would not read otherwise is a good idea, as it encourages those children to undertake a learning activity that they would not do in the absence of the reward.

Rewards do not have to be tangible, however. One of the most powerful rewards that a teacher can use is praise, although it is critical that praise be used well if it is to be effective, with Brophy (1981; see also Henderlong & Lepper, 2002) providing definitive guidance about how to do so:

- Like any reinforcer, praise should be delivered as soon as possible after the student does something that is praiseworthy.
- In delivering the praise, the teacher should make clear what the student did that was praiseworthy. Students should be told that they are competent and what they are doing is valuable (e.g., "You're a great reader, and reading National Geographic will fill your head with information that is important to know").
- Praise should be sincere. It should reflect that the teacher knows what the student is accomplishing.
- The teacher should let the student know that he or she can be successful in the future by continuing to exert appropriate effort (e.g., "Keep on reading. Everyone who is successful reads a lot. Ever notice that the President often has a book in his hands when he gets off his helicopter?").
- The teacher should remind the student about how enjoyable it is to expend the praiseworthy effort (e.g., "I know you really enjoyed finding out about Aslan as you read The Lion, the Witch, and the Wardrobe"; Lewis, 1997).

Praise is reinforcement that is richly informative to students. In short, teachers should provide lots of information to students about what they are doing well and why they should engage in the praiseworthy behaviors in the future. It is not easy for teachers to praise effectively, however (Brophy, 1981). Some teachers simply praise anything a student does, which can make the classroom atmosphere seem positive but does not provide students with critical information about what they should be doing. Other teachers simply do not expend the effort to praise at all.

In summary, a huge idea in the motivation literature is to reward behaviors that should be strengthened. Often, providing rewards does increase student motivation, although rewards can undermine intrinsically motivated behaviors. Perhaps most critical, rewards need not be tangible to be effective, with teacher praise a very powerful reward. Use of rewards can be combined with other approaches, with skillful rewarding a critical component of cooperative learning.

Cooperative Learning

Just as competition undermines motivation, cooperation increases motivation and achievement. In fact, cooperative learning, which involves several students working together rather than alone, consistently produces at least small learning benefits and sometimes quite large learning benefits.

A great problem with schools in the United States is that competition and individualism are so prevalent that there is relatively little cooperative learning, which ranges between 7 and 20% of class time in typical classrooms (Johnson & Johnson, 1985). David W. and Roger T. Johnson (e.g., Johnson & Johnson, 1975, 1979) have done more than others to increase understanding about when and how cooperative learning is effective. For cooperative learning to occur, learning has to be interdependent. That is, students have to be given tasks that are large enough that no one student can do it all, tasks that can only be accomplished by students working together. The Johnsons have produced quite a bit of evidence that small groups work better than large groups, that constructive and engaging interactions about academic tasks are more likely with three to four children working face-to-face than an entire class confronting a task.

Something that is absolutely essential, however, is that there be individual accountability. The groups and tasks cannot be structured so that everyone is rewarded if only one or two students work. What works especially well is when there are group and individual rewards (Slavin, 1985a,

1985b). Thus, perhaps a small group of students works on some type of arithmetic problems for the first 4 days of the school week. On day 5, there is a test, with students' grades determined not only by their own performance on the test but also by the performance of groupmates. Thus, a student getting 80% on the test would get a higher grade if his or her group's average was 85% versus 70%.

Cooperative learning is a very flexible mechanism that can be incorporated into a variety of content areas, used in kindergarten through college, and applied with diverse children. For example, it is right in the middle of some urban education reform efforts that are very effective in improving the academic achievements of inner-city students (e.g., Fantuzzo, King, & Heller, 1992).

Making Academic Tasks More Interesting

Some content is more interesting than other content. Also, individual students differ in their interests. In general, student academic motivation is going to be greater when content is intriguing, matched to student interests, or illustrated with examples that are exciting to students (e.g., Hidi, 1990; Renninger, 1990; Renninger & Wozniak, 1985; Shiefele, 1991). Perhaps particularly inspiring are reports of students with severe reading problems making much progress in literacy when permitted to read about topics that they are passionately interested in (Fink, 1995; Pierson, 1999). Unfortunately, it is not unusual at all for students to find the content they are asked to read to be boring.

More positively, content can be presented in ways that are more or less interesting. As far back as John Dewey's (1913) work at the beginning of the last century, educational theorists have recognized that student learning can be improved by increasing how interesting the lessons are. Consider this example. Several years ago we were in a school during the week when the first grade covered sex education. The state mandated that grade 1 students learn about how chickens hatch from eggs. One teacher bored all of her students with some poster charts of the hatching process, using the posters to lead question-and-answer sessions about what might be happening to the eggs and chicks in the pictures. Across the hall, another teacher constructed an incubator with actual eggs in it. In that classroom, math lessons for the week involved figuring out the right temperature for the incubator. Reading consisted of stories about chickens. Then students wrote about how the class had helped to construct the incubator and to figure out the right temperature. The students also wrote about what they anticipated would happen on the day of the hatching. The students were excited in this classroom about the lessons, in complete contrast to the students in the other class who recited answers to questions as the teacher pointed at the chart depicting the hatching process.

Incidentally, as part of the requirement, both classes actually attempted to hatch a dozen chicks. In the classroom with the more connected and motivating instruction, all 12 chicks hatched and survived; in the other classroom, only 3 made it. Interesting instruction was a matter of life or death for the chicks!

Reading researchers have studied carefully the various ways that content can be presented, especially in the context of reading instruction. What has become clear is that some approaches to elementary literacy instruction are more interesting to children and more motivating to them than other approaches.

Whole Language

Whole-language classrooms immerse children in authentic literature and writing experiences (e.g., writing in response to a literature reading). Whole-language classrooms are decidedly pupil-centered, for example, permitting much student choice in what is read and written. Students are encouraged to take reasonable risks (e.g., to read a book just a bit beyond current competence). They are encouraged to use multiple strategies to read words, in particular, during the primary years, the strategy of using semantic- and syntactic-context cues to recognize words, in addition to letter cues and sounding out.

Turner (1995) compared the academic engagement of grade 1 students in whole-language versus more skills-oriented grade 1 classrooms. The students in the whole-language classrooms were more involved in their learning than students in the skills-oriented classrooms. In addition, Turner's (1995) analyses revealed that particular whole-language practices, such as partner reading and reading of trade books, were more engaging for students than tasks more typical in skills-oriented classrooms, such as completion of worksheets.

Morrow (1992; Morrow & Sharkey, 1993) compared second grades that followed a whole-language approach with more skills-oriented second grades. Whole language promoted students' abilities to process text, as reflected in story retellings and listening comprehension assessments. The writing in the whole-language classrooms was better as well. Most critical here, however, was that the students in the whole-language class-rooms read more on their own and were more excited about literacy in general.

Beyond these global evaluations of the motivating impact of whole language (see also Sacks & Mergendoller, 1997, for evidence of the moti-vating qualities of whole language at the kindergarten level), there is growing evidence of positive motivational impacts of a variety of specific instructional practices that are strongly favored in whole language. These include providing children with access to books (Elley, 1992, 1994, 2001; Fractor, Woodruff, Martinez, & Teale, 1993; Gambrell, Codling, & Palmer, 1996; Koskinen et al., 2000; McGill-Franzen, Allington, Yokoi, & Brooks, 1999; Neuman & Roskos, 1993; Purcell-Gates, McIntyre, & Freppon, 1995) and allowing children choices about what they read (Flippo, 1998; Palmer, Codling, & Gambrell, 1994; Turner, 1995).

Concept-Oriented Instruction

More generally, John Guthrie and his colleagues at the University of Maryland have illuminated well just how such interesting, conceptually driven instruction can make important content come to life for children. The starting point for Guthrie's work on concept-oriented instruction was close study of classrooms using interesting conceptual units to drive in-struction. Thus, when Sally Trent was teaching ecology to her third-grade students, classroom visitors immediately noticed the bird nests that were in the room, as well as feather collections and displays, a pair of doves, and many, many books about birds (Guthrie, 2002). A variety of topics in science that relate to the concept of ecology were studied by the class. Part of the unit was accomplished by studying bird behavior, from their habitats (i.e., the nature of deserts, rain forests, grasslands, arctic regions, and temperate forests) to bird reproduction (i.e., by monitoring carefully the hatching of a dove's egg). The children considered how birds eat, compete with one another, defend their territories, move around their en-vironments, communicate, breathe, reproduce, prey on other animals, and adapt to environmental shifts.

The children especially focused on owls, with their study of this bird in-cluding dissection of owl pellets to gain insights about owl diets. As part of this activity, the students asked questions and then pursued the answers to their questions in information books. Because searching information texts is challenging, Ms. Trent supported students during their searches, provid-ing many mini-lessons about how information can be found in books. This included instruction about how information is organized in whole books and individual paragraphs. During interactions with the information books, Ms. Trent discussed many text conventions with students.

During reading instruction, the students read some stories about birds, and owls in particular. The students used the Internet and other computer resources to find additional information about owls and other topics related to the ecology unit. Ms. Trent taught the students strategies for reading information and narrative texts as they worked through the ecology unit, including when and how to skim and self-question during reading.

Such conceptually oriented instruction is engaging when teachers study topics with high intrinsic interest for children, and there are many such topics. Teaching with a conceptual focus includes opportunities to make learning concrete, thereby making ideas more comprehensible. That is, abstract concepts can be illustrated with interesting experiences for children. For example, students understood very well that owls are birds of prey after discovering the bones of small animals in the owl pellets. The students examined as part of the lessons how the owl's preying behavior maintained an important ecological balance: that is, how owls prevented the world from being overrun by mice.

For most important social studies and science topics that can drive conceptually oriented instruction, there are many informational and narrative texts that can be part of the mix of reading that the children experience. The search through and reading of diverse texts can include many opportunities for teacher–student and student–student collaborations, with such cooperative learning more lively than conventional social studies or science instruction (i.e., lecture-, textbook-, and workbook-driven instruction).

The evaluations of conceptually oriented instruction have been very positive. When teachers do it, there is always high engagement. Students get into the concrete activities, go exploring for information to answer the questions that occur to them, and read a lot as they also write extensively. Although there has only been limited controlled study of conceptually oriented instruction as Guthrie conceives it, what has been done confirms its potency: After a year of such instruction, students' comprehension skills seem to improve, conceptual knowledge increases, and, particularly relevant here, academic motivation is greater compared to students in classrooms experiencing conventional instruction (Guthrie et al., 1998; Guthrie, Anderson, Alao, & Rinehart, 1999; Guthrie, Wigfield, & VonSecker, 2000).

Conceptually oriented instruction involves a number of components (see Guthrie & Knowles, 2001). The concept being explored should be interesting to students as they undertake a range of collaborative explorations, from concrete experiences with actual artifacts to library research about the topic being explored. The concept should permit across-curriculum connections (e.g., the owl unit permitted contact with both social studies and science, with students doing much reading and mathematics as they carried out the many activities associated with the unit). Students are taught strategies for finding information and for understanding it. Students make many choices along the way as to what aspect of the topic they will explore, what they will read, and how they will communicate about the topic. (See Meece and Miller, 1999, for additional evidence of the motivational potency of such a mix of components.) Guthrie and his colleagues do not believe that much happens by mobilizing single motivational mechanisms in classrooms; rather, motivating instruction is the result of converging and complementary instructional elements that are well articulated. This is just the first encounter in this volume with instruction that is filled with multiple motivational mechanisms, reflecting that classroom teachers can and should articulate a variety of motivational mechanisms in their classrooms. If they do, students are likely to find instruction engaging.

A Warning about Making Instruction Interesting

Not all efforts to make content more interesting are going to increase student learning. For example, sometimes teachers or textbook writers attempt to make content more interesting by including extremely intriguing anecdotes or seductive details (e.g., Garner, 1992; Wade, Schraw, Buxton, & Hayes, 1993), although ones not essential to understanding the content. Thus, a section of text about Gerald Ford's presidency might include that he played football at the University of Michigan and on election night cheered the Michigan cheer "Go, blue" because the networks used blue to represent the states where he won. Unfortunately, such an interesting detail has the potential to distract attention from much more important facts about Ford's presidency, for example, that he was not elected but rather took office after Nixon's resignation, and that he never recovered politically from pardoning Nixon, watching many more states be colored red (i.e., the color for states won by Jimmy Carter) rather than his beloved Michigan blue on that election night. A replicable finding is that adding seductive details to a text can reduce learning and memory of more important information in the text (Garner, Alexander, Gillingham, Kulikowich, & Brown, 1991; Wade & Adams, 1990).

Educational software often suffers from interesting distractions that can reduce attention to the material being taught (Lepper & Malone, 1987; Malone & Lepper, 1987). For example, a math drill program set up as an arcade game can be filled with many flashing lights, bells, and whistles. If the game is programmed to end once the student has mastered the skill and content covered in it, some students may intentionally provide incorrect answers so that they can continue playing the game!

In short, although making educational experiences interesting has the potential to be very motivating, the trick is to make certain that interesting distractions are not being added. Such well-intended distractions are far too easy to find in many classrooms, however. Teachers should be alert to whether students are attending to the content to be learned (and the big ideas in the content) or distractions (i.e., tangential details), doing everything possible to orient students to the critical ideas and away from the tangential details. In some cases that might mean extreme action—for example, replacing a computer game that only elicits pinball arcade reactions from students in favor of one that causes greater reflection on content.

Availability of Books

There are consistent associations between reading achievement and the availability of books in the child's environment. Thus, doing all possible to assure that the classroom library and local public libraries are well stocked seems important. See Chambliss and McKillop (2000) for a review of the literature supporting the conclusion that the presence of books can increase children's motivation to read, and hence their achievement.

Beliefs about Achievement and Intelligence

What people believe about their achievement and intelligence can go far in affecting their motivation. A number of researchers have provided theory and research substantiating that beliefs affect motivation, work that is at least suggestive that instruction can be more motivating by persuading young learners to think about themselves and their accomplishments in particular ways.

Attribution Theory

When students either succeed or fail, they can explain their successes or failures in a variety of ways (Weiner, 1979). Students can attribute their performance to ability ("I did well because I am smart" or "I'm dumb at math"). They can attribute it to the difficulty of the task ("I did well because this was an easy test" or "No one could have done well on a test this hard"). Sometimes students think that luck accounts for their performances ("I really was lucky on that test" or "I received a 'D' because this was not my lucky day"). The problem with all of these explanations is that the students are attributing outcomes to factors that are out of their control. No student can control God-given ability, the difficulty of the exam the teacher creates, or the random factors that produce luck!

In contrast, consider ability attributions. When students do poorly and attribute their failures to ability (e.g., "I'm just dumb"), what incentive is there to try hard? None, because being innately dumb is not something that a student can remedy with effort. Ability attributions undermine motivation just as certainly when students succeed, however. Thus, when students conclude they did well because they are very smart ("Math comes easy to me because of my high IQ"), there also is no incentive to work hard. Rather, the student believes that achievement is about being smart rather than working hard.

Alternatively, students can attribute their performances to a factor that is under their control—personal effort (e.g., "I did well on this test because I studied hard" or "I should have done better and would have done better, if I had studied the night before the exam"). Attributing outcomes to effort motivates those who succeeded because of effort to exert such effort in the future. This is why Brophy (1981) urged teachers, when praising students, to remind them of the efforts that resulted in such praise. Attributing failure to lack of effort motivates the student to do more in the future in order to avoid failure.

Often students are taught strategies that require effort to carry out. Students are more likely to use these strategies if the teacher makes it clear that the strategies guide one's efforts in ways that permit task accomplishment (e.g., Carr & Borkowski, 1989). Once the student is successful, then the good teacher praises the success and reminds the student about how use of the strategy resulted in the success, that is, how effort paid off (e.g., Deshler & Schumaker, 1988; Graham & Harris, 1996).

As a general point, when people believe they can control their outcomes, there is greater motivation to try (e.g., deCharms, 1968; Martin &

Martin, 1983). This perspective is explicit in Weiner's (1979) attribution theory, but it is also present in other theories that specify the importance of learner beliefs in academic motivation.

Incremental Theory

Some people believe that they inherit a fixed level of intelligence, which determines how well they will achieve academically (i.e., they believe that they're either smart or not). Others perceive that their intelligence can change as a function of experience—increasing with rich academic experiences and decreasing if they do not work hard to learn the ideas and skills that smart people know. Carol Dweck and her associates (Dweck & Leggett, 1988; Elliott & Dweck, 1988; Henderson & Dweck, 1990) and others (e.g., Meece, Blumenfeld, & Hoyle, 1988; Wood & Bandura, 1989) have provided substantial evidence that believing intelligence is changeable by one's intellectual efforts and experiences in fact motivates academic efforts, especially when students experience failure. Following failure, students who believe intelligence is God-given are more at risk of giving up, believing there is nothing they can do to improve. Students who believe that intelligence can increase with effort are more likely to keep plugging away despite failure.

Possible-Self Theory

We believed for a long time that we could be authors before we actually were authors. In fact, that is what it is like with all high achievers. Most lawyers believed for a long time they could become lawyers, and doctors envisioned themselves as doctors for years before they began their professional educations. Such high achievers have ambitious possible selves and have had them for a long time. In contrast, many drug dealers believed for years that there was little chance that they could become productive. Many people living on welfare lived with parents on welfare who created in their offspring beliefs that living on welfare was inevitable. Possible selves can be positive and inspiring or negative and discouraging of effort (Cantor, Markus, Niedenthal, & Nurius, 1986; Markus & Nurius, 1986).

In the primary grades, teachers can encourage students to think about the long term (e.g., "Someday, you might be a doctor"), the medium term ("You're going to be ready for middle school"), and the short term ("You can be a great reader, someone who is reading the level 16 books"). Although we could wish for more research to confirm the long-term benefits of creating positive possible selves in students, to the extent that researchers have appraised possible-self theory, they have produced support for it (Day, Borkowski, Dietmeyer, Howsepian, & Saenz, 1992).

Summary

Student beliefs can either motivate academic efforts or undermine them, both in the short term and long term. The message from this body of theory and research is that teachers should encourage students to believe that they can produce academic success through effort, thereby becoming smarter and being successful in school and, ultimately, in the world beyond.

Success

Success motivates. One of the ways it does this is by increasing students' self-efficacy, their understanding that they can do particular tasks (Bandura, 1977, 1986; Schunk, 1990, 1991; Schunk & Zimmerman, 1998; Zimmerman, 1989a, 1989b, 1990a, 1990b). When students do well in math in second grade, they come to believe they can do math. Such self-efficacy beliefs motivate efforts both during current math lessons and in the future. As students read increasingly difficult books in first grade, they believe they can become better readers. Believing one can read in turn motivates more reading and trips to the library (e.g., Marsh, 1990; Zimmerman, Bandura, & Martinez-Pons, 1992). The strong connections between success, beliefs about ability, and subsequent academic efforts are now well understood and established (see Boekaerts, Pintrich, & Zeidner, 2001; Borkowski, Carr, Rellinger, & Pressley, 1990; DiPerna, Volpe, & Elliott, 2002; Zimmerman & Schunk, 2001).

In addition to personal success, there are other factors that influence self-efficacy. It helps to be surrounded by people who are able to do tasks. Thus, if other students in the class are figuring out how to to do the problems covered in math lessons, a student is more likely to believe he or she can learn as well (e.g., Schunk, 1990, 1991). Encouragement by others also can increase a student's self-efficacy. If teachers tell students they can do math or be readers, the students are more likely to believe it (Schunk, 1990, 1991).

One approach to increasing success would be to give students only easy tasks. In fact, that does not increase self-efficacy and student motivation as much as giving students tasks that are moderately challenging— not so easy they can be done with little effort, nor so difficult that they cannot be performed even with great effort (e.g., Harter, 1978; White,

1959). Indeed, when students are in environments where they experience moderately challenging tasks on a regular basis, they come to like appropriate challenge rather than fear it (Miller & Meece, 1999). In contrast, tasks that are easy are seen as boring because they require so little thought (Miller & Meece, 1999).

The risk in giving students moderately difficult tasks is that sometimes a student may be stumped. Rather than leave the student to flounder when confronted with a task that he or she cannot do, the teacher can "scaffold" him or her (Wood, Bruner, & Ross, 1976), providing enough support so that the student can begin to make progress. That is, the teacher does not do the task for the student but provides hints, prompts, and enough instruction so that he or she can forge ahead. Students can almost always have success with moderately difficult tasks with sufficient support—that is, with the kinds of tasks that allow them to see they can solve challenging problems and come to understand challenging material.

Just as success motivates, failure undermines motivation, especially when failures are persistent and salient. For example, students who experience difficulties in reading during the first few years of school typically are not motivated to exert academic effort in the middle grades.

They have come to believe they are dumb and that there is nothing they can do to increase the likelihood of academic success (Jacobsen et al., 1986; Pearl, 1982). Those struggling learners who can hold on to the belief that they can do better if they try hard, are more likely to make academic progress than students who have come to believe that there is nothing they can do to affect their achievements positively (Kistner, Osborne, & LeVerrier, 1988). Unfortunately, years of failure and the hurt feelings accompanying failure more typically produce feelings of personal incapacity and learned helplessness (Covington, 1987; Dweck & Licht, 1980). The result is that such children often would prefer to do nothing academically, rather than try and fail again (Covington & Omelich, 1981, 1984). Teachers who motivate their students do all they can to assure success for their students on demanding academic tasks. Above all, they make certain that students do not get caught up in a pattern of persistent and consistent failure.

Beliefs about the Value of Academic Tasks

Success can increase students' self-efficacy and, thus, expectations that they can succeed at academic tasks. Is that all there is to motivation? Not really. For example, one of us expects that he could succeed in producing a putting-green surface on his lawn with appropriate effort. Why doesn't he do so? Because he does not value having a lawn that looks like a putting green, but, rather, feels fine about the lawn he has. In order to work hard at something, there has to be some value in it for the individual expending the effort.

Thus, even though a student may be confident of doing well in math, this subject might not receive much effort if the student does not see the point of learning it ("When would I ever use this?"). In fact, both self-efficacy with respect to academic content and valuing of the content are necessary for high achievement (Berndt & Miller, 1990). Thus, an important motivational element of teaching is to provide students with understanding that what they are learning is very valuable now and in the future.

Teacher Caring

Nel Noddings, an educational philosopher, has heightened awareness of the role of teacher caring in student motivation and performance. Of course, the caring teacher is motivated to work hard with students, to teach them well. For example, the teacher who consistently scaffolds students must care a great deal to do so. Scaffolding requires great effort. The teacher must consistently monitor students and size up situations to decide the type of assistance that would help a particular student at a particular moment. Then, the teacher has to provide just enough support to get the student started. The goal of the caring teacher is not to control the student but to help him or her be able to do educational tasks, to encourage all students to feel they can accomplish academic tasks in a self-regulated fashion.

Noddings sees teacher caring as a centerpiece of teaching that produces competent students, as she expressed it in her 1984 book:

> The teacher works with the student. He becomes her apprentice and gradually assumes greater responsibility in the tasks they undertake. This working together, which produces both joy in the relation and increasing competence in the cared-for . . . needs the cooperative guidance of a fully caring adult. . . . [The caring teacher] has two major tasks: to stretch the student's world by presenting an effective selection of that world with which she is in contact, and to work cooperatively with the student in his struggle toward competence in that world. (Noddings, 1984, pp. 177–178)

The wonder of such care is that excellent teachers manage to do such teaching with all of their students, even if they have large classes. The teachers featured in this volume work very, very hard to monitor and provide support for all of their students. Noddings's point in the quotation is that only a very caring teacher could exert such Herculean effort.

Summary

Motivational theorists and researchers have produced a great deal of work that has increased understanding about what can be done by teachers to increase academic motivation. A main message of this chapter is that many, many approaches to increasing student motivation have been identified. The coverage in this chapter was anything but exhaustive. Michael McKenna (1994, 2001) has done more than anyone to document the many ways that teachers can positively impact students' academic attitudes, especially their attitudes toward reading. He notes that there are quite a few approaches that enjoy at least a little bit of research support. These include not denigrating students for their reading or their reading-group placement (Wallbrown, Brown, & Engin, 1978), using high-quality literature (Morrow, 1983), activating prior knowledge in students by asking questions about what they are about to read (Jagacinski & Nicholls, 1987), reading aloud to students (Herrold, Stanchfield, & Serabian, 1989), connecting ideas in text to the lives of students (Guzzetti, 1990), teaching children to be more aware of their reading (i.e., whether they are understanding what is being read; Payne & Manning, 1992), conducting literature discussions (Gambrell, Mazzoni, & Almasi, 2000; Langer, 1995, 2001; Leal, 1993), having children correspond with college students about their reading (Bromley, Winters, & Schlimmer, 1994), cross-age tutoring (Leland & Fitzpatrick, 1993/1994), and reading (McKenna & Watkins, 1995) and writing (Karchmer, 2001) electronic texts. What McKenna (1994, 2001) has done is alerted teachers to the possibility that there is a huge menu of techniques with potential for affecting students' attitudes toward reading and their academic motivations, which often will result in increased academic engagement.

In the chapters that follow, case studies of engaging teachers will be highlighted. In every case study, the teachers used many of the mechanisms discussed in this chapter. We hypothesize based on the association between engaging teaching and motivational flooding that we observed in our work—as well as by the association between less engaging teaching and little use of motivating teaching techniques—that primary-grade teachers should be employing the many motivational approaches validated by educational researchers. That is, a major hypothesis that emerges from the research work reported in this book is that primary-grade teachers can produce much greater academic engagement in their classrooms by using many different motivational mechanisms often—by flooding their classrooms with motivating instruction.

We are certainly not the first to offer this recommendation, however. Jere Brophy of Michigan State University has propounded this perspective since the middle 1980s (Brophy, 1986, 1987; see also Gambrell & Morrow, 1995). To make the point that there is very much that can be done by the classroom teacher to promote academic engagement, we conclude this section with a paraphrase of Brophy's list of what teachers can do to motivate students:

- Model interest in learning. Students should see a teacher who likes reading and math, and finds science and social studies content interesting. Communicate to students that there is good reason to be enthusiastic about what goes on in school. The message should be that what is presented in school deserves intense attention, with the teacher doing all that is possible to focus students' attention on important academic content.
- What is being taught, in fact, should be worth learning!
- Keep anxiety down in the classroom. Learning should be emphasized, rather than testing.
- Induce curiosity and suspense, for example, by having students make predictions about what they are about to learn.
- Make abstract material more concrete and understandable.
- Let students know the learning objectives so that it is very clear what is to be learned.
- Provide informative feedback, especially praise when students deserve it.
- Give assignments that provide feedback. Thus, if students cannot do a set of problems, it signals that they have not yet mastered the ideas in the math lesson.
- Adapt academic tasks to student interests and provide novel content as much as possible (e.g., not covering material that students already know simply because it is in the district-mandated curriculum).
- Give students choices between alternative tasks (e.g., reading book A or book B, covering topic X or Y in science).
- Allow students as much autonomy as possible in doing tasks. Thus, to the extent students can do it on their own, let them do so.

- Design tasks to include an engaging activity (e.g., projects, discussions, role playing, simulation), product (e.g., a class-composed big book), or game (e.g., a spelling bee).
- Tasks should be moderately challenging.

An overarching message in Brophy's recommendations and a clear implication of our recommendation to use many motivational mechanisms is that teachers must be good classroom managers. Only a terrific classroom manager could accomplish all that is necessary to use the many motivational mechanisms recommended in this section and throughout the book. If a teacher relies on only a few of these approaches, there is a clear risk of the techniques becoming monotonous in a hurry. By using the many well-validated mechanisms discussed in this chapter, it is possible to keep motivation fresh and effective.

If the teacher is successful in developing literacy in students, the very success will be motivating to students, for they will be able to function much better than before they were literate: They will be able to organize and carry out their lives better (e.g., from being able to make lists to reading signs in their environment). They will be able to communicate in ways they previously could not (e.g., write and read letters and e-mails). They will be able to experience new forms of pleasure (e.g., being able to read on their own the books and stories they like). Life will be better because they learned to read and write (Barton, 2001). Furthermore, they will have a sense of competence that empowers them to do things academic in the future, knowing that they are capable of what others their age are capable of (e.g., Covington, 1992, 1998).

WHAT'S AHEAD?

In the past several years, we have carried out three studies, at grades 1, 2, and 3, respectively, that have started as searches for motivating primary-grade teachers. We did intensive observation and interview investigations of some classrooms in all three studies. In each of the studies, one or two classrooms stood out as producing greater academic engagement in students.

What do we mean by academic engagement in this volume? At one level, our approach to engagement is very behavioral. Basically, engaged students are busy at academic work in school—reading, writing, and problem solving. In the studies reported here, classroom observers were constantly assessing the percentage of students who were working hard academically. In the most engaged classrooms, this translated as 80% of the students, 80% of the time. In addition, we were also sensitive to whether the work was challenging and required thinking by the students or was very easy. For a classroom to be considered engaging, we required that the students be doing work requiring thought.

In each of the most engaging classrooms that we encountered, the teacher used numerous motivating tactics with students. In contrast, the less engaging classrooms were staffed by teachers doing much less to motivate the children they taught. The next chapter reviews the methods used in the three investigations, presenting one study in some detail and providing a general summary of the results of all three studies. The outcomes at the three grade levels support the perspective developed in this chapter, that there is much teachers can and should do to increase student motivation.

Chapter 2 is followed by three chapters, each of which is a case study of a primary-level teacher who oversaw an exceptionally engaging classroom. The cases will make clear how a teacher can use a wide variety of mechanisms to promote student motivation. However, we emphasize that there are very few teachers who flood their classrooms with motivating instruction. Those who do capture better the attention of their students, with more compelling evidence of learning occurring during every classroom visit. Sadly, classroom teachers who do little positive to motivate their students often do much that potentially contributes to undermining student attention and academic commitment. For most teachers to be transformed into more motivating teachers, they must learn how to motivate as well as how to stop behaving in counterproductive ways that weaken the motivation they hope to foster.

The final chapter is a set of reflections on this research effort. It will place in perspective how motivating instruction is just one part of excellent teaching, albeit a very large part of it. Thus, each of the case study teachers is also an excellent classroom manager and superb at coordinating diverse approaches to curriculum and instruction to meet both curriculum demands and student needs. In arguing that motivation works in tandem with excellent classroom management and diverse curriculum and instruction, we are convinced that effective classroom management and many curriculum and instruction practices are potent, at least in part, because of their impact on student motivation. Hence, we consider the possibility that transformation of classrooms for the better might go far by focusing on motivation, expecting that focus also to result in changes in classroom management and curriculum and instruction. That is, by the end of this book, we will be advancing the hypothesis that there is very good reason to evaluate whether instruction in classrooms in the United States would be much better if great efforts were made to teach teachers to flood their classrooms with motivation, including reinforcing class-room management as well as curriculum and instruction that really grabs students' attention and maintains it. In the final chapter, we will invite primary-level teachers who are reading this book to give it a try—to flood their classrooms with motivating instruction and watch what happens. The concluding chapter also provides a set of suggestions for teachers who want to begin to transform their classrooms into more motivating educational environments.

CHAPTER 2

How Do Primary-Grade Teachers Motivate Students?

The first chapter reviewed a great deal of thinking about educational motivation that has been informed by substantial educational research. In particular, there have been many experiments in the past 30 years providing evidence to support the motivational mechanisms discussed in the chapter. Most studies of educational motivation have focused on single mechanisms, have utilized an experimental design involving at least two conditions, one in which the mechanism operated (e.g., reinforcement was provided) and another in which the mechanism was absent (i.e., the control condition).

In the past decade, however, our research group has used a different research tactic. We have carried out grounded theory analyses (Glaser & Strauss, 1967) of effective elementary instruction. This type of research involves extensive observations of teaching as it naturally occurs, complemented by interviews of the teachers who are observed. The observations occur over a long period of time, with the researchers determined to describe the instruction in detail, for example, in the work reported in this book, to identify the motivational mechanisms used by the teachers observed. Observations and interviews continue until the researchers are confident that they have the whole story, that is, until no new conclusions are emerging from observations. This chapter summarizes three studies (albeit one in much more detail than the other two), all of them grounded theory analyses. This work was conducted between 1999 and 2002.

METHODS USED IN THE RESEARCH

The three studies were carried out in grades 1, 2, and 3. The main purpose of the research was to find out how primary-grade teachers motivate their students.

Basically, in each study, teachers in the same Midwestern United States community were observed (i.e., seven grade 1 teachers, nine grade 2 teachers, and nine grade 3 teachers). (The first-grade study was conducted first, followed by the grade 3 research, and concluding with the observations of grade 2 teachers.) Researchers visited each teacher's classroom on multiple occasions, typically in the morning, when instruction is most academically focused in the primary grades. Consistent with grounded theory methodology, the visits continued until the observers felt they understood what was occurring in the classroom, especially with respect to the teacher's approach to motivating students. A particular strength of these studies was that multiple observers visited the classrooms, with the conclusions presented here reached by all the observers. That is, most visits involved at least two and sometimes more observers. Across visits, every teacher was observed by at least three researchers. After making observations, each observer catalogued the motivational mechanisms that were observed in the classroom. The various observers then compared their categories, with the final list of motivational mechanisms used by a teacher containing only those that all observers agreed occurred in the classroom.

In addition to coding how the teacher motivated students, the observers were also attentive to the academic engagement of the students. That is, they were constantly monitoring the percentage of students who were academically engaged—actually doing what the teacher wanted them to do. Every 15 minutes or so, the observer would look around and code the percentage of students who were productively working, doing what was expected of them. In all three studies, the observers noted that in some classrooms, students engaged in tasks that were very easy, requiring only that they go through the motions of doing the task without any real thinking. In contrast were classes in which the students engaged in tasks that required they do some thinking, expend some real cognitive effort. A highly engaging classroom was one where most of the students (i.e., at least 80%) were on task most of the time (i.e., 80% of the time), doing tasks that were definitely of great academic worth (e. g., reading appropriately challenging books, writing, problem solving).

The researchers kept visiting, observing, and coding their data until there was agreement between them. Basically, the observers developed summaries of what they saw, trading their summaries and checking them against each other. Discrepancies were resolved by discussion informed by a thorough search of notes to substantiate or refute points of disagreement. When the observers could not agree that certain categories of behavior occurred in a classroom (which was rare), no final conclusion was reached, so that the conclusions offered in what follows are biased in a conservative direction: The evidence was overwhelmingly supportive of every point made in this and later chapters.

The researchers came to this research project with the goal of being as open-minded as they could be as they observed and analyzed the data. That is, consistent with grounded theory approaches (Glaser & Strauss, 1967), the observations were open-ended, with the researchers determined to let the data drive their conclusions rather than evaluating a priori hypotheses. The researchers were determined that their expectations about what should or could occur in the classrooms would not determine what they saw! By having multiple observers who kept visiting classrooms as long as there was any mystery left about how the teacher was motivating students, the researchers felt they succeeded in letting the teaching speak for itself.

A primary goal from the outset of the research was to determine if academic engagement would covary with the teacher's attempts to motivate students. That is, would the teachers doing the most to motivate students actually produce students who were more academically engaged? If that were the case, it would make a great deal of sense to detail especially well the teaching of teachers who were doing much to motivate their students, for their teaching could go far in providing information about how to make primary-grade classrooms more motivating. Thus, although all teachers were seen multiple times, we expected to sample very completely the teaching of teachers who were producing high engagement, especially if that engagement might be due to their efforts to motivate students. (Not to get ahead of the story, but the teachers who did the most to motivate their students did have students who were more academically engaged.)

Multiple visits to the classes increased the likelihood that the observers were seeing teaching as it typically occurred in the classrooms. Our experience over years of doing research in elementary classrooms is that sometimes teachers can be on best behavior for a single observation or perhaps two or three. However, the teacher eventually becomes more comfortable with the observers. If the teacher is faking good behavior, it is impossible to keep it up for weeks and months, and as visits continue, it becomes apparent what the classroom is really like.

While doing observations, the researchers typically sat in different parts of the room, watching the teaching. That is, if two observers were present on a day, one might sit at the back of the classroom and one at the side. As instruction continued, sometimes the observers would get up and walk around as unobtrusively as possible, often to observe better how the students were responding to the instruction. The observers noted classroom artifacts, from sticker charts recording student accomplishments, to notes sent home to parents, to class-composed big books. The observers noticed not only artifacts in the classroom but also ones in the hallway, the work that the teacher chose to show off to the rest of the school. Sometimes the observers would have brief conversations with the teachers during the visits to clarify what was happening, although the observers made every effort to be as unobtrusive as possible.

As visits proceeded, the observations also became more focused. As the researchers came to know the classrooms, their observations increasingly were aimed at nuances missed in previous observations. Sometimes coding the notes from previous visits clarified elements of instruction that were puzzling (e.g., Why does the teacher have so many boxes in every nook and cranny of the room? Why does the teacher read stories that are so much more mature than typically are read to primary-grade students?). On subsequent visits, observers often tried to solve such puzzles, either through observations or brief questions to the teachers.

After all observations were completed, each teacher was interviewed in depth, with the specifics of the teacher's interview driven by what was observed in his or her classroom. The interview always included presenting the teacher with a summary of the instruction observed, including the motivating tactics used by the teacher. The teacher commented on and corrected the description, with every teacher both generally agreeing with the description generated by the researchers and agreeing with almost all of the particular points made in the description. That the teachers felt the descriptions were honest accountings of their teaching validated the observations.

Beyond evaluating the descriptive summary, the interview included general questions (e.g., What is the role of sticker charts in your class?). The interviewer probed specific aspects of each teacher's instruction that remained puzzling to the researchers (e.g., How is the student of the week selected? How are books selected for the students to take home?).

In summary, across 3 years, classroom motivation in primary classrooms was studied in depth, using both observational and interview methodologies. The approach permitted only a relatively few teachers to be observed at each grade level, although across the 3 years of research, the researchers saw a great deal of teaching. Most importantly, there was great consistency in the results across the 3 years, with clear understandings about motivation in primary-level classrooms as a result of this research.

The next section presents the study conducted at the grade 2 level. The outcomes in that investigation are representative of the detailed results obtained in each of the studies.[1] We chose to present this study in the greatest detail for several reasons. Most importantly, second grade was observed in the third year, after we had vast experience observing primary classrooms with respect to motivating instruction. We were maximally sensitive at that point to instructional practices that potentially would impact student engagement. Hence, if anything, our analyses during the year of grade 2 observations were probably more complete than the previous analyses. (If practice in doing a type of research does not make perfect, it makes better!) In addition, during this third year of study, we came to some important insights that had eluded us during the first 2 years, the most important of which was that there were some tasks that were not very challenging that nonetheless produced high on-task behaviors. The results were more fine-grained, and we think more insightful in this second-grade study than in the previous years efforts.[2]

THE SECOND-GRADE STUDY

In early September of the 2001–2002 school year, letters of invitation to participate in the project were sent to 22 schools. Then each principal who received a letter was contacted by phone. After a principal identified a second-grade teacher as a potential participant, we contacted him or her by mail and phone. Nine teachers (8 female, 1 male) from six schools agreed to be observed and interviewed. The teachers had taught between 2 and 34 years (average = 15 years). Their experience at second grade

---

[1] For those who wish to read the grade 1 and grade 3 studies in their complete detail, they are published and readily available (grade 1 study: Bogner, Raphael, & Pressley, 2002; grade 3 study: Dolezal, Welsh, Pressley, & Vincent, 2003).

[2] The grade 2 study was Sara Dolezal's master's thesis in the Psychology Department at the University of Notre Dame.

ranged from 2 to 18 years (average = 6 years). Class sizes ranged from 15 to 26 students. The teachers taught mostly white children, with a few minority students. The classrooms served a wide range of socioeconomic levels, from classrooms in which most children lived in poverty to ones where all children were from upper-middle-class families.

On-Task Behavior

There were clear differences between teachers with respect to the involvement of their students. Academic engagement begins with on-task behavior, with students considered to be on-task in our studies if they were doing what was asked of them. In the second-grade investigation, students in the classrooms of two teachers, Ms. Squint and Ms. Davidson exhibited a high amount of on-task behavior.[3] That is, all three observers agreed that most students in these classes (i.e., at least 80% on average) were on-task most of the time (i.e., 80% of the time).

The three observers also agreed that four of the teachers had classes where on-task behavior was low. That is, the majority of the students (half of the class or more) were off-task the majority of the time in the classrooms taught by Ms. Ames, Ms. Boone, Ms. Davenport, and Ms. Carroll. In the three remaining classrooms—ones taught by Ms. Farley, Ms. Eldridge, and Ms. Humboldt—on-task behavior was somewhere in the middle, described in what follows as moderate task engagement.

Thoughtfulness

In addition to on-task behavior, the observers noted physical, emotional, auditory, or cognitive expressions of students as they worked on assignments, participated in class activities, or bid for answers. Some students seemed obviously interested and excited about what they were learning— thinking deeply, making connections, and carefully considering the information presented by the teacher. The students in Ms. Davidson's and Ms. Squint's classrooms were the only students judged to be consistently thoughtful. In these classes, 80% of the time, 80% of the students were

---

[3] Consistent with our use of the actual names of the outstanding teachers featured in the case studies in Chapters 3–5, we use the actual names of the two highly engaging teachers in this chapter, with their permission to do so. The other seven teachers are referenced with pseudonyms. Because the grade 2 study included only one male teacher, to protect fully that teacher's identity, all of the teachers in this investigation are referred to as "Ms."

emotionally connected to, positively interested in, and obviously think-ing about their academic work.

Cognitive Demands of Tasks

Some teachers assigned a very high proportion of easy tasks, ones requir-ing little thinking or connecting to other learning. For example, the re-search team saw many easy worksheets requiring the cutting and pasting of word pictures into a blank to complete a sentence. Students did the word completion quickly, although cutting and pasting the pictures into the correct blanks took much more time. On other occasions, some teach-ers assigned worksheets to the class, but only had the students copy the answers after the teacher had written the correct responses on the over-head projectors. We also observed many easy classroom activities, such as students outlining words in different-colored pencils after they had copied them down from the classroom word wall. Similarly, we saw a great deal of round-robin-type reading, during which the students would take turns reading a story, but the teacher rarely stopped to check for students' un-derstanding or to make connections to their previous learning. Addi-tionally, the art component of the activity would often become the main focus instead of the writing and reading that it was supposed to comple-ment. Yes, the students would work on these tasks until they were fin-ished, and thus be scored as on-task, but it was also apparent there was no challenge and probably little learning for many tasks we observed. The tasks seemed consistently unchallenging in four classrooms: those taught by Boone, Ames, Davenport, and Carroll.

In contrast, we saw some activities that did challenge students but did not overwhelm them. One example was a science unit on whales in which the teacher had taken a story from the basal reader and used it as an introduction for a series of student-directed lessons on whales. The stu-dents helped generate a list of questions they wanted to answer about the animal. The teacher then helped the students, as a community of learn-ers, decide what resources to use and where to locate them, how they would present their findings, and how they would celebrate their learning successes. The teacher and students worked through a wide range of skills involving the use of the library, comprehending nonfiction texts, using the Internet, and improving their reading, writing, and drawing skills. At the end of the unit, each student had put together a book about whales, full of his or her own informational and fictional writing, illustrations, and list of resources. The class then made a bulletin board for the hallway as a means of communicating their success and learning with the rest of the school. Throughout their whale unit, the students were asked to connect skills in science, reading, writing, and speaking. They were given an authentic activity where their personal choices and interest drove the curriculum. The students were challenged to think about the process of asking questions, locating the important information, and communicating their findings. In the activity, the students were asked to behave like true scientists, even to the extent of going to a "whale convention" with other students to share their ideas. The students were engrossed as they completed this unit and came to credible conclusions about how whales function in their environment. Their engagement was almost palpable as the students worked together, shared their ideas, and expressed their amazement at some of the whale facts. Often during our visits, we would hear lots of "cool" and "wow" comments as students read material, listened to whale sounds on tape, or found sites on the Internet.

Clusters of Teachers: Low-, Moderately, and Highly Engaging Teachers

Summarizing across the on-task, thoughtfulness, and cognitive demands data, there were three clusters of teachers. There was consistently low on-task behavior, low thoughtfulness, and low task-demand in four classrooms—those headed by Ms. Ames, Ms. Boone, Ms. Carroll, and Ms. Davenport. These teachers will be referred to as low-engaging in the commentary that follows. There was better on-task behavior but low thoughtfulness and consistently low task-demands in three other classrooms— those taught by Ms. Eldridge, Ms. Farley, and Ms. Humboldt. We refer subsequently to these teachers as moderately engaging. Finally, in two classrooms, those headed by Ms. Davidson and Ms. Squint, on-task behavior was consistently high, with students consistently thoughtful about tasks that were appropriately challenging for them. These teachers will be described as highly engaging.

Observed Instructional Practices with Potential to Impact Academic Motivation

Over the course of our study, we observed 102 practices that would be expected to support and 72 practices that might undermine student motivation, based on the body of motivation literature reviewed in Chapter 1 as well as our previous work in grade 1 and grade 3 classrooms (Bogner, Raphael, & Pressley, 2002; Dolezal, Welsh, Pressley, & Vincent, 2003). In examining the practices, however, it was evident that some were closely related and could be more appropriately combined into more general categories. Thus, the practices of "allows students to self-correct" and "teacher probes for answers" were both combined into one category: "checking for understanding." In that way, the 102 practices that support motivation were reduced to 79 categories, and the 72 practices that undermine motivation were condensed into 55 categories. The categories are defined in Tables 2.1 and 2.2, along with supporting references. The motivational practices observed for each teacher are summarized in Table 2.3.

What is most striking in Table 2.3 is that the most engaging teachers used more motivational mechanisms than would be expected to increase engagement compared to the moderately engaging teachers, who in turn used more such mechanisms than the teachers who produced low engagement. In general, the number of behaviors that could undermine motivation covaried inversely with the number of positively motivating practices. In fact, in the most engaging classroom (Ms. Davidson), we observed very few practices that would undermine her students' motivation as compared to the other teachers. The attractiveness of the instruction in the most engaging classrooms comes through in the brief case studies that follow, when contrasted with the case studies of the moderately engaging teachers, but especially in contrast to the classrooms with low engagement.

Variations in Motivating Instruction as a Function of Variations in Student Engagement

The classroom descriptions that follow have been collapsed across several classrooms to provide portraits of low-, moderately, and highly engaging teachers. Greater detail is provided about the highly engaging teachers, those teachers who were able to grab student attention and maintain high levels of engagement. After a brief summary of the common teaching practices for each group, specific characteristics and unique practices are highlighted for each teacher.

Low-Engaging Teachers

The first group of teachers—Ms. Ames, Ms. Boone, Ms. Carroll, and Ms. Davenport—used few positively motivating practices. We observed gener-

TABLE 2.1. Elements Promoting Academic Motivation in Grade 2 Classrooms

---

Positive classroom physical environment and psychological atmosphere

Physical environment

- The classroom is filled with books at different reading levels for students to use (Gambrell, 1996).
- The teacher reads aloud to students on a regular basis (Trelease, 1995).
- The teacher uses literature that is highly regarded in terms of its writing and illustrations for children (Morrow, 2002).
- The teacher introduces new books to the students and displays them in a designated area in the classroom (Gambrell, 1996).
- The classroom is decorated with brightly colored signs and posters. The charts, maps, and posters hanging are useful teaching tools. The bulletin boards are changed with the passing months and seasons and are neat and well kept. Student work is prominently displayed in the classroom (e.g., Doyle, 1986; McVey, 1971).

Psychological atmosphere

- The teacher has high expectations, making certain that students are aware that they are expected to learn and perform in school and are accountable for doing so, including to their parents, who are made aware of their student's progress (e.g., Brophy & Good, 1986).
- The teacher emphasizes quality, communicating to students that they are to do their best work all the time (Brophy, 1987).
- The teacher communicates to students that it is important to give their best efforts. He shows students that their successes are due to their hard work. That is, the teacher encourages effort attributions (e.g., Weiner, 1979).
- The teacher creates community of learners in the classroom. A cooperative atmosphere is fostered as students and teacher relate to each other and the larger community in positive ways (Cheng, 1994; Ugwoglu, & Walberg, 1986).
- The teacher and students work together to create and accomplish learning tasks (Noddings, 1984).
- The teacher believes students can learn, communicating that they can be successful with challenging activities (Brophy, 1985, 1987).
- The teacher consistently finds ways to complement and encourage students for their good behavior, learning success, and helpfulness in the classroom (Brophy, 1981).
- The teacher praises students in a timely manner, communicating to them what behaviors were praiseworthy and why (e.g., Brophy, 1981).
- The teacher encourages students to help the less fortunate, do good deeds for others, and act responsibly for society (Lickona, 1991).
- When students give incorrect or incomplete answers, the teacher communicates to them that mistakes are a normal, understandable, and natural part of the learning process and that most learning comes from understanding why the mistake was made and then correcting it (Oldfather & Dahl, 1994).
- The teacher encourages students to take responsibility for their actions (e.g., Lewis, 2001).
- The teacher encourages students to be proud of themselves, to be confident in their abilities and accomplishments, and to realize they have special gifts and talents to share with others (Coopersmith, 1967).

(continued)

- Students "own" work (Oldfather, 1991). For example, students can decide whether their compositions can be put on display.
- The teacher creates curiosity, interest, and excitement, grabbing students' attention by providing activities that pique students' curiosity and that are interesting and exciting (Hidi, 1990; Lepper, 1988; Raffini, 1993).
- The teacher is available to students, constantly interacting with them, providing a lot of individual and collective attention (Finn, Fulton, Zaharias, & Nye, 1989).
- The teacher creates an atmosphere of warmth, care, and concern for students. He or she uses humor in a positive way, models enthusiasm for learning, and has a positive attitude toward all students (e.g., Noddings, 1984).
- The teacher interacts in a positive, caring way with students (Noddings, 1984).
- The teacher fully enjoys being with the students. He or she communicates to them how much he or she cares for them and wants them to succeed (e.g., Noddings, 1984).
- The teacher takes advantage of many opportunities to give constructive feedback to the students. Feedback is immediate and specific to their accomplishment. The teacher uses these opportunities to encourage and gently push the students to thinking more deeply (e.g., Brophy, 1981).
- Student are given choices, including opportunities to choose aspects of their own learning (e.g., Deci & Ryan, 1985).
- The teacher stresses to students that it is important to read frequently, and to read many different types of books (Gambrell, 1996).
- The teacher affirms the different cultures and heritages of students. Different cultural ideas are infused throughout the curriculum (Webb, 1990).
- In planning lessons, the teacher allows students to be creative and think in novel ways (e.g., Nickerson, Perkins, & Smith, 1985).

Classroom instruction and content

- The teacher communicates the importance of schoolwork—that it deserves to be done carefully, including being checked and corrected (Brophy, 1987).
- The teacher checks for and monitors students' understanding of the material. He or she probes for answers, allows wait time for students to think before answering, and encourages them to self-correct their wrong answers (e.g., Tobin, 1987).
- The teacher gives clear directions in a precise, easy-to-follow way, checking for understanding as each step is completed (e.g., Brophy, 1985).
- The teacher creates cognitive conflict as part of teaching, devising activities and examples that challenge mistaken beliefs and provide cognitive dissonance (Chinn & Malhotra, 2002).
- The teacher creates activities that are concrete examples of the concepts the students are learning. The curriculum is both hands-on and minds-on, allowing students to create and explore as they learn (Stipek, 2002).
- The teacher emphasizes cooperative learning in the classroom. The students are encouraged to work together, help each other, and achieve success together (e.g., Johnson & Johnson, 1975; Nichols, 1989).
- Students engage in authentic activities—reading, writing, and completing other activities for purposes that are like real-world tasks. They are asked to think and act as scientists, writers, historians, or mathematicians (Spiro, Feltovich, Jacobson, & Coulson, 1992).
- The teacher provides activities and lessons that promote deep processing and higher-order thinking skills in students (e.g., Segal, Chipman, & Glaser, 1985).

(continued)

TABLE 2.1. *(continued)*

- The teacher assigns activities that are interesting and exciting to the students, ones that arouse the curiosity and anticipation of students (Guthrie & Wigfield, 2000).
- The teacher uses suspense and curiosity to get students' attention for an upcoming activity (Trelease, 1995).
- Over the course of the school year, the tasks and activities provided the students become more complex and appropriately difficult (Stipek, 2002).
- The teacher makes connections across lessons and activities as well as connecting what is being learned to the outside world (Guthrie et al., 1996).
- The teacher provides an assortment of books, audiotapes, videotapes, computer software, posters, pamphlets, or other learning items for students to use in their learning (Scardamalia, & Bereiter, 1992a, 1992b).
- The students use various large and small muscle movements to reinforce their learning (Trelease, 1995). For example, while doing the day's word wall activity, the students practice their words by snapping their fingers with each letter recited. They also clap, bang fists like cymbals, and make other movements to reinforce the letters in the word.
- Students are given many opportunities to use materials to assist them in their learning (e.g., Sowell, 1989).
- To teach a single concept, the teacher uses many different methods to deliver the lesson's content (e.g., Krajcik, 1991).
- The teacher spends time reviewing concepts with the students to solidify their understanding of concepts (Anderson, 1989). Content is reviewed in a meaningful way, employing many whole-language strategies, creating authentic products, using current events as context for learning, using hands-on strategies, and building excitement when introducing new material (e.g., Verhoeven & Snow, 2001).
- The teacher uses computers, tape players, overhead projectors, calculators, or other devices to assist student learning (Burbules, & Callister, 2000).
- The teacher uses activities with students that are interesting and engaging to teach the mandated state standards (Guthrie & Wigfield, 2000).
- The teacher uses games and playful activities in the lessons to reinforce a concept, review material, or make learning more enjoyable and concrete (e.g., Smith & Backman, 1975).
- The teacher values the role of the family in students' learning. He or she provides opportunities to communicate with the families and make them integral parts of the learning experience (Laseman & de Jong, 2001).
- The teacher gives students an overview of the activities for the day and week ahead, often listing them on the board, or in a classroom newsletter (Yopp & Yopp, 2000).
- The teacher uses small homogenous and heterogenous grouping for instruction (Morrow, 2002).
- Lessons are organized and well-planned. The students have enough materials for the activities and experience little "down time" between activities. The teacher is mindful of what the students have learned in previous grades as well as what skills they need to acquire at this grade level (e.g., Ginsberg & Wlodkowski, 2000).
- Students are given one-on-one instruction when necessary to clarify or extend the learning (Stipek, 2002).
- The teacher models and assists students when they are struggling to learn new material (e.g., Wood, Bruner, & Ross, 1976).
- The teacher pauses after asking students a question, allowing them time to process their thoughts and respond appropriately (Tobin, 1987).

(continued)

- The teacher provides many opportunistic mini-lessons at moments when the students' learning can be extended or clarified (Shavelson, 1983).
- The teacher provides appropriately challenging activities—individual and whole-group instruction and activities within students' zone of proximal development (i.e., the range of tasks that are too difficult for students to master alone but that can be mastered with the guidance and assistance of adults or more highly skilled students (Cheyne & Tarulli, 1999).
- The teacher gives students little reminders and hints to help them with an activity—that is, the teacher scaffolds instruction (Wood et al., 1976).
- The teacher encourages students to participate and affirms a wide variety of student responses (Collins, Brown, & Newman, 1989).
- The teacher uses explicit strategy instruction with students. They are taught many skills and strategies by the teacher modeling and thinking out loud his or her process and plan for attacking a problem or question (Pressley, Woloshyn, & Associates, 1995).
- Teachers provide explicit instruction of strategies that will improve students' understanding and comprehension of what they are reading (Pressley et al., 1992).
- The teacher talks aloud, modeling thought processes while demonstrating activities and strategies for students (Bandura, 1986).
- The teacher does dramatic and expressive read-alouds that are really engaging for the students. The use of different voices for the characters as well as facial expression and gestures add to the ambiance created by the teacher (Trelease, 1995).
- Students are encouraged to bid for answers, read chorally during story activities, and share their learning with others (Meyerson & Kulesza, 2001).

Classroom management

- The teacher keeps the class on schedule by allocating and monitoring enough time to complete activities throughout the day (Anderson, 1989).
- The teacher constantly assesses the students' engagement, understanding, and behavior during the course of the day. The teacher constantly monitors the entire class, even while working one-on-one with a student (e.g., Wharton-McDonald et al., 1998).
- The teacher uses parents and adults in the classroom to assist students (e.g., do guided reading with them). Adults are welcome in the classroom (e.g., Walker & Scherry, 2001).
- The teacher clearly communicates expectations for student behavior and what students are to learn (e.g., Brophy, 1985).
- The teacher and students discuss the reasons behind the activities, rules, procedures, and routines the students perform each day. The students understand why they are being asked to behave in appropriate ways and to learn new material (e.g., Brophy, 1985, 1987).
- When students are disciplined for their behaviors, the punishment that follows is a natural consequence for the transgression. If the punishment is a loss of a privilege, there is opportunity to earn the privilege back through good behavior (Anderson, 1989).
- The teacher provides extrinsic motivators for students as rewards for appropriate behaviors and activities. The teacher uses these extrinsic motivators not as bribes, but as a tool to extend learning (e.g., Bandura & Schunk, 1981).

(continued)

TABLE 2.1. *(continued)*

- The teacher uses classroom management techniques that are positive, constructive, and encouraging toward students. When the teacher needs to correct a student's behavior, he or she does so quickly and privately, getting the student back on task as soon as possible and with as little disruption to the rest of the class a possible (Evertson, Emmer, & Worsham, 1999).
- When the teacher has to correct a student's behaviors, the teacher's communications are positive and kind but firm (Anderson, 1989).
- The students are given responsibilities to help maintain the cleanliness and orderliness of their classroom (Anderson, 1989).
- The teacher has devised rules, procedures, policies, and routines for her students that are useful and provide smooth transitions within lessons and between activities (e.g., Evertson et al., 1999).
- The teacher and students move smoothly from one activity to another with minimal disruption (Anderson, 1989).
- Students are allowed to choose their own areas to work during designated times throughout the day (Morrow, 2002).

---

ally low student engagement in these classes, as the teachers used many negative classroom management practices and assigned students easy tasks.

During our observations in the classrooms of Ms. Ames, Ms. Boone, Ms. Carroll, and Ms. Davenport, we were first struck by the drabness of the classroom environment. The walls in these four classrooms included few colorful decorations, no informative bulletin boards, and few examples of student work or other accomplishments. Frequent management problems were common. Often the students were very noisy, restless, and disruptive, and the teachers had to warn them two, three, or more times to get settled. For example, in Ms. Ames's room, a frequent classroom management sequence would involve the students getting off-task and talking in loud voices. The teacher would then remind them to quiet down in a louder voice. The students responded by ignoring the teacher's plea and talking that much louder. The teacher then began screaming directions and commands to her students. "QUIET DOWN! I will not call on children who are screaming at me!"

Ms. Ames, Ms. Boone, Ms. Carroll, and Ms. Davenport often used critical and punitive tones with misbehaving students, criticizing and punishing publicly and then admonishing harshly. Ms. Carroll had the following exchange with a misbehaving student: "Student X, I'm not going to ask you to sit down again. I'm going to count to three . . . one . . . two . . . if you don't sit down, you'll be out in the hall . . . three." The student finally sat down after being threatened and publicly reprimanded.

TABLE 2.2. Elements Undermining Motivation in Grade 2 Classrooms

Unattractive physical environment and classroom atmosphere

Physical environment

- Few examples of student work, projects, or accomplishments adorn the walls of the classroom, making obvious to the class that they do not accomplish a great deal that is worthwhile (e.g., Brophy, 1985, 1987; Doyle, 1986).
- Some room environments are quite sparse, others are decorated for appearance's sake; few posters or bulletin boards are used during curricular lessons (e.g., Doyle, 1986).

Psychological atmosphere

- The teacher does not have a positive attitude or high confidence about students and learning. The teacher does not communicate to students that he or she has high expectations for their learning (Brophy & Good, 1970).
- The teacher gives messages to students that the work is difficult and that they may not be successful even if they put forth their best efforts. The students are not encouraged to try their best at all times (e.g., Weiner, 1979).
- The teacher communicates to the students that accomplishing the task and doing it correctly are more important than learning the material. There is little talk of learning from one's mistakes (e.g., Nicholls, 1989).
- The teacher's message to students reminds them the most important part of school is getting the correct answer or high grades (Ames, 1984; Nicholls, 1989).
- The teacher uses practices such as calling out of grades, posting papers with grades visible on bulletin boards, or displaying assignments in the room or hallway where grades can be seen by other students or adults (Ames, 1984; Nicholls, 1989).
- The teacher frequently reminds students that they are preparing for standardized tests and that what they are learning is only valuable because it will be tested (Murphy, Shannon, Johnston, & Hansen, 1998).
- The atmosphere fostered by the teacher is not cooperative. No sense of community is fostered where the students are encouraged to be helpful, respectful, and trustful towards one another (e.g., Cheng, 1994; Ugwoglu & Walberg, 1986).
- The students are asked to complete tasks where winning or being the best is valued rather than working together and improving (e.g., Nicholls, 1989).
- The teacher consistently reminds students that the work they are doing is difficult (e.g., Deci, 1975; Harter, 1978; White, 1959).
- The teacher communicates to students in a way that is pressuring to them. Often the teacher talking about the difficulty of upcoming assignments, tests, and projects without letting the students know that they will be supported in their learning. Often the tasks described by the teacher seem insurmountable to the student. This may increase student anxiety and fear of failure (e.g., Hebb, 1955).
- The teacher gives very little praise to students. The teacher does not call student attention to their good deeds, thinking, or participation in class. (e.g., Brophy, 1981).
- The teacher rarely checks to see if students understand the concept being taught, gives little help to struggling students, provides them with answers, or mostly uses the "initiate–respond–evaluate" strategy when asking questions (e.g., Mehan, 1979).
- The evaluative information the teacher gives students is often negative, emphasizing differences between students, embarrassing students by highlighting their mistakes in front of the class, or making accountability public (Skinner, 1953).

(continued)

TABLE 2.2. *(continued)*

- The teacher does not give students opportunities to have power over their own learning. Students do not have choices in their work (Deci, 1975).
- The teacher does not allow students to use their creativity or imaginations during assignments. The products the students make are to be the same as the teacher's model (e.g., Charles & Runco, 2001).
- Teachers do not actively promote excitement in their students, or they immediately quash any signs of excitement when they happen (e.g., Stipek, 2002).
- The teacher is very quick to react in a harsh, negative tone with students when misbehavior occurs (Chien, 1984).
- The teacher often communicates to students using a loud, negative, harsh, punitive, or angry tone (e.g., Skinner, 1953).
- The teacher does not clearly communicate with students, often sending them conflicting messages about his or her expectations and directions for assignments, or their performance (Llatov, Shamai, Hertz-Lazarovitz, & Mayer-Young, 1998).
- The teacher does not communicate the importance of reading or the value of books. The teacher sends students the message that reading is not a skill that they will find necessary or enjoyable (Brophy, 1987).
- Teachers do not provide situations and incentives for students to be honest, or they create situations in which students may be tempted to be dishonest (Miller, 1987).

Classroom instruction and content

- The teacher does not check that students are understanding what he or she is teaching, what they are reading, or what they are supposed to be doing (Evertson, Emmer, & Worsham, 2002; Wood et al., 1976).
- The teacher does not probe students for their background knowledge. The teacher automatically assumes that the students are familiar with the topic and proceeds with the lesson (Anderson & Pearson, 1984).
- The teacher does not give specific, focused directions for the students to follow when completing an activity (Evertson et al., 2002).
- The teacher does not have a focused plan for what the students are learning. Often the students are confused about what they are learning and why they are learning it (e.g., Evertson et al., 2002).
- The teacher rarely has students work together on assignments or projects. Most of their work is done individually, with little opportuntiy to cooperate with others (Johnson & Johnson, 1975).
- The activities and lessons assigned by the teacher are routine, boring, simplistic, or lack excitement and stimulation (e.g., Wlodkowski & Jaynes, 1991).
- The tasks and activities provided by the teacher are too easy for most students in the class. The activities are of a low cognitive level, demanding little of the students (e.g., Csikszentmihalyi, 1990, 1997; Deci, 1975; White, 1959).
- The teacher uses many initiate–respond–evaluate sequences with students, sounding more like a lecturer than a discussion leader (Stipek, 2002).
- The activities and lessons the teacher uses are not connected to prior learning, other subjects, or experiences of the students (e.g., Guthrie et al., 1996)
- The basal readers, maps, textbooks, and other materials are out of date (Martinez & McGee, 2000).
- The teacher does not use opportunities to connect lessons to other concepts in the curriculum, to previous learning experiences, or to the outside world (e.g., Guthrie et al., 1996).

(continued)

- The teacher does not provide opportunities to open the lines of communication between families and students. Parents may be seen as adversaries rather than partners in education (Laseman & deJong, 2001).
- The teacher has not properly planned and/or made full preparations for the lessons of the day. The students lack all the materials necessary to complete an activity, or are experiencing long delays as the teacher scrambles for the next lesson to teach (e.g., Evertson et al., 2002).
- The pace of the teacher and the class is too slow for the majority of the students (e.g., Kulik & Kulik, 1984; Southern & Jones, 1991).
- The teacher does not model the thinking process, or the steps to take in completing an activity. No concrete examples are given to students to follow (e.g., Bandura, 1986).
- Students are not given time to process questions and think about answes before they are called on by the teachers. There is also little opportuntity to self-correct wrong answers (e.g., Tobin, 1987).
- The teacher looks for the one answer that he or she feels is "correct" and dismisses all the other possible answers from students. Students are not validated for coming up with novel solutions or thinking "outside the box" (Collins et al., 1989).
- The teacher gives students information that is completely or partially incorrect (e.g., Steipek, 2002)
- The teacher does not help the students become independent learners. They do not know what they are to do after they finish an assignment early or have extra time for an activity. The students have to be prompted many times to find something to do (e.g., Zimmerman, 1990a, 1990b).
- The teacher does much of the work for students, giving them too much help and not allowing them to think for themselves or come up with their own answers (e.g., Wood et al., 1976).
- The teacher does not support students using the text to find answers to questions, think about new material, or stretch their imaginations (e.g., Stipek, 2002).
- The art component that is supposed to complement the learning activity actually becomes the focus of the activity, to the exclusion of necessary reading and writing (Allington, 1984; Calkins, 2001).

Classroom management

- The teacher does not check for the progress of students in their work. He or she fails to notice that students are off-task or are confused about the activity at hand, or allows disruptions to occur during classtime (e.g., Wharton-McDonald et al., 1998).
- The teacher does not keep track of time well, often allowing too much or too little time for an activity. The students are frequently late to their appointments (e.g., lunch, special classes; e.g., Anderson, 1989).
- The teacher does not allow or have adult assistants in the classroom; when the teacher does have adult volunteers, they are not used appropriately. For example, they are only used to prepare materials rather than work with students some or all of the time (e.g., Walker & Scherry, 2001).
- The teacher allows students or adults to interrupt his or her teaching (Weinstein & Mignano, 1997).
- The teacher uses a harsh tone of voice and reprimands students for misbehavior (Weinstein & Mignano, 1997).
- The teacher uses negative, punishing techniques to maintain order in the classroom. The teacher may be threatening, overly stern, or angry with students (e.g., Evertson et al., 2002).

(continued)

TABLE 2.2. *(continued)*

- The teacher uses a system of time-outs either within the classroom or outside of the classroom to control student behavior. The teacher may also seat students away from the rest of the classroom group for extended periods of time (Turner & Watson, 1999).
- The teacher makes grades, punishment, errors, or behavior public to all of the students in the class. The teacher often names and singles out one student to make an example of in front of the class, has the students call in their grades aloud, or posts grades on a bulletin board (e.g., Doyle, 1986; Hoffman, 1970).
- As a classroom management technique, the teacher tells the students that they will have to do extra school work as their punishment (Weinstein & Mignano, 1997).
- The teacher provides rewards (e.g., stickers, candy, tickets for later prizes, more free time) to reinforce a desired behavior. Additionally, the teacher provides rewards for an intrinsically motivating activity (e.g., the teacher uses rewards such as pizza certificates to encourage reading in students who like to read and read a great deal; Lepper, Green, & Nisbett, 1973).
- The teacher has not established rules or systems to accomplish tasks throughout the day, such as lining up, passing papers, collecting homework and so forth (e.g., Evertson et al., 2002).

TABLE 2.3. Number of Supporting and Undermining Motivational Practices for Each Grade 2 Teacher

Teacher	Number of supporting motivational practices	Number of undermining motivational practices
Low-engaging		
Ames	21	42
Boone	20	28
Carroll	19	25
Moderately engaging		
Davenport	26	17
Eldridge	38	15
Farley	37	10
Humboldt	25	3
Highly engaging		
Squint	63	9
Davidson	74	5

After regaining some control of a class, these four teachers often needed to stop additional times to warn or punish misbehaving students again. Students in these classes did not respond well to the management techniques used by their teachers.

One possible contributing factor for the management problems was the lack of student self-regulation and autonomy. These four teachers had not set up effective routines, procedures, and expectations for behaving and learning in their classrooms. The closest to self-regulation that was observed was when the students would sit at their seats and do nothing but wait for the next set of directions, after they had finished an assignment. In fact, Ms. Carroll frequently gave directions to the students to sit and wait when they were finished with their work. During one observation, a student told her that he was finished with his work and she replied, "Just sit and wait patiently until we are ready." With nothing to do that would sustain his interest or promote his learning, the student went back to his desk, started to bother his neighbors, and then began to wander around the room. Noticing this behavior, Ms. Carroll said the student's name harshly, gave him a warning, and repeated that he should sit and wait until the whole class was ready to continue. Several minutes later, when the student was again bothering classmates around him, the teacher gave him a time-out in the hallway. By not setting up routines, not giving students activities options, and not encouraging them to self-regulate their learning, the long amounts of time between activities gave students many opportunities to misbehave.

The large number of classroom management problems observed was concomitant with problems in lesson planning and instruction. These teachers often struggled to get through the objectives of a particular lesson, if there were objectives at all. Student engagement was severely compromised when the teacher had to stop every 3 or 4 minutes to get the students back on track and paying attention. During many of our visits, we observed lessons that were not planned or organized carefully. In one instance, Ms. Ames was passing out a set of reading test booklets the students had started the day before. The teacher passed out all of the booklets she had and then found out that some of the students did not receive theirs. She told the students that she lost them and gave them new booklets. One of the students was visibly upset, on the verge of tears. The teacher was totally oblivious to the student's disappointment and gave her directions to complete the tests that the class did the previous day. On other occasions, the teachers planned and organized lessons that did not seem to accomplish the curricular objectives. Often these teachers would plan activities with an art component that was to be accompanied by some reading and writing. In her class, however, Ms. Davenport commented, "Math, reading? We have no time for math or reading. We have to get these Christmas [projects] done." Allowing the students to color and decorate often became more important than academic coverage.

In these four classrooms, the lessons did not engage or excite students because of the low cognitive demands of the activities. The majority of the lessons required students to fill out worksheets or read from basal readers. Even lesson topics that had the potential to be interesting, promote critical thinking, and support students' learning were made trivial through the use of uninspiring workbooks and basal lessons.

For example, Ms. Carroll's class was reading a story in their basal series about a dinosaur becoming a family pet. Ms. Carroll had her students close their eyes and imagine finding a dinosaur in the backyard. The students were very involved in the imagination activity, and had difficulty keeping their eyes closed. Many of them put their hands up to share and were very excited about what they had thought about in their imaginations, but Ms. Carroll dismissed their participation, not wanting to take the time to hear what they had imagined, in order to start a workbook page requiring the students to write three reasons they would use to persuade their mother to keep the dinosaur. The students were eager to talk about their reasons, but the teacher again dismissed their enthusiasm and told them to write three sentences so they would be finished with the workbook page before recess. The teacher diminished an activity that engaged the students and could have been a terrific catalyst for student writing. She also elevated a frustrating, tedious workbook exercise. Publisher materials drove the vast majority of activities in the low-engaging classrooms.

In the low-engaging classrooms, the observers watched many undemanding, whole-group lessons, experiences that did not challenge, produce interest, or motivate students. In Ms. Ames's class, for example, the students often remarked that the lessons were too easy. She would reply, "I don't like it when you say that," instead of taking the students' comments as a hint to increase the demand of an activity or change it entirely to something more engaging.

When Ms. Ames, Ms. Boone, Ms. Carroll, and Ms. Davenport were giving their students instructions, the methods were often in the form of the initiate–respond–evaluate pattern. They usually accepted only one correct answer or interpretation. Often these teachers would simply tell students if they were wrong and move on to another volunteer. For example, Ms. Boone was helping her students correct the punctuation and capitalization on some sentences she had written on the board. Student Y gave an answer that Ms. Boone accepted as correct, and she moved onto the next sentence. A few minutes later, Ms. Boone realized that Student Y had made an error. She then said, "On number 5, you made a mistake, Student Y. You were wrong." She then encouraged the members of the class to capitalize on Student Y's mistake and fix the sentence, instead of allowing the student to think about the sentence again and fix it himself.

Additionally, this group of teachers did not stop regularly to check for understanding, or did not allow students some wait time to think about what they were saying, and did not grant the time required for students to self-correct wrong answers. These four teachers gave very little praise, no scaffolding, and quite a bit of ineffective feedback. They were stern, negative, punitive, and publicly critical of students, often making the children in their classrooms aware of their failures. The atmospheres in these classrooms were quite negative and competitive. The teachers emphasized getting the correct answers rather than student effort. The goal at most moments of the day was to satisfy the teacher's demand; longer-term goals also did little to inspire students, such as preparing for standardized tests.

Students in these classrooms displayed passive attention at best, with more than half of the students typically not participating in the lessons. When assigned seatwork, the majority of the students were off-task, not using strategies the teacher taught. The children were often chatty, restless, or doing other things (drawing, reading, fiddling around in their desks, bothering their neighbors) as these teachers presented their lessons. Teachers and students in these classrooms generally were not enthusiastic about lessons, activities, and being together in the classroom.

In addition to the commonalities among the teachers in this low-engaging group, each also had unique ways of undermining motivation. Thus, we consider each low-engaging teacher individually.

Ms. Ames. Ms. Ames had twice the number of practices undermining motivation (42) as those supporting motivation (21). Much of the chaos in her class was due to ineffective room arrangements, negative classroom management techniques, problematic lesson planning, and discouragement of student effort. During one observation, the students' desks were pushed into a circle around the perimeter of the classroom. The desks were facing the walls, away from the center of the circle. Ms. Ames then stood in the center of the circle and yelled at the students for not looking at her when she was talking. She also frequently shushed students, tapped on the overhead projector to get their attention, and clapped loudly when tapping on the projector did not work. Comments such as the following were frequent: "Ssssshhhhhh!" [*tapping on the overhead*], "Focus here, guys. Sssshhhhhh!" "I can't teach when you're talking." "Student Z, Student Y, stop talking." Then, Student Z might say he was not talking and tattle on another student as the culprit! Ms. Ames frequently became very angry, for example, yelling "Boys and girls, open your books. Raise your hands." She also relied on singling out, publicly criticizing, and humiliating students. During one observation, the research team noted a message written on the board above one student's desk. "Student A, you left a mess for me to clean up. I don't like it! Ms. A" As a result, when the student entered the room in the morning, he not only knew that his teacher was upset with him, the rest of the class did, too. We were somewhat taken aback during her interview when she claimed, "Positive discipline is the big overall thing that I try to do. Trying to emphasize the positive, trying very hard not to have so much exterior stuff, but have natural consequences happening to kids." Although she seemed to believe she was being positive with her students, her methods were not successful, and were extremely negative in tone and content.

Ms. Ames also had difficulties planning and organizing her lessons. She frequently taught lessons that had vague and confusing objectives, gave worksheets to students that were disconnected from anything the students had learned, and discouraged student creativity. During a math lesson using geo-boards and rubber bands to construct shapes, the students discovered many different ways to stretch the rubber bands to make regular and irregular polygons. Ms. Ames became very upset at their discoveries and demanded that they make the exact triangle shapes that she was making on her board. On another occasion, a student had written a poem and asked Ms. Ames to read it. The teacher told her that it wasn't a poem because it was too long and did not rhyme. She emphasized to the student that all poems rhyme, or they are not considered good poems. There were many instances such as this in which Ms. Ames gave negative feedback, discouraged students' efforts, and communicated little praise and encouragement to her students.

Ms. Boone. Ms. Boone had similar problems creating lessons that were appropriately challenging and engaging. We observed 20 practices supporting and 28 practices undermining motivation in her classroom.

Ms. Boone used many out-of-date materials, including maps with the USSR still prominent and basal readers from the early 1980s. Although her school adopted several new basal series since then, she commented that "They're [the 1980's basal] in bad shape, but I've never found a book that's better for teaching what I want to teach them." In her reading lessons, Ms. Boone created a bit of excitement when she introduced a new story, but then focused on decoding words and round-robin-type reading instead of comprehending and connecting the story to personal experiences or previous learning. Her focus was so narrowly on decoding that the class frequently read a selection two or three times in a row so each student had a chance to read aloud. During these reading sessions, little emphasis was placed on comprehension of other than the main idea. After reading one fable, she posed a question about the main idea and said, "Let's see how many of you can answer this question. [Nine students out of 16 raised their hands.] Only nine of you can tell me how the bear has lost its tail? Then I guess you didn't read, because if you did, then you would know." Such negative comments were made in this classroom on a regular basis.

The main emphasis of Ms. Boone's classroom was getting the right answers, getting high grades, and preparing for the standardized tests. Although Ms. Boone did allow for some student choice, she always constructed the choices so that they followed her agenda. She consistently reminded her students what she was "looking for" (i.e., question marks, punctuation, spelling, neatness) as they completed an assignment. She made the announcement after winter vacation about a new grading policy. "You have now spent $1\frac{1}{2}$ years writing. Words not correctly capitalized will have a point taken off." Similarly, she said during another language arts lesson that "I need you to write five sentences, because five sentences will give me 30 points to grade." During that same lesson, one student brought her paper to the teacher for feedback. Ms. Boone said, "You didn't follow directions. I told you. You have to have someone talking in your sentences. [The teacher then erased all the work on the student's paper.] You didn't understand the lesson. We have been over this a dozen times. You didn't listen. Now you don't know." The teacher then sent the student back to her seat without an explanation. Although she made students aware of their mistakes and shortcomings, she occasionally gave them a bit of praise and encouragement, such as "It's not how many red marks you put on your paper, but did you make marks so that you know where your mistakes are?" The observers felt that the little positive in such remarks was overwhelmed by the overwhelmingly negative messages the teacher provided.

Ms. Carroll. Ms. Carroll tried to create interesting lessons that were connected to previous learning. The researchers observed 19 practices that might support motivation in her classroom. Some of the lesson previews generated excitement: "I'm working on a surprise for you. Our new science kits came, so we can start new science lessons tomorrow." Also, the students often were engaged in listening to Ms. Carroll read stories from big books, which permitted them to see the text and pictures clearly.

Unfortunately, the observers also witnessed 25 practices that might undermine motivation. In general, the tasks in Ms. Carroll's class were very undemanding and uninteresting to students, with artwork, rather than reading and writing, the focus of many activities. Additional problems with the lessons in Ms. Carroll's classroom involved her style of direct instruction. Often the students would be interested in learning about the topic that she had introduced, but became restless and off-task as she talked on and on about it. The lessons were not interactive, her view seeming to be that the students should be sponges, absorbing the information in her lectures. With her unapproachable demeanor and rigid classroom management style, she quashed the excitement that she did create with interesting activities. For example, during a science lesson dealing with the principles of balance, the students were working cooperatively to build a mobile out of straws, paper clips, and paper of various shapes, sizes, and textures. Realizing that his mobile was finally balanced, one student jumped up and down calling, "Ms. Carroll, Ms. Carroll!" to have her come over and see his success with the project. Instead of looking at his mobile and affirming his accomplishment, she shushed him, told him to calm down, and ignored his mobile. The student, visibly dejected, went back to his group and sulked on the floor with the rest of his group. Situations similar to this, in which a student accomplished something and Ms. Carroll ignored the student, were common.

The most problematic practice observed in Ms. Carroll's classroom was her frequent punishment of students for their misbehavior. During the majority of the visits to her classroom, two students would be seated at either end of a long, rectangular table in the back of the room. These students were in perpetual time-out, given many scoldings by the teacher, and virtually ignored by the other students. Ms. Carroll isolated other students by having them spend time in the hallway when they acted out in class. There was a great deal of negativism in this classroom.

Ms. Davenport. With 26 practices that supported and 19 practices that undermined motivation, Ms. Davenport was more positive in tone than the other three low-engaging teachers, but had similar problems with classroom management, content and instruction, and task difficulty. The strength of Ms. Davenport's teaching was her ability to connect with students, encouraging them to be happy about school and themselves. She had many nicknames for her students (e.g., My Friend, Kiddo, Darlin') and was affectionate with them. Ms. Davenport communicated many messages that built students' self-esteem: "This is sooooo tough, but not for you, because you are genius children." She gave the students tons of encouragement and praise! The students received literal pats on the back and hugs at their request. (This was a school where patting children on the back and hugging them was acceptable.) It was obvious to the research team that she valued her students and wanted them to be successful. One day a student brought two medals from his father and grandfather who had fought in the Gulf War. Although the show-and-tell of the medals disrupted class, Ms. Davenport gave her undivided attention to the student and talked with him about the medals and the pride the student had for his family. The second graders obviously adored their teacher and desired her attention and approval, but Ms. Davenport did not use this to her advantage to get them excited about their reading and writing.

In addition to her care for her students, Ms. Davenport was incredibly entertaining. Her sense of humor was clearly evident. The week before break in November was known as "Thinksgiving." When questioning students, she acted more like a game show host than a second-grade teacher: "I have a question, for twelve bazillion dollars or his and her ski boats, what is a noun?" In getting their attention, she would announce, "Ladies and germs, boys and gorillas, listen please." She also tried to make learning exciting by being overly dramatic. During one lesson on the life of an octopus, Ms. Davenport faked crying, "Now this is the sad part, when the eggs hatch, the octopus dies." The students went absolutely nuts for her play-acting and sense of humor. Unfortunately, rather than getting them excited about learning and interested in the material, Ms. Davenport's tactics only seemed to increase off-task behaviors. Consequently, Ms. Davenport spent more time reminding the students to be quiet and pay attention than she did instructing the class.

Much of the time was spent quieting the students. Consequently, Ms. Davenport sometimes took a half hour to complete one worksheet on the overhead projector (i.e., so that students only had to copy answers, rather than do the worksheet themselves). Worked-out worksheets were typical of very low cognitive demands in this classroom. The bulk of the lessons were filled with workbook pages, art tasks, cut-and-paste activities, and the like, with students receiving help even to do easy activities: "I'm sort of giving you the answers anyway. Put in whatever you want. If you don't have an idea, you can copy mine." That she had spent many years teaching preschool and kindergarten was evident in her "playtime" style and low task-difficulty. The students seemed to be in a holding pattern for third grade, with no real academic improvement apparent during our year of observations.

Summary. In the classrooms of the four low engaging teachers, we found classroom management problems, poor instructional methods, and negative classroom atmospheres. These teachers assigned very easy, undemanding tasks. The many classroom management problems combined with tasks of low difficulty. As a result, these teachers' students were often off-task and rarely cognitively engaged. Although each of these teachers encouraged academic motivation in some ways, their teaching also undermined motivation in other ways. The undermining aspects of their instruction did more to determine the engagement in their classrooms (or more precisely, the lack of it) than did their attempts to motivate their students.

Moderately Engaging Teachers

The second group of teachers—Ms. Eldridge, Ms. Farley, and Ms. Humboldt—were more able to engage their students and use effective methods of classroom management than the low-engaging teachers. The three teachers in this group created learning environments for their students that were generally positive, warm, and caring. For example, Ms. Humboldt gave much encouragement: "I have seen lots of people who have not raised their hands, and I have a feeling that they know the answer." In addition to a positive classroom atmosphere, the teachers in this group organized their rooms to be "student" friendly, with desk arrangements, learning centers, and reading areas that promoted cooperation, exploration, and student participation. During the latter part of the school year, Ms. Farley created a tree house with her students in their reading corner. With cardboard boxes, brown construction paper, a little paint, and a sign that read "Magic Tree House, Members Only," the class had made their version of the tree house featured in a series of books by Mary Pope Osborne. In these classrooms, the students were often seated in pairs or table groups to encourage working together and assisting each other. The teachers created areas for reading that were comfortable, inviting, and packed with many books for students to enjoy. The bulletin boards, walls, and hallways were covered with decorations, posters, signs, artwork, and other symbols of student achievement. These rooms were colorful and cheerfully decorated as the seasons and holidays progressed during the year. Ms. Eldridge, for example, had a garden growing in her classroom with plants lined up on the windowsill and in every corner of the room. "This is one of my homes," she said during her interview, "I spend more time here some days than I do in my real home. The kids do too." Ms. Eldridge's classroom, and the other classrooms in this group, were inviting, safe, comfortable places, much like a home.

Another commonality among Ms. Eldridge, Ms. Farley, and Ms. Humboldt was a system of classroom management focused on everyday routines and procedures. The teachers encouraged their students to be self-regulated and helped them make choices about their learning. In Ms. Eldridge's class, the students automatically pulled out other work to complete, chose a book from the classroom library, played a game with a partner, or observed at the science station when they finished their work. Some days the students were so excited to get to their other activities that they had to be reminded not to rush through their seatwork. From the daily chores of turning in homework and transitioning between activities to procedures such as sharpening pencils and lining up for restroom breaks, the students in these classrooms understood what they were supposed to be doing at the appointed time and how to accomplish their tasks. The morning rituals in each classroom were quite organized and elaborate. In Ms. Farley's room, the students arrived in the classroom, hung up their coats, moved their sticks on the lunch count poster, put away their homework folders in the designated basket, moved their stick person on the "People Graph" chart, put away their materials from home, sharpened their pencils, took out their writing journals, and started their journal entry for the day. What was even more impressive was that the students completed their morning jobs without any reminders and in less than 5 minutes!

In the classrooms of Ms. Humboldt, Ms. Farley, and Ms. Eldridge, the students became self-regulated because they practiced these daily routines at the beginning of the year until they became second nature. If reminders were needed, the teachers used gentle tones, and as a result, the students were generally appropriate in their reactions. Because of these well-developed routines and procedures, there were many fewer instances of teacher correction of a student's behavior compared to the classrooms overseen by low-engaging teachers. The moderately engaging teachers established goals for their students, made their expectations clearly known, provided detailed directions, checked for student understanding of directions before activities began, and made smooth transitions from one lesson to the next. These classrooms were quite organized, and for the most part ran very smoothly.

In developing lesson content, Ms. Humboldt, Ms. Farley, and Ms. Eldridge provided curriculum lessons that made many connections between the learning activity of the day and the students' previous knowledge, real world events, or cross-curricular topics. During the month of February, Ms. Eldridge's class studied the government of the United States and the presidents. Each student chose a president and was able to get books, look up information on the Internet, and have his or her family help to create a short report and project celebrating that president's life. One student even sculpted a bust of Jimmy Carter using a recipe for Rice Crispy treats. The bust was so creative (not to mention mouth watering) that Ms. Eldridge helped the student write a letter to the Carter Museum to see if they would accept his entry for an exhibit. Lesson topics like these were meaningful, interesting, and filled with effective integrations of the curriculum.

Despite the positive classroom environments, effective management, and interesting curriculum topics, often task and assignment difficulties were low in these classrooms. Ms. Humboldt, Ms. Farley, and Ms. Eldridge had many tasks and assignments with a fun or game-like twist. These activities often "grabbed" their students' attention by providing opportunities to use manipulatives, play a game, or design art. For example, Ms. Farley frequently had a "Making Words" activity (Cunningham & Hall, 1994). The students were very excited when the letters began to be passed out and the teacher cleared the wall pocket chart. The activity was a wonderful method of studying words, spelling, and building vocabulary. Unfortunately, the words that Ms. Farley chose were much too easy for her students. The class figured out the words quickly and accurately. They did not stretch their minds to make connections between words. The activity itself encouraged student participation, on-task behavior, and some engagement, but the low difficulty level did not further the students' word recognition or vocabulary skills.

In addition, these three teachers relied on textbook exercises, basal readers, and easy-to-complete worksheets. Some worksheets were so "minds-off" that they could be completed without even reading any of the accompanying material. After a small-group reading meeting, Ms. Eldridge told her students, "Don't worry if you haven't finished reading the story. You can complete the worksheets without having read it." The students then raced through their assignment, disregarded the story, and found something else to do with their time (e.g., activities like reading a book of their choosing or finishing a piece of writing).

Although these teachers were able to gain initial interest in these activities due to their ease of completion, engagement was not sustained throughout lessons. Students in these classrooms often became bored, restless, or off-task. In comparison to the low-engaging teachers, Ms. Humboldt, Ms. Farley, and Ms. Eldridge were better at managing their classrooms, creating interesting lessons, and providing support for student learning. The activities assigned to the students, however, required little thought. These three teachers were happy and enthusiastic about being with their students and supporting student success, albeit often with respect to easy tasks.

Despite their similarities, the three moderately engaging teachers had distinct differences. As with the low-engaging teachers, we review each teacher's strengths and weaknesses.

Ms. Humboldt. Ms. Humboldt was only able to participate in this study for a brief time at the beginning of the school year. The research team was able to make two visits in her classroom, spending about 3 hours of observation time. They were able to document 25 supporting practices, however, as compared to some teachers in the low-engaging group who had fewer positive practices observed over the course of the entire year. With only three questionable practices noted during those observations, Ms. Humboldt had gotten her students off to a great start.

We saw the students in Ms. Humboldt's classroom composing and illustrating a number of stories that were displayed in the hallway. The students wrote coherent stories of two to six pages in length, with three or four sentences on each page, with few errors in mechanics and usage. The students were also reading many books, most at grade level or above. Each student's desk had a neat pile of books to read after the child had finished his or her seatwork.

Ms. Humboldt provided her students with many authentic, hands-on experiences. Many of these activities connected science and language arts. In the fall of the year, her students were working on their nature-spying activity. The students constructed a journal of what they observed while walking around the school grounds as well as in their yards and neighborhoods. Ms. Humboldt then used their journals in science lessons about the seasons and how animals and plants prepare themselves for winter. In her interview, Ms. Humboldt commented that she would revisit the journals at the end of the year, having the students make similar entries about winter changing to spring. By also using high-quality literature, like *Four Stories of Four Seasons* by Tomie dePaola, Ms. Humboldt made additional connections between the nature-spying activity, the students' experiences, and the enjoyment of the different seasons.

Ms. Humboldt used a very positive, calm tone with her students. She was quite effective in her classroom management, with little public criticism of students. When she corrected a child, she went to the student, whispered words in his or her ear, and reminded the student what to do. Ms. Humboldt praised and encouraged her students. She communicated to them that their efforts were important, that she could see they were thinking, and that they could succeed and do well. Ms. Humboldt also communicated, by her words and example, that kindness is important. For example, Ms. Humboldt took time to talk with her students about something they could do to help the community. One day she announced that the students could bring food to school to be distributed to the poor. On Veterans Day, the class attended a schoolwide patriotic service. Then the class discussed relatives who were veterans and ways they could thank them. By her lessons, positive management, and example to her students, Ms. Humboldt sent the message that learning was connected to others and all people are valued.

Despite the connections Ms. Humboldt made between curricular areas, the tasks she assigned were often undemanding. After reading the dePaola book aloud, Ms. Humboldt handed out copies to all the students. As a whole, the class made a list of the nouns in the book, and the teacher wrote them on the board. The students then went through the book to find the words on the board, circling them. After that was finished, they colored the pictures. This task was pretty easy for the students, and many of them rushed through the circling to begin coloring. The teacher did not ask the students to re-read the story, a task that would have been more demanding and could have produced more understanding of the story and fluent reading of the words in the text.

Ms. Farley. Ms. Farley created a very warm, positive classroom atmosphere through her demeanor and classroom management practices. The researchers observed 37 practices supporting and 10 practices undermining motivation in her classroom. Above the chalkboard a sign read "Because Nice Matters!" This sign seemed to be the motto and rationale for everything that occurred in Ms. Farley's classroom. She used a very soft-spoken, pleasant tone with her students, often reminding them to give "gentle reminders" to each other if they forgot something or were misbehaving. She encouraged students to think about their actions and take responsibility for their learning. When two boys were being disruptive during an activity on the rug, Ms. Farley said, "Boys, you need to make a decision. You are responsible for you." The students then chose to move to different spots on the carpet, on opposite sides from each other. After they were settled, Ms. Farley thanked them for making a good decision, and then immediately included them in the next part of the activity.

In addition to these gentle behavior reminders and an emphasis on kindness, the classroom ran very smoothly because of its dedication to routines and procedures. In addition to their morning routine, the students knew how they were to get in line, how to find an activity to do when they had completed work, and how to care for the class pets. One interesting routine occurred after Silent Sustained Reading (SSR) time. When the students were finished with their individual reading, they grouped themselves with one or two other students. Each student then took turns telling the group about the book, a favorite part, or an interesting character. Another member of the group then said, "I heard you say . . ." and filled in the sentence to show the presenter that he or she had understood what was said. The presenter then corrected the student if there was a misunderstanding, and then another student presented what he or she had read. This practice encouraged speaking and listening skills, as well as made students accountable for what they were reading during that block of individual reading time.

Ms. Farley often allowed students to choose their own places to sit in the room during work time. The flexible seating was one way students made choices and took responsibility for their learning.

Ms. Farley's classroom was well organized, with a place for everything and everything in its place. Plastic containers were filled and labeled to make it easy for students to find what they needed and to put away their materials.

Most impressive were the containers filled with books the students had written, illustrated, and published. The books were an integral part of the classroom library, and students were often seen reading books that other students had written during reading time. The students were made to feel like real authors as they completed the writing process with the "publication" of their book so that it was available for other students to read. Some of the stories were more complex and mechanically correct than others. The norm seemed to be about two sentences per page with fair mechanics.

The lessons that Ms. Farley planned were interesting, engaging, and connected to other content and previous learning, although often undemanding. For example, in their basal readers, the story *The Air Is All Around You* by Franklin Mansfield Branley is featured as a connection between science and literature. Ms. Farley connected science to ths story by setting up an experiment for the students to discover some of the properties of air. After demonstrating the experiment, Ms. Farley had the students read the story in pairs and complete one worksheet listing their questions about the experiment and the story. The students then read the story and took turns doing the experiment, which was playtime because Ms. Farley failed to monitor the activity. When the students finished the story, they were given a packet of five worksheets to complete. That is, Ms. Farley took an engaging, hands-on task capable of producing extraordinary learning and dumbed it down. One student even told her that he had a question the story did not answer. She told him that the worksheet only required him to write down his favorite part of the story. That is, she did not encourage at all students' inquisitiveness.

The pace of instruction was often slow in Ms. Farley's classroom. The students took a long time completing the activities and were rarely urged to complete tasks efficiently. Ms. Farley usually failed to monitor student progress or check for understanding. During one of her lessons with a reading group, Ms. Farley introduced the story to the students, helped them do a picture walk, make some predictions, and start reading silently. After a few moments, the teacher left the group to monitor other students and did not return to check on their progress, help them with their comprehension, or give them a follow-up activity to extend their learning.

The observers were bothered by how Ms. Farley isolated students. There was one extreme case. For the majority of the year, one student was placed in the back corner of the classroom facing the wall. He was so isolated from the whole class that often when the teacher or students were passing out materials or papers, they would forget to give him what he needed, and he had to retrieve the items himself. This practice of isolating students seemed to demoralize them and devalued their contributions in the eyes of classmates.

Ms. Eldridge. Ms. Eldridge had 38 practices that supported and 15 practices that undermined motivation in her classroom. She jammed her room with lively displays, bulletin boards, posters, plants, and books.

There was stuff everywhere and no escaping something to read in her classroom, for there were books and print everywhere. Even so, there were few postings of student work samples, other than a reminder chart, recording who had been turning in homework.

Ms. Eldridge used many school projects to connect what the students did in the classroom with their family life. She often linked content coverage to the world outside of school. During the World Series, and again in the spring, she used baseball and concession stand prices to relate adding, subtracting, and money. In April, the spelling challenge words were about tax day and the government. Frequently she used students' names in language sentences and writing prompts.

Ms. Eldridge was very caring, with a positive demeanor. She was quite happy all the time. On several occasions, a student called her "Mom" by accident. The teacher smiled, giggled, and said, "I'm not the mama." In addition, she gave the students clear rationales for everything they did, from assignments to classroom rules. These reasons helped the students know she cared about their learning and their safety. She communicated that she valued their questions and their place in her classroom. Her second-grade students definitely showed that they wanted her attention, praise, and time. For example, they made a beeline for her whenever she announced that she was going to be working at the back table. The table was overflowing with students wanting to work and sit next to her.

One reason for students desiring to be in close contact with Ms. Eldridge was that she gave them many extrinsic rewards (prizes) and much verbal praise. In fact, her system of classroom management was saliently driven by rewards.

Sadly, it was also driven by a great deal of public criticism of students. Controlling noise was Ms. Eldridge's most obvious management problem. Disruptions and noisy work were noted with a check on the board, which led to lost recess time. "You know it is getting loud again, and you already have three marks on the board." The class then quieted down. Other marks were given to individual students for quiet work, resulting in a chance to get a reward out of the prize box at the end of the week. Ms. Eldridge also used candy to acknowledge success. After students had finished their minute-math drill, the teacher asked students to report publicly how many items they had gotten correct. The students who had perfect papers were given a handful of gummy bears, and other students received one or two. The Turn-a-Card chart, tally marks on the blackboard, prize box, and food rewards for achievement made the students dependent on her judgments of their behaviors and accomplishments. Students felt proud when they pleased Ms. Eldridge, not when they learned more or improved their skills.

In her classroom, Ms. Eldridge emphasized grading and standardized testing. During one observation, a student asked a question about an additional section of his worksheet. Ms. Eldridge replied, "I'm not concerned with you knowing that. It's not an Indiana second-grade standard, so we don't have to know that." During another observation, as she was giving a reading test, she commented, "If you don't know something on this test, I can help you. This is not like those horrible tests we took before [referring to the standardized test]." Later she added, "Standardized tests are more trouble than they are worth." These comments sent the message that schoolwork was driven by tests that are not really valuable. Nonetheless, skills and ideas not appearing on the test are not valuable!

Many of the activities Ms. Eldridge planned for her class were undemanding and repetitive. She had a heavy reliance on worksheets and other reproducible materials. Often the worksheets were completed without embedding them in other reading or writing activities. Other worksheets were disconnected activities provided with the basal series. She gave a small reading group a series of workbook pages and then remarked, "If you haven't read the story already, you should do that later, but don't worry because the workbook page has nothing to do with the story." Many times the students would race through these easy worksheets to be able to self-select a book, game, or writing project that was more engaging to them.

All things considered, the students in Ms. Eldridge's classroom were on-task and engaged a fair amount of time. They were eager to shout out answers during whole-class lessons, complete their worksheets, participate in their minute-math quizzes, observe at the science station, and play social studies games. Every one of these tasks was easy for the students, however! And, all too often, it seemed the kids were doing it for Ms. Eldridge's approval, prizes, or the candy.

Summary. The many motivational mechanisms found in these classrooms produced high levels of on-task behavior. Ms. Humboldt, Ms. Farley, and Ms. Eldridge had more effective classroom management techniques, focused instructional methods, and positive classroom atmospheres compared to the low-engaging teachers. Despite these teachers' ability to "grab" student attention, they were not able to maintain engagement as well as some teachers we observed who were highly engaging.

We hypothesize that the difference between the moderately and highly engaging teachers was in the level of the task demands in the moderately versus highly engaging classrooms.

Highly Engaging Teachers

This group of teachers—Ms. Squint and Ms. Davidson—created warm, caring environments that encouraged students to take risks, push themselves to think deeply, and challenge their abilities. They saturated their teaching with many different, positive motivational techniques. Often, during our observations, so many things were happening at once that it became difficult to note all that was occurring. The tasks assigned by these teachers were complex and cognitively demanding. During our observations in the classroom, we saw many supporting motivational practices for each teacher and few practices that would undermine student motivation.

Ms. Squint. Ms. Squint succeeded in motivating her students to be consistently on-task and engaged in all learning activities. The researchers identified 63 practices in her teaching that supported student motivation and only 9 practices that might undermine it. Her lessons were well planned and executed so as to minimize downtime and transition problems. Students were always eager to discover what was to happen next in Ms. Squint's classroom. They enthusiastically participated in discussions and volunteered when she needed a helper. Additionally, the students cooperated and worked well together, always willing to help their neighbors and friends. Ms. Squint created a warm, supportive environment where students were excited about learning and consistently involved and engaged in their work. Ms. Squint used quality literature with her students to make connections between what was in the basal reader and other books about the same theme, of the same genre, or by the same author. The classroom was full of books, and the students did a great deal of reading each day.

The activities Ms. Squint shared with her students were authentic, engaging, and cognitively demanding. Her students truly felt like authors, historians, scientists, and mathematicians in the classroom. Daily, they experienced being poets, novelists, researchers, and writers. Students worked on a variety of writing projects, revising until their work was publishable. Much student writing was displayed in the hallway. That writing had improved over the course of the year was obvious from reviewing the student writing on the hallway walls. In science, the students performed many different investigations, exploring the properties of magnetism and electricity, fulcrums and balances, mealworms, and various plants. These hands-on activities encouraged students to question the world around them and be involved in their surroundings. Many lessons connected across the curriculum, with most of the science, in particular, connecting to reading and writing.

Ms. Squint took the concept of daily oral language (DOL)—where students correct the errors in punctuation, usage, spelling, and capitalization of sentences—to a more cognitively demanding level. While some teachers have students just correct the mistakes, and other teachers have the students give reasons for the corrections they make, Ms. Squint's students did more than language as they worked on writing mechanics. The sentences the students corrected were always connected to a recent learning experience in the class. For example, one day the sentence read, "on Monday how did we make gas in a bag." The students corrected the sentence and responded to the question. Thus, Ms. Squint simultaneously assessed student knowledge of writing mechanics and also their knowledge about the science experiment. The students were challenged to think carefully and use their knowledge in many different ways.

Ms. Squint used every opportunity to give feedback, encouragement, and praise to her students. She made it clear that it was all right to make mistakes. During one lesson, a student volunteered to answer a question and was called on, but responded, "I just had it, and I forgot it." Ms. Squint replied, "I know, I do that too." She then waited a minute and had the student choose a helper to whisper a clue in his ear. "Oh yeah," the student replied, and gave the correct answer. She was constantly checking for student understanding and gave plenty of opportunities for students to think before asking for bidders. When teaching a lesson, Ms. Squint frequently used many signals (i.e. thumbs up, hands up, touch your nose, flap your arms like a bird) to gauge the student's understanding of the material. "How many of you are saying, 'Hey, we don't need any more of these. I understand'? Please raise your hands." Often Ms. Squint took advantage of teachable moments and used them to scaffold student learning and model strategies. When reading a book about animals and what they eat, the story turned to predators and their prey. "What is 'prey'? Does that mean get down on you knees?" The students and teacher then discussed the difference between the two words. Then she said, "Wait a minute, I just thought of something. If cows eat grass, is grass 'prey'?" The discussion then continued with the students explaining to her what they know about predators and their prey before continuing with the book.

Ms. Squint also affirmed and demonstrated the value of each student in her classroom by encouraging multicultural connections. During the school year, Ms. Squint had four children who spoke Spanish in her classroom. She used these students as helpers to teach the other classmates about their culture, families, and language. The students even helped Ms. Squint label the furniture and objects in the room with their Spanish names. As a further testament to her willingness to embrace these students and their families, Ms. Squint enrolled in a night class to brush up on her Spanish in order to better communicate with the students and their parents. In this way, all of her students were valued and reminded that they were a special part of the classroom community.

Ms. Squint displayed a few practices that undermined her students' motivation, however. When students became disruptive or off-task, she would use punishment to correct their behavior. At times, Ms. Squint would isolate such students from the group, for example, asking them to return to their seat during an activity on the rug or placing them in the hallway for a time-out. In addition, Ms. Squint would turn out the lights to gain the students' attention, asking them to be totally silent and watch the clock for a minute to calm down or put their heads down until they were settled. The observers also had concerns about the pace of instruction in this classroom. Although Ms. Squint planned interesting, engaging, appropriately challenging tasks, the activities were completed with such speed that the researchers were often left wondering what skills or knowledge the students had taken away from the lesson. It may have been more appropriate to cover less material in a more thoughtful, deeper fashion to ensure that all students were learning the objectives and making improvements. Ms. Squint used center-based learning in her classroom to teach in many of the curriculum areas. Although these centers were organized to be challenging and thought provoking, monitoring students was sometimes difficult, and the centers turned into play areas that allowed students to learn only surface level concepts without gaining more complete understandings. Despite these reservations, however, the observers definitely concluded that, for the most part, Ms. Squint created a challenging and positive place to learn.

Ms. Davidson. The most highly engaging teacher in this second-grade study, Ms. Davidson, had 74 practices that supported student motivation and only 5 practices that undermined it. The on-task behavior and engagement of students in Ms. Davidson's class was much greater than in the classrooms of any of the other teachers in this study. During every observation made in this class, the students were nearly 100% on-task nearly

100% of the time. Students were quiet and focused when the activity called for intense concentration, but were boisterous and enthusiastic in situations that called for expression and playfulness.

Ms. Davidson's classroom environment was so saturated with evidence of student work and accomplishments that it spilled out into the hallway. Projects, writing assignments, artwork, class posters, and signs had all made their way into the hallway as the class finished a unit and moved to another topic. By the end of the year, the evidence of student work from this one classroom was displayed down both sides of the corridor for its entire length. Each piece of student work was carefully evaluated by the teacher with lots of feedback, praise, and congratulatory remarks penned on the student papers. Inside the classroom, the furniture, learning centers, and student desks were organized for smooth transitions between activities and centers and for the distribution of enough materials and supplies for every student. Ms. Davidson even used the ceiling for eye-catching displays. With arrows taped to the floor and ceiling, a banner on the ceiling read "Follow me to the dinosaur fossil sites." The arrows led the students to the computer center that was decorated with dinosaurs, books on the topic, directions for the Internet sites, and other materials for students to work on their projects. In addition, on the ceiling above the students' desks were torn paper self-portraits that the students had made the first week of school. The pictures and accompanying "FRIENDS" banner reminded the students that they were a community of learners.

Probably the most striking aspect of Ms. Davidson's classroom was the books. This classroom was literally jammed with books on tables and shelves, display cases, and chalkboard ledges, inside students' desks, on top of the teacher's desk, and so on. These books varied in readability, assuring that each student could find interesting books at his or her reading level. The books were often grouped according to the theme the class was currently studying. One display case had over 25 books, both fiction and nonfiction, for students to read as they were studying dolphins.

The friendly, inviting environment of Ms. Davidson's classroom added to the spirit of cooperation and positive atmosphere. Ms. Davidson clearly valued her students and built a community of learners. She spent a few minutes at the beginning of the day affirming their experiences outside of the classroom. After the students returned from a 4–day break because of a snowstorm and power outage, Ms. Davidson took some time to meet with her students to share their experiences during the break. The students were eager to share how their families coped with the storm. The

discussion was lively, affirming, and fun. She took advantage of many opportunities that arose to teach the students about how electrical poles
work and why ice collects on the wires, and to discuss questions that students posed about the weather. Ms. Davidson also asked about the books
they had read over break (and all of the students had read at least one
book). One student asked about her experiences, and she gladly shared
them with the students, for example, telling them about toasting marsh-
mallows in the fireplace. The teacher and students built a community
where student contributions were valued and student strengths built
upon.

Ms. Davidson was very involved in the lives of the students' families.
She kept her students' parents well informed about what was happening
in the classroom, including them in their child's learning. During a social
studies and language arts lesson, the students were learning about communities. Ms. Davidson asked that the students go to their homes and neighborhoods and bring back five objects depicting what their neighborhood
was like. With the parent's help, the students brought some terrific items
and shared them with the class. After they were finished, the class constructed a quilt made from the objects and drawings of each student's
neighborhood. Ms. Davidson used the lesson to affirm the students' life
outside the classroom and teach the class about neighborhoods and communities.

Activities such as this were common in Ms. Davidson's classroom as
she encouraged student participation. Each morning, the class would have
their math meeting and review many real-world math problems related to
the day, month, season, temperature, time, and so on, completing about
15 different skills in a 20–minute period. Each day one student would lead
the class through the activities. Every Tuesday was "Teacher Tuesday,"
when one student got to be the teacher during the basal activity. On
Monday, Ms. Davidson would introduce the basal story and read it with
the students, completing a comprehension activity. She had taught her
class how to look at her teacher's edition, finding the questions the
teacher was to pose as students read the text. The next day, as the students were reading the story again, a student would be selected as the
teacher to ask these questions. The class thoroughly enjoyed this activity
and participated in reading the story and answering questions. By encouraging student participation, students were allowed to make choices in
what they were learning and how they would learn the material. Student
participation was also apparent in the transitions between activities. The
teacher or student chose a song that the class sang as a group as they

moved from one activity to the next. Songs about the days of the week and the months of the year were common, as well as counting to 100 by multiples of 2 or 5, forwards or backwards. These group chants and songs helped the students focus and move quickly into the next activity.

Ms. Davidson introduced excitement, suspense, and interest through her enthusiasm about upcoming activities: "We have something very special to do today. But before we start, lets share our journals." The students were then eager to finish something so they could move onto the other fun activity. On another occasion, as she introduced the story and the activity, "It's going to be so fun! It won't even seem like it's work today."

The activities in Ms. Davidson's classroom were appropriately challenging and connected to other content. She often stressed the building of vocabulary and background knowledge when linking literature and science or social studies. To enable her students to think more like scientists, historians, and so on, she taught the jargon that was appropriate to their activity. By connecting their background knowledge and building their vocabularies, the students were better able to think deeply about many topics and use their reasoning skills. For example, during a morning math meeting, she connected real-world concepts about coin flipping and probability, grocery shopping and making change. Even putting up a new month on the calendar could be a lesson for reasoning and decision making for students as they determined the first day of the month, how many days were in the month, and the pattern of dates in the calendar (i.e., the number of weeks with the full cycle of Sunday through Saturday). All of the thinking resulted in students feeling ownership with respect to their learning and thinking—that is, they knew they were figuring out things rather than being told things!

Ms. Davidson was extremely well organized. She planned lessons carefully and noted where there could be connections between lessons, taking advantage of teachable moments. During the unit on whales, the teacher reviewed some of what they had learned, including what the different whales ate. "What are they called?" The students answered, "Krill." Ms. Davidson said, "How do you spell it?" The students then spelled the word. The teacher responded, "How many other words do we know that sound like krill?" The students offered thrill, bill, spill, and many more "-ill" words. Ms. Davidson acknowledged, "You see, that's how we can remember the word. Now for the big question. What is krill?" She provided plenty of wait time to allow students to think before they would raise their hands or to correct themselves after an incorrect answer. Because Ms. Davidson monitored student understanding and progress during question and answer sessions (as well as during every other activity), she was able to make good judgments about teachable moments and when the students needed clarification or additional information.

In addition, Ms. Davidson used feedback, praise, and scaffolding to encourage students to extend their knowledge. In giving comments like "Isn't that an interesting question. What do you think? How could we find the answer to that question?" the teacher encouraged students to persevere in their learning. When teaching a lesson or having a discussion with the class, Ms. Davidson promoted higher-order thinking by encouraging students to evaluate, predict, come up with new ideas, and ask further questions. This type of questioning, which contrasts with the initiate–respond–evaluate cycles common in classrooms (Mehan, 1979) kept students engaged and thinking hard about the topics they were covering. Ms. Davidson also promoted cognitive conflict in her students by encouraging them to use their "I Wonder Journals" in science to write questions and work with the teacher individually and on group projects to discover information. To assist her students with their learning, Ms. Davidson provided lots of support. She continually modeled strategies, scaffolded student learning, and encouraged students to take risks and challenge themselves.

Ms. Davidson taught her students how to be self-regulated not only in their learning, but also in the ways they praised themselves. For example, the class had many types of silent cheers that the teacher and students used. When the class solved a difficult math problem together, Ms. Davidson asked them to do their silent "ketchup bottle" cheer (left hand in a fist, right hand flat hitting the other hand, like getting ketchup out of a bottle). While students were working, you could see times when the students would give themselves such a silent cheer for accomplishing a goal.

While Ms. Davidson used a myriad of motivational practices to encourage on-task behavior and engagement, she had a few instructional practices with the potential to undermine motivation. There were instances when Ms. Davidson used extrinsic rewards with her students, specifically to promote good behavior and reading skills. Thus, Ms. Davidson had a bulletin board for the "Reading Wheel of Fortune," a game taking place each day in the classroom. Rewards were listed with a blank for each letter. Ms. Davidson chose one student each day for having a great day, or at least a great portion of the day. The student then chose a letter to add to the word and make a guess for the reward.

A second problem the observers noticed was the public display of grading. Having many examples of student work posted was wonderful.

Despite the positive comments on much of the student work, student grades were there for everyone to see.

The third problem the researchers observed occasionally was negative tone when students misbehaved. Every so often, she threatened to use schoolwork as punishment (although never delivering on this threat): "Excuse me. I'm beginning to lose patience. You are not sitting very well today, and we have been taking too much time to finish. It looks like a great play-in-the-snow day today. Do you want extra homework because you did not finish this in time?" Such negative comments to correct students' behaviors were the exception, however. For the most part, Ms. Davidson was very positive and encouraging to students.

Summary. In the two most engaging classrooms, the motivational instructional practices were interconnected, constantly occurring and recurring in coordination with other motivational instructional practices. For example, in Ms. Squint's classroom, the students read a selection about the octopus out of their basal reader. With this as an introduction (building excitement), the students were asked to do a report on an animal (engaging content). They were allowed to pick the animal that interested them the most (allowing for student choice) and do research on that animal (using many resources). Ms. Squint both provided questions to guide research and permitted the students to generate their own. That is, the teacher and students cooperated as the research was occurring. While doing the research, the students with the same animals were paired (cooperative learning). The students took almost the entire week to brainstorm, research, take notes, organize their thoughts, write, edit, revise a draft, draw illustrations, and publish their reports. What we emphasize here is that students in Ms. Squint's class were always doing multicomponent tasks with the various subtasks motivated in multiple ways. Ms. Squint effectively wove engaging instruction that resulted in students learning a great deal.

In comparison, a less engaging second-grade teacher similarly had her students write a report about animals, but because the basal selection was about the octopus, the students were all asked to write the report on that animal (not allowing for student choice). They used only their basal story for references (no use of outside materials or quality literature), made a small idea web, and wrote reports without scaffolding. The writing task was especially difficult for these children because the teacher's directions about what the students should be doing were unclear and seeking clarification from classmates was not an option, as student cooperation was not permitted. The report writing lasted about 20 minutes. The majority of the students handed in only one or two sentences, many of them with ideas copied directly out of the story. The differences between the teaching in this classroom and Ms. Squint's classroom were striking, as were the differences in the qualities of the final products.

Discussion

There were clear outcomes in this study. First, teachers who did much to motivate their students had more engaged students, with their students working on tasks that produced admirable academic achievements (e.g., the writing was better in such classrooms, the content being covered was more conceptually advanced). Second, teachers who did little to motivate their students positively often also did much to undermine the motivational levels of their students. The most extreme example in this study was a teacher who had twice the number of undermining practices (42) as she did practices supporting motivation (21).

Third, teachers could be separated into three groups based on their number of motivational mechanisms, student engagement, and task difficulty. Ms. Ames, Ms. Boone, Ms. Carroll, and Ms. Davenport had low levels of motivational practices, student engagement, and task difficulty. Ms. Humboldt, Ms. Eldridge, and Ms. Farley had higher numbers of motivational mechanisms, and more student engagement, but low task difficulty. Ms. Squint and Ms. Davidson had high levels with respect to all three characteristics.

Given the current national obsessions with standards and accountability, we were struck by how the highly engaging and less engaging teachers prepared their students for standardized tests. In the less engaging classrooms, we often saw teachers set aside time to review concepts and prepare students specifically for taking upcoming standardized tests. These sessions often met with complaints and moans from the students because the time was usually spent on worksheets, practice books and tests, and similar uninspiring tasks. These teachers often emphasized remembering specific content because it would be on the test. Such constant reminders and practice sessions made students feel anxious and worried.

In contrast, Ms. Davidson, one of the highly engaging teachers, had different tactics. Ms. Davidson's students learned the standards through appropriately challenging, hands-on activities. For example, one of the district standards was that second graders be able to write a letter using complete sentences and good mechanics. The district assessment required that the letter answer three specific questions about their behavior, how they were learning in school, and what they like best about school. A few weeks prior to this assessment, Ms. Davidson and the class had been studying the books about Arthur written by Marc Tolon Brown. They had read almost the entire Arthur series, learned to draw the characters in the book, and had written, illustrated, and published their own stories with Arthur as the character. The teacher then sent copies of the students' books to the author and was waiting for a reply.

On the day she was to introduce the assessment to the students, Ms. Davidson began the morning announcements by telling them that she had a surprise during their language arts time. The students were visibly excited as they did their morning calendar and math routines. The teacher led them to their circle time and had one student go to her desk and retrieve an envelope. She then told her students that she received the letter in the mail at school yesterday after they had gone home, and she had been unable to sleep that night because she was so excited to share the letter with the class. This pumped the class up even more. A student was then asked to read the letter, which was written by Arthur himself! . . . with some help from Ms. Davidson. The class was visibly and audibly excited that Arthur had written them. The letter thanked the students for the books they had sent, praised their efforts, and encouraged them to write letters back to him. In the letter the students were to write, Arthur wanted to know something special about them, what subjects they liked in school, how they were behaving, and how they liked to learn best. After finishing the rest of the letter, the teacher took a poll of the number of students that wanted to write back to Arthur. The vote was unanimous!

The teacher then took some time to explain the contents of their letters a little more, and reviewed the format of a letter and addressing an envelope from previous lessons. She wrote directions on the board so that the students had a visual reminder. She checked their understanding of the task before asking them to write a sloppy copy, edit with a buddy, and then come to her for help and final editing. The teacher also informed them that their final drafts would be on special gold stationery with Arthur's picture on it. The students practically ran to their desks to get started. They worked extremely hard on their letters, many of them writing paragraphs, and a few writing multiple pages. The final drafts had good mechanics and were clearly written, definitely the sort of excellent work the teacher had hoped for in this assessment. In speaking to us after the observation, Ms. Davidson told us that she was going to take each letter home, and, after the scoring, was going to write back to each of them personally as Arthur and send the letter to their home addresses to include the families in the process. By using many different motivational mechanisms during a single lesson, this teacher was able to make the assessment activity meaningful and enjoyable for her students. Effective teachers transform tasks that are dreaded in other classrooms into eagerly anticipated events, and, in doing so, get much from their students.

In summary, the good news was that we found some classrooms where engagement was high. In those classrooms, the teachers did much to motivate academic involvement of students, and they succeeded. The bad news is that only two of the nine teachers studied were impressive in their motivation of students. These results at the grade 2 study were generally comparable to the results that we obtained at the grade 1 and grade 3 levels. Those outcomes are reviewed in the next section of this chapter.

THE RESULTS ACROSS INVESTIGATIONS

First, there was striking convergence across the three studies, across the three primary grades. The teachers who did much to motivate their students and succeeded in engaging their students were distinctly in the minority at each grade level. There were two such teachers (of seven total) in the grade 1 study, two in the grade 2 investigation (of nine total), and one in the grade 3 work (of nine total). The teaching in these most engaging classrooms was just saturated with motivation. Hardly a minute went by when the teacher was not doing something to motivate one student or a few students or the entire class. Their motivating teaching often was so intense that it was difficult to record everything that was occurring. Each of these most engaging teachers were observed using more than 40 different motivating mechanisms that have been documented as effective in the educational motivation literature (e.g., Anderson, Shirley, Wilson, & Fielding, 1987; Bandura & Schunk, 1981; Block & Mangieri, 1994; Brophy, 1981, 1985, 1987; Brophy & Good, 1986; Clifford, 1991; Cooper & Valentine, 2001; Deci & Ryan, 1985; Dewey, 1913; Doyle, 1986; Eisner, 1998; Evertson, Emmer, & Worsham, 1999; Ginsberg & Wlodkowski, 2000; Gump, 1982; Guthrie, 1996; Johnson & Johnson, 1975; Krajcik, 1991; Lantieri & Patti, 1996; Laseman & de Jong, 2001; McVey, 1971; Nicholls, 1989; Nickerson, Perkins, & Smith, 1985; Noddings, 1984; Pressley, Woloshyn, & Associates, 1995; Segal, Chipman, & Glaser, 1985; Smith & Blackman, 1975; Sowell, 1989; Tobin, 1987; Verhoeven & Snow, 2001; Walker & Scherry, 2001; Weiner,

1979; Wharton-McDonald, Pressley, & Hampston, 1998; Wood, Bruner, & Ross, 1976; Zimmerman, 1990a, 1990b, 1998). The motivational mechanisms observed in the most engaging classrooms in all three studies are summarized in Table 2.4. The table includes the mechanisms common to two teachers who were showcased in the previous section of this chapter (i.e., the grade 2 highly engaging teachers) and three highly engaging teachers who will be showcased in Chapters 3–5.

On every visit to each of the three classrooms covered in Chapters 3–5, we saw most of the mechanisms summarized in Table 2.4, many of them repeatedly. We did not just see them every visit; we saw many of them every hour of every visit. Many individual minutes of instruction included several of the mechanisms. The really motivating teachers were always emphasizing their students' efforts, always praising, and always presenting instruction that grabbed students. In contrast, other teachers we studied used these mechanisms relatively rarely, never using the majority of them. That is, no matter how often we visited their classes, the vast majority of teachers used only a few of the mechanisms in Table 2.4, although the specific set of approaches varied from teacher to teacher.

Does this mean that the behavior of the not-so-engaging teachers was without motivational implications? Hardly. In fact, the not-so-engaging teachers often acted in ways that would be expected to undermine student motivation. Table 2.5 summarizes the behaviors that can undermine student engagement that were observed during the 3 years of research informing this chapter.

THE CASES STUDIES AHEAD

Chapters 3–5 summarize the case studies of three teachers: two grade 1 teachers and one grade 3 teacher. These were the most engaging teachers observed at the grade 1 and 3 levels, respectively. The cases provide expansion of the general claims made in the previous section, with each of these teachers flooding their classrooms every minute of every day with motivating instruction. Nonetheless, each classroom had a unique personality, and each teacher had unique emphases. We want readers to leave this book with the strong impression that we did not discover a one-size-fits-all model in our work. What we found was that motivational flooding can work with a wide variety of teaching.

That said, it cannot be missed in these studies that the literacy instruction, which is much of primary education, was excellent—a strong

TABLE 2.4. Motivating Teaching Behaviors by the Most Engaging Teachers in the Three Primary-Grade Studies

Positive classroom physical environment and psychological atmosphere

Physical environment
- *Books.* The classroom has many books, spanning a range of difficulties and topics.
- *Classroom environment.* The classroom is decorated with brightly colored signs and posters. The charts, maps, and posters hanging up are useful teaching tools. The bulletin boards are changed with the passing months and seasons and are neat and well kept. Student work is prominently displayed in the classroom.

Psychological atmosphere
- *Accountability expectations.* The teacher makes certain that students are aware that they are expected to learn and perform in school and are accountable for doing so, including to their parents, who are made aware of their student's progress.
- *Attributions of performance to effort.* The teacher communicates to the students that it is important to give their best efforts. He or she shows students that their successes are because of their hard work.
- *Clear expectations.* The teacher communicates clearly his or her expectations for their behavior and what they are to be learning.
- *Cooperation encouraged/competition downplayed.* The teacher emphasizes cooperation in the classroom. The students are encouraged to work together, help each other, and achieve success together.
- *Students told they can do challenging tasks.* The teacher communicates to the students that they can be successful with challenging activities.
- *Encouragement/praise.* The teacher consistently finds ways to compliment and encourage the students for their good behavior, learning success, and helpfulness in the classroom.
- *Positive feedback.* The teacher takes advantage of many opportunities to give constructive feedback to the students. Feedback is immediate and specific to their accomplishment. The teacher uses these opportunities to encourage and gently push the students to think more deeply.
- *Encourages prosocial behavior.* The teacher provides opportunities for the students to do things helpful to those in need. In addition, the teacher leads discussions about why doing considerate things for others is important and necessary.
- *Encourages risk taking.* The teacher encourages students to take chances and try new things. The students get the message that when they try new things the teacher and classmates will be there to support their efforts.
- *Encourages persistence.* The teacher encourages stick-with-it-ness, that often it takes a while to accomplish something worthwhile and that initial failures sometimes occur.
- *Encourages independence.* The teacher communicates to the students that there are many things they can do on their own, without the teacher's direct assistance. The students know that they are to do as much as they can before asking for help.
- *Modeling interest and enthusiasm.* The teacher models interest in academic matters and enthusiasm for what is being covered in class, communicating that academic tasks deserve intense attention.
- *Positive atmosphere.* The teacher creates an atmosphere of warmth, care, and concern for the students. He or she uses humor in a positive way, models enthusiasm for learning, introduces excitement, and has a positive attitude toward all students.

(continued)

TABLE 2.4. *(continued)*

- *Student choice*. Students are given opportunities to choose aspects of their own learning.
- *Values students*. The teacher fully enjoys being with the students. The teacher communicates to them how much he or she cares for them and wants them to succeed.

Classroom instruction and content

- *Attention to school work*. The teacher communicates the importance of schoolwork, that it deserves to be done carefully, including being checked and corrected.
- *Encouragement of student understanding and reflection*. The teacher monitors the students' understanding of the material. He or she probes for answers, allows wait time for students to think before answering, and encourages them to self-correct their wrong answers.
- *Monitoring*. The teacher constantly assesses the students' engagement, understanding, and behavior during the course of the day. The teacher constantly monitors the entire class, even while working one-on-one with a student.
- *Clear directions.*The teacher gives the directions in a precise, easy-to-follow way, checking for understanding as each step is completed.
- *Clear, realistic goals and objectives*. The teacher makes clear the goals and objectives of lessons and units, and these are realistic goals (i.e., challenging, but can be accomplished with appropriate effort).
- *Cognitive conflict*. The teacher encourages students to see that their expectations are sometimes violated and that, when they are, there is an opportunity for learning to occur (e.g., estimations about relative weights of rusty and nonrusty nails as an opportunity to learn about what rust is).
- *Concrete activities*. The teacher creates activities that are concrete examples of the lessons the students are learning. The curriculum is both hands-on and minds-on, allowing for students to create and explore as they learn.
- *Connections across curriculum*. The teacher uses many opportunities to relate the current lesson to previous lessons, to other curriculum activities, and/or to the outside world.
- *Cooperative learning*. The teacher uses cooperative learning strategies and lessons in the classroom.
- *Critical thinking*. The teacher explains, models, and provides opportunities for students to develop and use higher-order and critical thinking skills.
- *Curiosity and suspense*. The teacher stimulates student curiosity and suspense (e.g., You'll never guess what is going to happen in the next chapter!).
- *Depth favored over breadth*. The teacher covers topics in greater depth versus covering of a large number of topics (e.g., teacher reading a long novel rather than a different story every day).
- *Engaging, interesting content*. The teacher provides lessons, activities, and tasks that arouse the curiosity and anticipation of students. The class reviews content in meaningful ways, employs many whole-language strategies, creates authentic products (e.g., classroom-written big books), uses current events as context for learning, and experiences hands-on strategies. The teacher builds excitement when introducing new material and exposes the students to excellent literature.
- *Games/play/fun*. The teacher uses games and playful activities in the lessons to reinforce a concept, review material, or make learning more enjoyable and concrete. In general, the teacher makes learning and school fun.

(continued)

- *Home–school connections.* The teacher values the role of the family in the students' learning. She provides opportunities to communicate with the families and make them integral parts of the learning experience.
- *Learning by doing.* Students are given opportunities for hands-on learning.
- *Multiple representations of tasks.* To teach a single concept, the teacher uses many different ways and methods to deliver the lesson's content.
- *Lesson planning.* The teacher is well planned and organized for the lessons each day. The students have enough materials for the activities and experience little "down time" between activities. The teacher is mindful of what the students have learned in previous grades as well as what skills they need to acquire at this grade level.
- *Manipulatives/concrete representatives.* Students are given many opportunities to use materials to assist them in their learning.
- *Scaffolding.* The teacher models and assists her students when they are struggling to learn new material.
- *Stimulates cognitive thought.* The teacher provides activities and lessons that promote deep processing and higher-order thinking skills in students.
- *Stimulates creative thought.* In planning lessons, the teacher allows students to be creative and think in novel ways.
- *Strategy instruction.* The teacher uses explicit strategy instruction with the students. They are taught many skills and strategies by the teacher modeling and thinking out loud his or her process and plan for attacking a problem or question.
- *Value of education emphasized.* The teacher communicates with the students the value of learning and school.

<u>Classroom management</u>

- *Appropriate pacing.* The teacher monitors the pace of the lesson, mindful of the range of abilities in the class. He or she does not go too fast or too slow for the majority of the students.
- *Classroom adult volunteers.* The teacher uses parents and adults in the classroom to assist students. Adults are welcome in the classroom.
- *Explanation for decisions/rationale.* The teacher and students discuss the reasons behind the activities, rules, procedures, and routines the students perform each day. The students understand why they are being asked to behave in appropriate ways and learn new material.
- *Extrinsic motivators.* The teacher provides extrinsic motivators for students as rewards for appropriate behaviors and activities. The teacher uses these extrinsic motivators not as bribes, but as a tool to extend learning.
- *Positive, effective classroom management.* The teacher uses classroom management techniques that are positive, constructive, and encouraging toward students. When the teacher needs to correct a student's behavior, he or she does so quickly and privately, getting the student back on-task as soon as possible and with as little disruption to the rest of the class as possible.
- *Rewards that stimulate.* The teacher gives rewards to students that produce learning (e.g., an opportunity to do some free reading).
- *Routines/procedures.* The teacher has devised rules, procedures, policies, and routines for the students that are useful and provide smooth transitions within lessons and between activities.
- *Self-regulation.* The teacher has provided ways for students to monitor their learning and transition independently to some activities after they are finished.

TABLE 2.5. Teaching Behaviors with Potential to Undermine Academic Motivation Observed in the Three Primary-Grade Studies

<u>Unattractive physical environment and classroom atmosphere</u>

Physical environment

- *Sparse decorations, posters, and so forth.* Some room environments have little decoration. Others are decorated for appearance's sake, with the few posters or bulletin boards not used during curricular lessons.
- *Few displays of student work.* Few examples of student work, projects, or accomplishments adorn the walls of the classroom, making obvious to the class that they accomplish a great deal that is worthwhile.

Psychological Atmosphere

- *Ability attributions.* The teacher communicates that success depends on innate intellect rather than effort.
- *Luck attributions.* The teacher attributes student successes to good luck and student failures to bad luck.
- *Task difficulty attributions.* The teacher attributes student successes to easy tasks and student failures to difficult tasks.
- *Competitiveness/lack of cooperation.* The students are asked to complete tasks where winning or being the best is valued rather than working together and improving. The teacher emphasizes student differences in performance.
- *Low task-difficulty.* The tasks and activities provided by the teacher often are too easy for most students in the class. The activities are of a low cognitive level, demanding little of the students.
- *Overly difficult tasks.* The tasks assigned by the teacher sometimes are much too difficult for the majority of the students to be successful and learn the concept.
- *Ineffective/negative feedback.* The teacher rarely checks to see if students understand the concept being taught, gives little help to struggling students, provides them with answers, or mostly uses the "initiate–respond–evaluate" strategy when asking questions.
- *Teaching style encouraging inattentiveness.* The teacher includes activities that are distracting (e.g., rewarding class by allowing them to do jumping jacks, which requires a great deal of time for students to settle down after completion).
- *Uninspiring/boring instructional practices.* The activities and lessons assigned by the teacher are routine, boring, simplistic, or lack excitement and stimulation.
- *Negative classroom atmosphere.* The teacher fails to establish a warm, caring environment in the classroom. The teacher may exhibit favoritism or irritation toward students, fail to encourage students, or make negative attributions.

<u>Classroom instruction and content</u>

- *Task completion emphasis.* The teacher communicates to the students that accomplishing the task and doing it correctly are more important than learning the material. There is little talk of learning from one's mistakes.
- *Lack of monitoring.* The teacher does not check for the progress of the students in their work. He or she fails to notice that students are off-task or are confused about the activity at hand, or allows disruptions to occur during class time.

(continued)

- *Lack of connections.* The teacher does not use opportunities to connect lessons to other concepts in the curriculum, to previous learning experiences, or to the outside world.
- *Discourages curiosity and suspense.* When students express curiosity (e.g., asking "What is this unit going to be about?"), the teacher discourages them (e.g., responding "Don't get ahead of yourselves!").
- *Poor/incomplete planning.* The teacher has not properly planned and/or made full preparations for the lessons of the day. The students lack all the materials necessary to complete an activity, or are experiencing long delays as the teacher scrambles for the next lesson to teach.
- *Lack of scaffolding.* The teacher does not provide assistance, modeling, or help to students struggling to answer a question or learn a skill.

Classroom management

- *Slow pacing.* The pace of the teacher and the class is too slow for the majority of the students.
- *Extrinsic rewards for intrinsically motivated behaviors.* The teacher provides rewards (e.g., pizza certificates) for behaviors that students would do without reward (e.g., pizza certificates for reading to children who are already avid readers).
- *Negative classroom management/feedback.* The teacher uses negative, punishing techniques to maintain order in the classroom. The teacher may be threatening, overly stern, or angry with the students, making them very aware of their failures.
- *Lack of routines and procedures.* The teacher has not established rules or systems to accomplish tasks throughout the day, such as lining up, passing out papers, collecting homework, and so forth.
- *Scapegoats students.* The teacher singles out individual students as blameworthy, especially for a group failure (e.g., "None of us can go out for recess because of what X did") or scolds a single student as an example.
- *Public grading/punishment.* The teacher makes grades, punishment, errors, or behavior public to all of the students in the class. The teacher has the students call in their grades aloud, or posts grades on a bulletin board.

---

balancing of skills, literature, and composing experiences. It also cannot be missed that the other content areas were inspiring. We were struck that in most of these classrooms there was really interesting science teaching occurring, much more interesting than in other classrooms we observed during our visits to primary classrooms during the past 3 years. Furthermore, the instruction across literacy and the content areas was always connected, with reading, writing, math, science, and social studies flowing into one another. Excellent instruction and motivational flooding seem to go hand in hand. We return to that theme in the final chapter of this book.

An important theme in this book, revisited in the final chapter, is that the flood of motivating instruction observed in engaging primary classrooms is filled with the instructional practices supported in the research reviewed in Chapter 1. In short, what engaging teachers are doing is definitely defensible based on the best of educational research pertaining to academic motivation. In contrast to many educational researchers who have focused their attention on one motivational mechanism at a time, engaging primary teachers fold many motivational mechanisms into their teaching. Thus, what emerges from the work summarized herein is a new hypothesis about how to motivate academic commitment in primary classrooms, an inclusive hypothesis: Primary teachers should do all that is known to increase academic motivation and avoid doing all that is known to undermine motivation. Engaging teachers are doing something to motivate their students positively every minute of every school day! This is the unique contribution to the educational motivation literature that emerges from our recent efforts.

CHAPTER 3

Nancy Masters' Grade 1 Teaching

To get to the school where Nancy Masters teaches requires passing through light industrial areas, working-class neighborhoods, and a few blocks filled with homes in disrepair. The school serves the children of these neighborhoods, with Nancy's class of 24 students a mixture of children from poor, working-class, and middle-class families. The school itself is in excellent condition; it is obvious that there has been attention to its maintenance for the past three quarters of a century. On entry to the school, it is striking that the building is clean, bright, and appealing.

As often as not, the first person to say hello to a visitor to the school is the principal, a middle-aged woman who spends much time in the hallways interacting with students and their parents. Her greetings are always friendly. She also ducks into classrooms quite a bit. This principal definitely knows what is happening in her school. She is respected by students, their families, and the teachers, and recognized as successful in overseeing with care a safe, orderly, and friendly school, recognized as stimulating an environment where students receive much attention.

Nancy Masters has taught for 11 years. Seven of those years were at the high school level, consistent with her college preparation as a secondary social studies teacher. The last 4 years have been spent in grade 1.

Nancy received her undergraduate degree from a distinguished 4-year women's college, later earning a master's degree at a large public university serving her hometown. Nancy is an extremely active member of the community where her school is located. Many of her students are her neighbors.

Nancy's students always are motivated and eager to learn. Misbehavior just does not seem to occur in this classroom, with reprimands the rare exception rather than a daily routine. Students always seem to know what they should be doing and do it. Transitions between tasks are very smooth. The students mix well together; it is impossible for the casual observer to pick out the two students who receive free/reduced lunch. Although the class is predominantly white, the Hispanic and African American children are treated by their peers as part of the gang, one that is obviously interested in school and generally gives rapt attention to their teacher.

Nancy perceives that most of her students began the school year ready for first grade. At midyear, she felt that the majority was performing at or above first-grade level, which was confirmed by standardized test performances. There were some English as a second language (ESL) students, however, who continued to struggle with basic literacy skills. Nancy was concerned about these children, and she liked them, referring to them as "sweet as can be."

Nancy believes that all kids can learn. She hoped to develop her students into independent readers, writers, and thinkers. To do so, she created an upbeat and happy classroom, filled with a variety of enjoyable activities. Nancy's classroom was structured to permit exploration. For example, in February, "Tiny Town," a student-constructed representation of a working community, dominated the middle of the classroom, spread out over a large part of the floor space. Tiny Town supported a writing workshop activity. Also, there were big books the class had composed (e.g., *Our Book of Titles*, *Our Visit to Mrs. Lamie's Kindergarten*, *Our Great Halloween Costumes*), which could be read and reviewed by students on their own. A memorable display was the slab of concrete made by the students and a builder who had visited the class during the unit on careers. The dynamism of the classroom was apparent, for displays changed often, reflecting that Nancy led her class through an always-renewing journey of ideas.

There were various centers in the four corners of the room. The reading center contained a variety of books, color-coded by reading level. Science projects were in another corner, with many science-related books also in that center. For example, in January there were students' "ocean in a bottle" projects on display, surrounded by several books about the ocean.

In summary, Nancy Masters teaches in an established, urban school, one serving some poor families but mostly working-class homes. The school is an attractive place, headed up by a dedicated and likable principal. Nancy's class meets in a spacious classroom, consistent with early

20th-century American school architecture, which favored very large classrooms. The classroom is filled with artifacts that support student literacy and learning activities, and which serve as props for Nancy's vibrant and dynamic teaching. From the moment of arrival in Nancy Masters' classroom, students experience an enthusiastic and caring professional, someone who communicates often that what happens in first grade is important, as are the first graders themselves. We emphasize the general positiveness of Nancy's classroom by reflecting additionally on the specific mechanisms used by Nancy to accomplish such positiveness.

A GENERALLY SUPPORTIVE ENVIRONMENT

Nancy's classroom was a supportive environment. She frequently praised her students, acknowledging that they were doing a good job (e.g., "I'm proud of you boys and girls. You really understand the story"; "Good job. You are making me so happy"). Students were well scaffolded as they attempted challenging tasks.

For example, during a test, Nancy reminded students of the connection between a story on the test and their current science project (i.e., both the test story and the ongoing carrot observation project were about growth).

Nancy always urged her students to try hard and "do their best" in every activity. Effort was emphasized above all else. Thus, when the students received their report cards, Nancy reassured them that their most important grade was for effort.

Although she downplayed ability as an explanation of success, Nancy expressed confidence in her students' abilities. She frequently asserted to her class that they were the smartest class in the school. Nancy repeatedly told her class, "I know you guys can do this."

When Nancy's students experienced difficulties, she attributed it to her teaching rather than blaming the students. On one occasion, Nancy related to her students how she reacted to their poor performance on a worksheet about contractions. She informed them after seeing their papers that she had walked around the house, feeling like she was a terrible teacher, that she had made a mistake in her teaching of contractions, a mistake that needed to be fixed. She consulted with the resource teacher, getting some ideas from her about how to teach contractions better. Nancy told her students that she became determined to teach contractions to the class because there was nothing too difficult for her students. The end result was a creative and successful lesson on contractions.

DIRECT INSTRUCTION

There is a never a day in Nancy's classroom when there is not a great deal of modeling and explaining. Nancy modeled sounding out of words as thinking and problem-solving processes. She actively made predictions as she read stories aloud, demonstrating for the class how good readers anticipate what might be in a story. She made clear to her students that understanding what they read would be part of reading for the rest of their lives.

During one visit, Nancy provided her class with a detailed explanation of her goals in reading. Before doing so, she praised her students for the goals they had achieved in the first half of the school year (i.e., learning to sound out words). Then she urged her students to strive for new goals during the second half of the school year, focusing in particular on learning to read with expression.

Nancy modeled many other strategies for her students as well. We observed her as she taught about reviewing for tests as a coping mechanism. She demonstrated repeatedly how to look up words in the dictionary. Nancy taught her students to double-check work, look at pictures to increase understanding of stories, brainstorm before writing, and use story grammar strategies to increase comprehension of stories (i.e., pay attention to setting information, then the problems encountered by the characters of the story, followed by attention to the problem solutions). Nancy emphasized the value of these strategies, stressing how strategies helped students learn and perform well.

Nancy was always explaining her actions to the class. On one occasion we witnessed her explaining the reason for the students' putting up privacy folders during the spelling test—so she could be sure that the students knew their spelling words. This was consistent with a larger, consistent message in Nancy's class that tests were to help the teacher know the students better.

On other occasions, explanations were given to make students aware of the relationship of various tasks to one another. Thus, we saw Nancy explain to students that, after she finished reading A Christmas Carol to them, they would watch the movie version so that they could compare it with the book.

COOPERATIVE LEARNING

Nancy believed in a cooperative learning environment, reporting during her interview that she set up her classroom deliberately to avoid competition between students because she disliked competition so much. For example, she seated her students in rows rather than small groups because she felt small-group seating encouraged competition. To stimulate cooperation, Nancy assigned collaborative book reports and projects, frequent small-group reading and writing, and partner reading and discussion.

One science project represented well the cooperative spirit in Nancy's classroom. The project involved observations of carrot tops as the carrots grew. Small groups of students monitored the growing of their group's carrots, complemented by whole class observations of the growing carrots and class discussions about the growth of carrots. During one such discussion, Nancy explained the definition of "prediction" and provided examples of silly versus real predictions. She also inserted a cooperative message in the lesson: "When we observe in science, there are no wrong answers. . . . Even if we are looking at the same carrot, you may not see the same thing as I see. . . . Everyone's observation is valued." To stress further the importance of accepting each other's observations, Nancy told a story to the class about a group of students from a few years ago who judged another group's observations to be in error, claiming they could see the actual carrot. In fact, that group could see the yellow of the carrot, which was above the soil line.

Cooperation occurred during reading groups as well. For example, on one day, the members of the class were assigned to several small reading groups, with each group reading a different book (e.g., *Great Frogs, Grasshoppers and Ants*). Students partner-read and discussed what they read during the small group. Nancy emphasized to the students to concentrate on reading with expression and using story comprehension strategies that the class had been discussing. She was emphatic that reading partners should encourage these skills in each other: "The point is . . . you should be helping your partner." To communicate this attitude completely, Nancy pointed out that she still bounced ideas off her husband. On that day, cooperation was apparent as Nancy read with the students as well as when the partners read with each other. The students continued to cooperate as they wrote in their journals about what they had read.

CONNECTIONS

Perhaps the most salient feature of Nancy's teaching was its connected-ness. There was a variety of connections made in her class.

Cross-Curricular Connections

There were numerous cross-curricular connections, especially between literacy and content-area instruction. In fact, Nancy seemed to take advantage of every possible opportunity to make a curricular connection.

Thus, science instruction and literacy development intertwined. Each week, there were new science projects in the classroom, with each surrounded by relevant books, and each tied to books read in class or by the class. As students consumed books like *Pumpkin Pumpkin* and *My River*, they created science projects related to ideas in the readings (e.g., the carrot top observations could be understood through ideas in *Pumpkin Pumpkin*; the ocean in a bottle project related to concepts in *My River*). The stories and activities prompted many discussions pertaining to science, from commentaries about the nature of scientific observations to the lifestyles of beavers and the natural history of rivers.

Connections within content areas were common as well. For example, while students worked in small groups reading and writing about African American heroes during Black History Month, they reviewed ideas about civil rights that were covered previously in social studies. The Black History Month project also permitted connection between reading and writing, with students reading from two sources (book and Internet) to research important African American historical figures. They then collaboratively wrote paragraphs about these figures during writing workshop.

Ethical Connections

In Nancy's school, the ethical development of students was a major issue. Nancy skillfully connected content learning to issues of moral and ethical development. For example, during Black History Month, Nancy read *The Story of Ruby Bridges* to the class. During the story, she explained why she felt sympathy with the characters of the story and for African Americans who were affected by the Jim Crow laws. Later, during a discussion of the Black History Month book reports written by students, Nancy explained civil disobedience and contrasted it with some rules of society that should not be broken.

The discussion of ethics in relation to literature occurred during the reading of Dickens' A *Christmas Carol*, which extended over a number of weeks during the fall. Nancy engaged the class in discussions about the author's background and how Dickens' experiences shaped his writing. In addition, Nancy linked ethics to the story by explaining why Scrooge should not be hated, with students expressing sympathy for Ebenezer in subsequent commentaries.

While discussing another story, *Franklin and the Tooth Fairy*, Nancy reminded the students of a previous lesson on good hygiene as well as pointing to an ethical lesson about celebrating the differences among people. This prompted the students to think about "What would this world be like if everyone was the same?" When the class read *My River*, Nancy praised her class for picking up the trash on the ground during the previous day's field trip, reflecting with her students about how they understood better than many adults their responsibility to care for the earth.

Home–School Connections

Nancy often connected with her students' homes. For example, she praised her students for working hard on schoolwork with their moms and dads. Parents were heavily involved in Nancy's room; she relied on them for help with classroom tasks, such as administering standardized tests, supervising writer's workshop, and going on field trips.

Personal Connections

During recess, Nancy entertained her students by singing, dancing, and playing popular music for them. Even when she was not feeling well, she played football and hopscotch with the students at recess. Nancy cared about her students, and it showed. She wrote get-well cards to sick students, made sure that new students in her classroom felt comfortable, and was supportive of families during times of tragedy (e.g., raking leaves with her students for a family whose father had died).

Nancy personalized instruction every day, relating aspects of her life to the students to make points. In particular, Nancy used stories about her personal experiences as tools for introducing new skills and ideas. For example, she encouraged her students to use comprehension strategies they were learning by telling them, "I still do it." On another occasion, she encouraged students to make images in their heads of what they were reading, informing them that making images helped her to remember what she read. Nancy told lots of stories about her family to increase her students' understanding of ideas.

For example, as a metaphor for writing instruction, Nancy began by pointing out to students that "someone needs to show you how to do complicated things." She then told a story of her father learning to fly an airplane by spending a great deal of time in the cockpit with an experienced pilot, watching him fly. She connected this to writing by explaining that "sometimes you need to see what good writing is."

On another occasion, she related a story of her son using the side of the crib to learn to walk because he wanted to reach a rocking horse a few feet away. Nancy explained, "That was a strategy," and then reminded the students about a writing workshop strategy they could use (i.e., using a personal dictionary to look up words).

She also provided warnings about the consequences of not being appropriately strategic by telling the class about her son's performance on the state achievement test. He had not done well when he failed to read problems carefully or check his work. Nancy implored her students: "My concern is that you are going to be like my son, Jim, who works ahead and makes mistakes." In this way, she was able to make her point about her students seeming to rush through their work without accusing members of the class of this shortcoming directly.

One day Nancy told the class about her husband breaking his leg and needing crutches. This was a lead-in to her explanation about why she was removing alphabet strips from the students' desks. She concluded by telling the students "Eventually, you have to get off the crutches."

By telling stories that connected with the lives of others—about her sons, last year's class, or "the other first grade"—Nancy managed to provide a lot of information to her own class about how smart people make their way about the academic world successfully.

Nancy connected to her students' lives through the community. For example, one way that she kidded her students was to tell them that she would talk about them with their mothers in the summer as she read books by the community pool.

Connections to the Future

Nancy's teaching often connected to what students might become. For example, in a unit focused on careers, community members came to the class to discuss their jobs (e.g., attorney, nurse, builder) with the students. The members of the class responded to these presentations by creating stories and pictures about themselves in the future.

In general, Nancy was very mindful of her students' futures. She aspired to teach her students to become independent readers and writers by the end of the year. There was much discussion in her class about how first grade is relevant to later years in school. Nancy explained to her students the expectations in second grade. For example, she introduced the standardized test taken in grade 1 as practice for the tests coming in later grades: "This is to give you practice. ... I need to make sure that you know how to do these kind of tests for second and third grade." She made very clear to her students that they would be capable of upcoming demands. Thus, during the grade 1 test, she told the class how difficult the test was and that she was proud of how well they were doing. One way that she concretized to her grade 1 students that they would be equal to the demands of the higher grades was to challenge the grade 7 students to an academic quiz. The game was structured so that the grade 1 students did quite well, with the first graders actually winning. (The grade 7 students graciously consented to be the losers.) Nancy was effusive in her congratulations to the first grade on their victory over grade 7, making the point that the grade 1 students were equal to the academic tasks ahead of them in the school.

Nancy was thinking about her students' futures even before they arrived in her classroom. She arranged a partnership with the kindergarten teacher so that Nancy and her class visited kindergarten. The kindergarten and grade 1 students collaborated in the writing of stories during this visit. A clear intention of this activity was for the kindergarten students to get to know Nancy, so that grade 1 would not seem like a frightening experience.

ENCOURAGING COGNITIVE CONFLICT AND ENGAGEMENT

Nancy asked many questions intended to get the students thinking. Students were often asked "why" during class discussion. She encouraged predictions by probing: "What's the story going to be about?" "Does everything we read always have a problem?" and "Are we reading this book because of a problem or to give you information?" When students seemed vague about a critical concept, for example, "prediction," Nancy would pose a question designed to increase the focus of attention on the concept, such as when she asked, "Is this a prediction? 'These carrots are going to turn purple and fly around the room.' " Students eagerly responded to Nancy's questions, and their answers often reflected great thought.

In general, Nancy's students were engaged by what went on in class. For example, they were raptly attentive during story time. Although in other classes in this study we had observed story time as just a way to pass the time during snack, this was not the case in Nancy's class. Story time in Nancy's class was full of excitement and challenge, with a strong emphasis on good literature. A highlight of every school day was Nancy's reading from a classic book to the class (e.g., *Black Beauty*, *A Christmas Carol*, *Charlie and the Chocolate Factory*, *The Call of the Wild*, *A Tale of Two Cities*). The students eagerly participated in discussions of these stories, enchanted by the stories themselves as well as by Nancy's enthusiastic and expressive rendering of them. During a very expressive reading of *Pumpkin Pumpkin*, Nancy proposed questions such as "What do you think this story is about?" "How do you know?" and "What do we know about ladybugs?" Nancy increased the excitement about the stories by revealing her personal feelings about them (e.g., talking about her sympathy for the characters in *The Story of Ruby Bridges*). She also increased interest in stories being read by relating them to upcoming class activities, such as when she related the upcoming science project involving the growing of carrots to the *Pumpkin Pumpkin* story.

Nancy made clear to us during her interview that it was her intention to motivate students during story time, to get them interested in all of the elements of reading (e.g., authorial intention). Thus, during several stories (e.g., *My River*, *A Christmas Carol*, *A Tale of Two Cities*), Nancy stressed the importance of understanding the author's experiences in order to comprehend the story. Nancy explained on one occasion, "Authors write about two things: what they know and what they feel like inside." She continued, "Who's been to Mexico? Could you write about Mexico?" She went on to make a connection to the story then being read by asking students, "Why do you think Dickens wrote about poor people?" What really increased students' interest was that this lesson about authoring connected directly to writing that afternoon, when students were asked during writer's workshop to become authors and write about something they know.

SUMMARY

The students in Nancy's classroom make clear that they love her! We encountered several parents of Nancy's students when we were doing the study. They loved her, too. Why not? The students are busy and happy, always working hard on obviously worthwhile academic tasks. The parents can be confident that their children are well taught, for Nancy keeps them in the loop: Parents often help in the class. Notes go home frequently. Nancy sees the parents in the community.

Nancy's reading of classic literature to her students is almost legendary in the community, with parents often lobbying to increase the odds that their kindergarten students will be in Nancy's grade 1 class. Such parents told us and tell the principal that they want their kids to experience the wonderful books that Nancy reads aloud. They also told us that they wanted the opportunity to interact with Nancy more themselves. Nancy's appeal is to the entire social world where her school is situated; she is someone that parents value enough to want to know better. The connections and cooperation that characterize Nancy's classrooms characterize her life in general, making her someone that many want to know.

Nancy is always getting the students thinking, asking them questions that they really have to ponder. In taking a stab at such questions, students often get conflicting perspectives on the floor, with Nancy managing to relate every one of the perspectives to one another so that students can feel their ideas are valued. She is always pointing out how something being covered or discussed at the moment relates to ideas encountered previously. As we close this case study of Nancy, we emphasize the word "always." Every minute of every day, Nancy is doing something to motivate someone in her classroom. Every minute of every day she is teaching—sometimes the whole group, sometimes small groups, and sometimes in response to individual student needs. Nancy never lets up in creating a positive, instructive, and informative world for her students.

In flooding her classroom, Nancy uses virtually all of the positive motivational mechanisms detailed in Table 2.4. Also, she rarely if ever does anything that could undermine a student's motivation (i.e., none of the elements of instruction in Table 2.5 occur in Nancy's classrooms). With so much support for academic engagement, it is not surprising that we observed every one of Nancy's students attentively engaged for every minute of every visit made to her classroom.

CHAPTER 4

Angel Shell's Class

This is the story of another grade 1 classroom—one where motivation also was very high, as reflected by student engagement in reading and writing. Like Nancy's classroom, this one was observed by Bogner and colleagues (Bogner, Raphael, & Pressley, 2002), with the researchers concluding that this classroom was better than most in the study with respect to stimulating students' motivations to read and write. Many students had little difficulty with the assignments in the class, which often provided just enough challenge that students could do them with a little bit of thinking. When students were more challenged, Angel or an aid provided assistance that permitted them to make progress.

Just as composition seemed a telling indicator of accomplishment in Nancy's class, so it was in Angel's class. By the end of the year, many students were writing stories that involved multiple sentences (i.e., one to two pages of writing), with the stories having reasonable coherence. Although mechanics were far from perfect, the writing of many students reflected knowledge of the most important capitalization and punctuation conventions as well as the correct spellings of many high-frequency words. Low-frequency words typically were good invented spellings. Of course, these same strengths were reflected in the stories that the class created, including one that connected with a science unit (*Is It Alive?*).

We review in some detail in this case study how Angel Shell motivated her students to read and write. What will become apparent is that there was some overlap in the approaches taken by Angel and Nancy, although there was also much that distinguished the two with respect to their approaches to motivating literacy engagement.

THE SETTING

Angel Shell teaches at a school serving a suburban-like area of the small Midwestern city where the studies summarized in Chapter 2 were conducted. The school is in excellent condition, clean, bright, and welcoming. Every day students are greeted by friendly faculty and staff as they enter the building. When a visitor comes by the school office or staff room, there are lots of hellos and smiles from the principal, secretary, staff, and volunteer parents. During the year when Angel was observed, the principal received an award from the community for her dedication to the school's students. The school has a reputation as a caring place, and the warmth was apparent to the observers throughout their year of contact with the institution. The school is fully enrolled, with a substantial waiting list for admission to most grades.

THE TEACHER AND HER CLASS

Angel had been a teacher for 5 years at the time of our observations. Four years had been spent teaching first grade; Prior to that, she taught art at the upper grades for 1 year. She had been an elementary education major at a university well known for its excellent elementary education program.

Angel knew her school community well, for she had been a student in the school when she was a youngster. In fact, the current principal had been one of her teachers. Throughout the year, we heard many remarks by Angel to students in her class and other classes, staff members, and parents that reflected deep knowledge of the community (e.g., comments about a student's older brother or sister, questions about whether a baby had been born yet).

A general impression of the observers after a year was that Angel's classroom was a fun and caring place, where there was never any tension. Misbehavior rarely occurred, with students always on-task and usually aware of what was expected of them. When interviewed at midyear, Angel felt that the current class had been well prepared for first grade. At midyear, Angel was very positive about her students' reading but concerned about their writing; she felt that they needed more practice in sounding out words to write them. She felt that many students were so concerned about spelling words absolutely correctly that it was negatively affecting their creativity and expressiveness in developing compositions.

Hence, Angel encouraged her students to take more chances with their spelling, making the case to them that learning to spell correctly is a by-product of writing a lot. The observers heard frequent remarks such as, "Try writing it out on your own. I bet you guys will do a great job. Don't worry about the spelling. I'll fix it."

Angel reported during her interview a complete commitment to the philosophy that every student can learn, and she was committed to guiding students through the learning process. She saw it as her job to create a classroom that supported and motivated learning. In fact, even before a student entered the room, the visitor knew that much effort had gone into making the most of the classroom space. The desks were clustered in small groups so that each group would have access to a display relevant to the current science project (e.g., butterflies in terrariums, with each small group having their own display). There were student mailboxes for the day's homework assignments that were to be taken to Mom and Dad, and in-boxes for returned homework. The teacher's desk was in a recessed space near the door, permitting private conferences with students while simultaneously taking up only a small area. With this arrangement, there was lots of space for students to move about the room, which they often did as they wrote and worked on projects.

A SUPPORTIVE ENVIRONMENT

Angel rarely seemed in anything except a good mood, reflecting the effect the students had on her. During an interview with the observers, Angel related that when she felt it was a tough day, she would sit back and watch the kids because they would make her laugh. Her pleasant temperament translated into exclusively positive communications with students, including lots of good-natured teasing by the teacher. Such teasing accomplished much, including making discipline more tolerable. Thus, when she spotted a student using a pen, which was not permitted in the grade 1 curriculum, Angel snatched the pen from the student, remarking "I love pens [exaggerating the word 'love' as she said it], but you can have it back at the end of the day." It was apparent the student understood the teacher's intention, quickly retrieving his pencil with no sign of distress over the encounter.

In another incident, when Josh went off-task, Angel bent over quietly and said to him, "Josh, here's your warning. I need you to calm down so we can learn about phonics." It worked, with Josh on-task the rest of the class. A favorite phrase for Angel was "You accidentally got one wrong," which consistently prompted students to recheck their work, with students so prompted always seeming determined to find the accident in their work! In these interactions and many others, the observers perceived a teacher who tried to interact with her students at their level, all the while making clear to them that they were smart and capable.

Angel cared about her students, which was apparent through her exceptionally kind interactions with them. Thus, when there was a misbehavior, Angel asked the student to stay in at recess to "talk" with her, with the talks always a gentle reflection with the student on his/her misbehavior, how the misbehavior negatively affected the classroom and the student, and how the student might behave more constructively. When a student was off-task—for example, cleaning out his or her desk instead of doing an assignment, Angel reminded the student of the morning's assignments and offered to help him or her get organized and get going. In a matter of a few seconds, the student was back on-task for the rest of the morning. When the whole class got a little noisy on one occasion, Angel simply stated in a very positive way her concern and offered a reasonable alternative: "I hear a lot of yib-yabbing. If you can whisper, that's fine." On another occasion when things got noisy, Angel asked the students to work quietly to show respect for the student who was reading to her. That is, she reminded the students about the consequences of the noisiness and the prosocial reasons for working more quietly. Angel knew how to get things under control quickly. Thus, when she wanted to move students out of small groups and into an individual activity, she simply said, "I need every little person to return to their seats," and it was a accomplished in a few seconds. The management was always gentle and effective.

Angel also adjusted classroom routines to meet individual needs of students, sometimes permitting unusual behavior if that seemed appropriate in a situation. Thus, when one little girl did not feel like participating in a class activity, Angel allowed her to sit under the teacher's desk and told the other students, "That is where she is comfortable right now." Angel's care came through as well as she reflected on particular students and sought help for them. For example, the observers witnessed a conversation between Angel and the resource teacher as they reflected on a student who had both emotional problems and was exhibiting mirror writing. When a student was not feeling well, Angel gave him a thermometer and asked, "Do you want to last until lunch? You could be sick because you're hot, wearing yourself down. Unbutton your shirt. Relax a bit."

Caring really came through when students did not understand something. Angel never put students down, instead finding a way for students to save face. Thus, when a student drew a flower on a worksheet directing students to draw an illustration of the Mayflower, Angel smiled and said, "It's OK. Lots of you drew pictures of flowers!" By the time the Thanksgiving Day lessons were completed, however, Angel managed to get across several more times that the Mayflower was the Pilgrims' ship! That is, student mistakes did not stimulate criticism from Angel, but rather guided her teaching and reteaching.

With respect to achievement, what was encouraged was for students to do their best. The message was consistent that effort paid off. As Angel put it on one occasion, "Never say that you can't do something. Chances are that you can. You just need someone to watch you." During difficult tasks, it was typical to hear Angel make remarks such as "This might be difficult, but you can do it. I want you to try." Angel praised students for trying difficult tasks, such as reading on their own or writing (e.g., "You have absolutely the best, best handwriting, which means you take your time. Pat yourself on the back"). She encouraged reasonable risks, such as guessing at new words encountered in text, assuring them that she believed they were capable of figuring out what the word might be. Similarly, she encouraged such risk taking during writing: "You guys, don't worry about spelling. This is the first time you're writing your own story. No need to get frustrated." Angel also praised her students for asking questions when they were unsure. She acknowledged that her students were doing a good job, frequently giving them stickers for good work, putting rubber stamps on their worksheets and journals, and telling the teacher aide loudly, "Oh, they are such good kids."

Although the school required letter grading even in grade 1, and Angel gave students letter grades on most assignments, the grades did not seem to be a big deal. At first, the observers had feared that letter grades might be prominent in the classroom because on the first visit they saw one display of the "A+" papers on a recent assignment. Even so, the display was in an obscure corner of the room, and no one seemed to notice it. Moreover, the same papers stayed up for months, which contrasted with other displays in the class that were always new, reflecting recent lessons. Even though there were letter grades in the class, no one noticed them much.

Rather than reinforce students for doing well, Angel reinforced students for doing better. For example, she gave students bonus points for trying more challenging tasks than ones they had tried previously. She also inspired students to do their best in writing by reminding them that their stories were going to be posted outside in the hallway. Yes, every-one's story was posted, but all the children were given incentive to make certain their stories were as good as they could be. There was never a hint of some stories being better than others, just that everybody's story was as good as it could be.

This supportive classroom was a lot of fun for students, which was one of Angel's goals, as she reported in an interview with the observers. Angel often addressed her charges as "little people," a reference that was recognized as affectionate by the students. She frequently pointed out to the students that they had a "goofy" teacher. Humor even occurred in what are often humorless first-grade tasks, such as doing the phonics workbook. For example, the students never had any difficulty with the workbook sheets, which Angel would emphasize by telling them, tongue in cheek, "These worksheets are so hard that you can't stand it." After students drilled on the sounds for *q*, *p*, and *b*, Angel told the class that they sounded like a bunch of bees. Her phonics lessons were often playful: "See how we change the word [i.e., when a long vowel sound occurs rather than a short vowel sound]. If you read the word, and it sounds goofy, maybe you are saying the wrong vowel sound." On another occa-sion, she characterized the letter *c* in human terms: "C is a sneaky guy that took someone else's sound." The "*q* and *u* connection" was probed with "Who is *q*'s best friend?" The playfulness continued as Angel monitored students doing their worksheets, figuring out who needed some encour-agement to reflect more on their work. Thus, the observers frequently heard remarks such as "Ohhhh! Some of us found our mistakes! If you said it wrong, you should look at it and correct it." In doing so, the students who did well were affirmed and the ones who were halfway there (i.e., seeming to be a little aware that what they sounded out didn't seem right) were encouraged to try some more. That fun was really important in this classroom was especially apparent on days when the weather was very nice. Even if it might make sense for a student to remain inside to com-plete work, Angel insisted that the children go outside and "just go play." As academically supportive as this classroom was, it was also supportive of children being children.

When Angel scaffolded writing one morning in late February, she told the students that they were writing just the way first graders should be writing. Angel had the students come to her desk for a writing confer-ence, which began with each student reading what he or she had written, with Angel then offering revision suggestions, sometimes to the point of rewriting the sentence into conventional English. Angel teased the students that she was helping them with their writing so that she could read it, too. Angel then went on to challenge the class to show their writing to Mom and Dad to see if they could read it. There were lots of messages in this set of exchanges, including clear indications to the students that their writing was good, something to take pride in (e.g., by showing their parents), but that it could and would be getting better.

COOPERATIVE LEARNING

In Angel's classroom, students cooperated, often working together. Angel recognized that her students enjoyed helping and teaching each other, so she encouraged them to work together as partners. Angel provided explicit instruction to her students about how to do such partner learning and teaching well. For example, it was typical to hear remarks such as "Help him read but don't tell him. Have him sound it out." Such cooperative learning was especially prevalent during science. Thus, during the millipedes unit, students observed the millipedes together and discussed their observations as they recorded them in their journals.

Even during whole-group instruction, Angel often asked the class to sound out words and letters together, telling the class that she needed to hear everyone say things together. Whole-group creative writing involved the students sharing ideas about what could be in the developing stories, with such writing almost always having a fun twist (e.g., when writing a story that connected with the science unit on insects, students pretended to be bugs and insects, writing from the perspectives of the creatures). Cooperative participation was prevalent, however, whether the instruction was whole or small group. For example, Angel monitored the peer tutoring, always stressing how the students were teachers in interacting with each other, giving them reason for pride in their partner learning and teaching efforts; she also monitored whole-group participation, moving quickly to encourage students who were not participating to get involved.

It should be noted that peer cooperative teaching and learning seemed more productive with the more capable students. Thus, weaker students had many interactions with the teacher's aide and parent volunteers as they did their work, with these adults providing much assistance in helping the weaker students understand tasks and how the work could be accomplished. Just as Angel's one to-one interactions had the feel of an adult working with students rather than talking at them, so it was with the teacher aide–student and parent volunteer–student interactions.

Rather than keep the good and weaker students segregated during partner learning, Angel frequently had stronger students partner with weaker students, again with the message that the students were working together rather than the stronger student providing the lead and the weaker student following. This was a classroom where people worked with one another. Cooperation was everywhere apparent in the room during every hour of observations.

INTERESTING CONTENT

Although there was a great deal of skills instruction, it was always carried out in an engaging fashion, as described earlier. Much of the skills work was clearly easy for the students, and never frustrating for most students. With the teacher, teacher aide, and parent volunteer providing support as needed for weaker students, frustration was avoided for the latter as well. If anything, the observers came to this study with the belief that skills instruction and practice would be boring for students. In general, this prediction proved wrong in Angel's classroom. The observers really saw nothing to suggest that students disliked or were bored by the skills work they were required to do.

Angel was really into science, with engaging science units all year. The students watched butterflies develop, studied centipedes, and planted gardens over the course of the year, with these activities complemented by content area instruction (e.g., coverage of metamorphosis during the butterfly unit), reading of thematically related literature (i.e., books and poems about butterflies), and writing (e.g., each student composing his or her own butterfly book).

Writing about particular topics was also a big deal in this class, with creative writing morning occurring quite often. During creative writing, Angel gave students the chance to be real authors, to have real ownership of their stories. Angel repeatedly told students as she scaffolded creative writing, "This is your story. We are making it up as we go along." Angel would make certain there was a lot of adult support in the room on such days, for many students needed it to develop their story ideas, organize the ideas into a draft, and then revise. Even so, creative writing was really exciting for the students. On one visit to Angel's classroom, the observers arrived during the beginning stages of drafting a story. The observers watched the entire writing process that morning.

The process began with each student selecting his or her favorite animal. Then, Angel continued, "You've chosen your favorite animal and have your reason. If you were that animal, what would your name be? What would your friends call you if you were a pill bug? It can be any name you want. Picking a name is really hard. I know when your mommies and daddies picked your name, it took a long time." Then, the students shared the names they selected with Angel, with everyone laughing at each other's choices. This creative writing started with fun and it continued that way until the students could read their stories to the adults in the room and their peers, beaming with pride as they did so. The creative writing topic cooked, with students assisted as needed so that everyone experienced success and the feeling of success. It was easy to understand why students in this class liked what Angel asked them to do.

During every visit, the observers were impressed that Angel's whole-group discussions had high participation rates. They were very traditional in the sense that the teacher posed questions and the students bid to answer. The number of bidders was consistently high and consistently enthusiastic, with students generally listening attentively as other students spoke. The discussions often required students to reflect on lexical subtleties, such as when students responded to Angel's questions about jack-o' lanterns:

> How can a jack o'lantern be good? Did he get all A's? Think about that . . .
>
> Can a jack o'lantern *have* feelings? Can it *show* feelings?
>
> Is it alive? What about when the pumpkin was attached to the vine? Was it alive then? If we cut the pumpkin off the vine and set it on the porch, is it alive?

The students could not wait to offer their insights about such issues. In short, even such traditional classroom discussions seemed interesting to students, with the students consistently excited about interacting with Angel and thinking about the things she found interesting. Discussions about even very abstract concepts—such as the nature of living versus nonliving things—which can be quite boring for grade 1 students, literally came to life in Angel's class.

Halloween was more than just a holiday party in Angel's class. It was a motivating curricular event. She read stories about Halloween, ones that motivated activities, which then drove discussions about Halloween. The students wrote stories about Halloween. Angel used Halloween to encourage reading, writing, and thinking, as her students immersed themselves in thoughts of a wonderful childhood experience.

Angel encouraged student interest in things academic. Thus, she often expressed interest in books students were reading, for example, asking a student what she or he liked about a book. When one little boy was reading a dinosaur book, Angel engaged him, "Do you wish you had a dinosaur? Do you see a picture in here of one you'd like?" When one was selected by the youngster, Angel reacted, "Ooh, that would be neat because you could fly on his back." Angel was always finding ways to let the students know that what they were reading and thinking about was intriguing.

BALANCING EXPLICIT INSTRUCTION, SCAFFOLDING, AND COGNITIVE CONFLICT

There was never a day when there was not a great deal of modeling and explaining of skills. Angel especially modeled how to sound out words. She encouraged other word-level skills as well, often modeling the process of looking up tricky words in the dictionary. As she thumbed carefully through the pages of the dictionary, Angel reported out loud to the class, "OK, guys, I have to look up 'leper.' Can you help me out? What does it begin with?" As she looked up the word, she sang the alphabet song, making clear that looking up a word was an alphabetic experience. She stopped the song when she came to the first letter of the word, remembering out loud the letter–sound relationship. Then she narrowed the search by singing the alphabet again until she came to the second letter, continuing letter by letter until she found the target word.

Angel also taught a lot of writing strategies, with these reviewed opportunistically. Thus, whenever students printed, Angel provided reminders such as to use finger spacing (if the child could not space without using the fingers as tools) and to make certain that letters touched the baseline. As students composed, Angel reminded students to sound out words that they did not know how to spell already and to use the dictionary if that helped. On completion of a draft of a story, Angel frequently reminded students to reread the story to see if it made sense and whether something might be added. She encouraged students to draw pictures to accompany their stories if that helped to make the story more sensible. The students were very well aware of the difference between a rough copy and a final draft when writing, with Angel providing lots of explicit teaching about how a final draft is the result of much planning, drafting, revising—all effortful processes.

Angel's teaching included lots of strategies to make certain that students understood what was required of them. For example, Angel provided numerous examples whenever she taught new content or a new skill, making the abstract more concrete for her students. She did a lot of teaching that involved students each using a very familiar word—her or his own name. Thus, the observers heard Angel ask students to tell her about the short and long vowels in their name, and they heard her prompt students to look at their name tags when trying to figure out how to write particular letters in their name.

Another teaching tactic was to ask lots of "why" questions, probes intended to promote cognitive conflict and encourage students to think hard about what they were doing. Thus, Angel asked students why they wrote certain words the way they did (i.e., eliciting explanations of invented spellings in terms of component sounds and the blending of sounds), why particular words looked the way they did, why students chose to include certain elements in a story, and why they enjoyed stories that were read in class. These questions typically reflected that Angel was monitoring a student's progress with a task and providing a question that prompted reflection on an emerging skill or understanding (e.g., Angel asked why a student spelled a word a particular way after watching the student carefully sound it out, perhaps getting most but not all of the word's spelling). Angel also sometimes asked questions about closely contrasting concepts and words. Thus, during a lesson on contractions, she asked her students about the difference between "here's" and "he's": "Could 'here's' be the same as 'he's,' since they both have 'he' in them?"

Angel often deliberately made mistakes or pretended that something was very tricky, with this approach to stimulating cognitive conflict in students always getting the students to think actively about the content being taught. Thus, often Angel would misread one or more days of the week during morning calendar, permitting the class to correct her loudly and with enthusiasm. Before covering some irregular words as part of phonics, Angel would tease the class about how some of the words in the lesson were really tricky. After teaching about contractions, Angel then wrote the word "cant" on the board, asking the students if it was correct. Many students shouted out that the word was wrong, with the students then pointing out where the apostrophe should go. By so making a point of challenging examples, Angel stimulated much processing in students and seemed to get them thinking a great deal about processing and learning of content.

When students asked Angel questions, she often turned it into an occasion for a process lesson. Thus, when a student asked her what "weeb" (her pronounciation of "web") meant, Angel's reply was "I don't know what a 'weeb' is either. Try saying it another way."

In short, Angel both taught explicitly and encouraged active thinking by students—modeling, explaining, questioning, and turning student questions around on them to stimulate a search for answers. She had many ways to encourage students to come to understand complex processes and hard content, including making subtle distinctions (e.g., "here's" versus "he's"). Once taught, however, new skills and knowledge must be used in order to be mastered. Angel assured that students experienced much success in using what they were learning through extensive scaffolding.

Scaffolding was facilitated in the class by seating the students most in need of support together. This permitted Angel, as well as the teacher's aide, resource teacher, and parent volunteers to spend more time with these students, while traversing little distance to move between those most likely to be struggling. These students certainly were not segregated from the rest of the class, however, as they were very much a part of the action during whole-group instruction and interactions.

When Angel scheduled activities that she knew would be especially challenging to the weaker students, she also scheduled in extra help in the form of the resource teacher and volunteers. Hence, although Angel scaffolded almost every task for struggling students as they worked (e.g., the worksheets that were so easy for most students were, in fact, challenging for some), scaffolding was more obvious during some activities than others, largely because of the number of adults in the room providing the support. Creative writing was one such activity, with the at-risk students needing more help with all phases, from planning to drafting to revising. Of course, that did not mean Angel ignored the at-risk students. In fact, she provided them with a great deal of support, much as she provided support to other students.

Consider this typical set of comments and questions from Angel while her students drafted their Halloween stories:

> "Tell me something about Halloween. What occurs after picking a costume? . . . (*turning to another student*) . . . 'I go trick or treating.' Is that how you say that? . . . (*turning to yet another student*)

... Think about how you feel, what you like about Halloween. (*then, another student*) ... Why didn't you think of little sentences first? Think of something short."

Angel was reading and reacting to her students' emerging drafts throughout the hour devoted to creative writing that morning. She never told students what to write, but rather provided hints, suggestions, and leading questions, such as "Instead of saying this, how about saying ... ?" "What does it begin with?" and "What letter should begin the sound?"

What was very impressive was that all the other adults who interacted with the students supported them in a style similar to Angel's, with the resource teacher just as adept at coming up with just the right comment to get students moving along. Although the teacher's aide and parent volunteers were not quite as able to provide such support quickly, they all worked well with individual students, consistently coming up with remarks that were helpful in encouraging more writing by students without telling the students what to write or doing the writing for the students.

In addition to making certain that students received supportive input and feedback as they wrote, Angel also assured success by having different goals for different students. Thus, at midyear, when she was urging the best writers to get four or five sentences in their drafts, other students in the class were urged to put together two-sentence drafts. Angel's goal was to make certain that each student's story was a little more impressive than the last story he or she wrote, with her current goal for each student informed by her knowledge of how the student had performed in the past. Expectations and demands increased gradually in this class, with every student on an upward trajectory.

CONNECTIONS

Angel made many connections intended to motivate her students. Connections were easy to spot during every day of observations.

Across the Curriculum

Of course, whenever Angel, the aide, the resource teacher, or a volunteer scaffolded a student so he or she would use a previously taught skill, there was a connection made across the curriculum; hence, across-the curriculum connections were frequent and tailored to student needs. The planned curriculum also was connected, however. For example, science instruction, which occurred every day, was completely intertwined with literacy. The butterfly unit included the reading of stories about butterflies and much writing. Thus, reading was definitely purposeful (i.e., students read to learn about science), as was writing (i.e., students wrote to communicate what they had observed in science). Students often read math problems aloud, with Angel probing to make certain they understood key vocabulary (e.g., "Do you add or subtract when something *becomes* bigger?").

With Students

Angel was genuinely interested in her students, frequently expressing her concerns about each of them. She asked about important events in their lives, from dental appointments to the birth of new family members. Students often shared their most recent accomplishments (e.g., the number of skip ropes one girl was able to do consecutively). Sometimes students stayed in at recess to tell their adventures to Angel, as when one little boy told her about an arrowhead he had found. Angel's reactions were always enthusiastic, with "Wow!" being a word that often came out of her mouth. Connections with students did not end when they graduated from Angel's classroom, with the researchers witnessing many visits from former students. For example, former students often marked their own birthdays by visiting Angel, who rewarded them with a sticker. Moreover, the start of the school year was not the beginning of Angel's connection to many of her pupils. For example, she sometimes visited with the kindergarten class, permitting some getting-acquainted time with her future students. Angel knew the children well, and her intense involvement during the grade 1 year was simply a widening in the road of their interaction. Students connected with Angel before they entered the school (the researchers witnessed a visit of school community members' babies to the grade 1 class, babies who very well might attend the school someday), while they attended the school, and after they departed (e.g., high school students who had previously attended the school sometimes volunteered as part of their service learning experience).

Home–School Connections

The most obvious home–school connection was the daily involvement of moms and dads with homework. Angel often praised students for the hard work they did on homework with their parents. She encouraged such involvement whenever possible. Thus, in November, the observers over-heard an Angel–student conversation: After Angel and the student worked awhile at reading a story, she urged the child to read the story to Mom that night, assuring the little girl that her mom would love to hear just how well she was reading. Angel's belief in the role of parents in edu-cation came through very clearly during the end-of-study interview, when she expressed the view that the parents were co-educators and, if any-thing, more important in the education process than the teacher. She ex-pected parents to read with their children and to check their homework, and, with a few exceptions, that seemed to occur.

The deep connection between Angel's classroom and the students' homes was especially apparent with respect to an activity involving a stuffed toy, "Lee the Lion." Lee went home every weekend with a class member, who wrote in a journal that accompanied the toy lion just what happened over the weekend. Angel read the journal aloud to the class on Monday and probed the student about the weekend's activities, with the class looking on (e.g., "Did Lee try and get your food?" "Where did he sleep?" "Did he chew on your pillow?"). Something that Angel sometimes pointed out to the class was that a student's older brother or sister carried the same lion home a few years before and wrote in the journal, with read-ing of that previous journal entry providing a connection between this first-grade classroom, its students and families, and earlier classes, over years. For example, Angel pointed out on one occasion how the journal permitted a child now in fourth grade to see how she used to write. The fourth grader recognized just how much growth there had been in the in-tervening years. In short, the Lee the Lion activity was more than just an inspired way to motivate literacy (i.e., writing). It was an effective way to make students in the class aware that they would continue to grow as lit-eracy learners and soon become as competent as the older students in the school.

CHOICES AND THE DEVELOPMENT OF SELF-REGULATION

It would be impossible not to notice that Angel's students were generally on-task, working hard. They were very self-regulated. An important part of self-regulation involves learning to make the right choices, and Angel definitely provided many opportunities for student choice. She created the clear message that making reasonable choices was expected in her classroom.

For example, the observers were present on a day when a student had many incomplete worksheets. Rather than permit the student to be overwhelmed, Angel counseled, "You just do one of them at a time. Which one do you want to do?" With that, she prompted self-regulation through choice and the construction of a manageable plan, with the child working away at the worksheets the rest of the morning. Similarly, Angel made certain that her students knew they had choices with respect to conduct. Thus, when a student was goofing off in his cooperative group, she informed the student that he could "choose to laugh," but there would be a consequence for not completing the task (i.e., it would have to be done later, when other students would have free time). On another occasion, a student was playing with his watch. Angel also gave that student a choice—to wear it and not play with it or put it in his bookbag—otherwise he would face the consequence that Angel would take the watch and send it home to his mom. These specific examples were just part of a routine in Angel's class, with the class usually assigned multiple activities during a morning. Students were free to choose the order in which they completed tasks, and they did.

Choice was everywhere in this classroom. Even when one group's mealworm died, the group was given a choice about what they were going to do with it! A sad moment for the group, one where they were confronted with an event out of their control, was turned into one during which the students were reminded of the control they still had of the situation.

Part of self-regulation is learning to self-reward. Angel encouraged such self-reward. Often, after the class did a particular task well, Angel would say something like "Good job, first grade, give yourself a hand," with the class then applauding itself. Of course, the researcher-observers recognized that no amount of applause could have been enough in Angel's classroom, for there was always something impressive occurring, every minute, every day. Angel's classroom is a place where children are motivated to do well, and they *do* do well!

SUMMARY

As the researchers walked down the hall to Angel's classroom, they knew that they were going to see a good day of schoolwork in Angel's class, for every day was a good one. Every day included Angel kidding around with the students as they thought about science, sounded out words together, and pulled together their reflections on the world into impressive compositions for grade 1 students. Angel's first grade is the first grade that all parents hope their child will experience.

Just as was the case in Nancy Masters' classroom, Angel Shell evidenced the entire range of positive motivating teacher behaviors summarized in Table 2.4, while avoiding the teaching behaviors summarized in Table 2.5 (i.e., those with potential to undermine student motivation). Angel floods every hour of every school day with motivating instruction. It is impossible to be in her room for even a minute without something positive happening to at least one child, more typically several children, and often the whole class. No wonder that many students would rather stay in the room with Angel during recess and many linger at the end of the day to have just a few more minutes with her.

CHAPTER 5

Chris Nemeth's Teaching

Ms. Chris Nemeth teaches grade 3. She does so in one of the most advantaged schools in the city, a private school with a long waiting list. The demanding parents who send their children there are very satisfied. As our research was occurring, the school was constructing a new wing, which included a state-of-the-art computer laboratory and a new library.

Of course, over the years of research on effective teaching, the team doing the research reported in this book has been in many schools with great resources and reputations. Extraordinarily effective teachers have been no more common in such schools than in less socioeconomically advantaged schools (Pressley, Allington, Wharton-McDonald, Block, & Morrow, 2001; Pressley, Wharton-McDonald, et al., 2001). Although Chris was the only teacher observed extensively in this particular school, the researchers were in the building a great deal, especially in the primary wing. They observed the students in Chris Nemeth's class to be more engaged than students in other classes in the school. For example, often when we passed the doorways of other classrooms, students would be off-task. That is, intense academic engagement is as rare a commodity in the school where Chris Nemeth teaches, as it is in other schools in the United States that our group has visited.

Consistently, every child in Chris's class was engaged in the academic tasks that she planned. There often was a lot of chatter, but it was about the tasks, reflecting substantial cooperation among the students. They were seldom off-task. The teacher and students laughed together as they worked through books, wrote great stories, and learned about the natural and mathematical worlds together. Although we never saw any concern in the class about preparing for standardized tests, the class scores were impressively high. As Chris put it, "Nationally, they went through the roof on their scores."

CURRICULUM AND INSTRUCTION

Chris Nemeth's students were always engaged. They were always academically focused, and it was rare to observe misbehavior. Chris's lessons were carefully planned, with materials ready to go at the start of the lesson. Chris delivered her lessons without a hitch.

Chris's classroom management was a mix of traditional and contemporary thinking. For example, the desks were arranged in groups of four, so that there were seven tables of four. That is, every student in the class had an assigned desk, but the desks are grouped to encourage cooperation, with many of the assignments involving cooperative learning by the students.

Concrete Manipulatives

In Chris's classroom, there were frequent hands-on experiences, with an outstanding collection of materials and equipment to support such instruction. Hands-on tasks occurred across the curriculum. For example, the researchers observed a number of lessons involving math manipulatives. During one math lesson, Chris taught the students how to fold a piece of paper to make a magic multiplier, which the students used to practice math facts (i.e., on the day we observed, the multiples of four). Chris covered an important math concept, operation in multiple ways, with the students experiencing and constructing multiple math representations during the lesson. Thus, Chris complemented the use of the magic multiplier to practice the multiples of four with a taped song that included the multiples of four. In addition, Chris provided flash card practice on the multiples of four and a homework page. Chris also took advantage of unexpected opportunities to reexplain various relationships or representations. Thus, when discussing that one-half of 10 was 5, Chris showed the students the equation $\frac{10}{2} = 5$. When mentioning the number 1,000, Chris reflected that it was the same as ten 100's. When discussing 0.8, Chris pointed out that this was equivalent to $\frac{8}{10}$ and that 80 cents was eight-tenths (0.8) of a dollar.

Chris's use of manipulatives always engaged the students. During an exercise on ordered series, Chris had them predict the weights of objects using their hands before they weighed the objects on a scale, with students placing the weights in a descending order from predicted heaviest to lightest. To make this exercise more interesting, Chris had the students bring their favorite toys as one of the objects to be weighed. The kids enjoyed doing this, but as they did their work, Chris led them to believe more fun was coming ("This is not even the fun part of the lesson, yet"). As an introduction to fractions, Chris had the students make a Fractional Person, a project which included having the students create a picture of themselves using equal squares of different colors. When the picture was complete, the students listed the colors and the fraction of the picture represented. The students then had to show that when all the different colored parts were added together, it equaled one whole person. By the end of the lesson the students seemed to understand the concept of fractions.

The students created multiple representations about literature as well. Thus, as the class read the novel *Sadako and the Thousand Paper Cranes* (Coerr, 1999), they also listened to a CD about the atomic bombing of Hiroshima, Japan. As they listened and read, the students constructed notes about the story in a special notebook developed by Chris. They also made paper cranes using origami. Of course, these materials-supported activities were just part of the encounter with the book: Chris provided an exciting preview by having students skim through the book, looking at the pictures. As the class read the novel, there were interesting class discussions, ones that permitted review of the plot but also related the story to the history of World War II and to ethics (e.g., a discussion of the horrors of nuclear war).

Concrete manipulatives also played a huge role in science instruction. During a lesson on how plants protect themselves, Chris brought in parts of plants for students to explore. There was no doubt that by the end of the lesson the students understood the protective role of thorns on roses and holly leaves. When the students covered the topic of insulation, Chris provided props like feathers, which permitted the class to experience firsthand the effects of an insulating material. Many of the science exercises were part of a science curriculum that Chris had selected because of its focus on concrete experiences and student experimentation. Science was exciting, a sensory experience, including opportunities for the students to amplify their senses through the use of real scientific equipment, most prominently the microscopes in the classroom. Equipment in Chris's room was used!

The most prominent set of concrete materials was a post office, with real equipment for stamp cancellation and delivery of mail (e.g., mail bags). Members of the class had real delivery routes in the school (i.e., the class wrote letters that were delivered to various people in the school). The classroom post office motivated student writing as well as permitting connections to math and social studies. Students wrote letters, performed calculations (e.g., to determine revenues produced by charging particular prices for stamps), and experienced lessons about how mail works through the national community as it moves from sender to recipient.

In summary, Chris's classroom was a place where students were immersed in multiple and deep representations, stimulated by concretely supported experiences. There was no doubt that these experiences were grabbers for students, as they were consistently engaged in math, science, and post office activities. The students received much practice relating the abstract to the concrete and then back to the abstract (i.e., the discussion of plant protection preceded the exercise with the rose and holly plants, which was followed by additional reflection on how plants protect themselves). The success of the activities was due, in large part, to extensive planning by Chris. She told us about how she ordered materials months in advance of specific lessons (i.e., ordering recipes online from a soybean company so the students could make hand cream and lip balm in a science lesson). The result was many quality lessons.

Scaffolding

Chris's class was filled with complex activities. Not surprisingly, students often needed assistance, and they received it. Chris, a classroom aide, and/or parent volunteers monitored individual student progress and offered assistance when students needed it. Often, when Chris observed several students struggling in the same way, she offered a mini-lesson or hints to the entire group, such as during a dictionary look-up exercise: "Sometimes we need to look for the base or root word." "What does *fidget* begin with?" "You're not using the guidewords. . . . Look at the first few letters. . . . Is it before or after the h? . . . Look at the guidewords."

Chris was especially attentive when students were off-task, often moving immediately to get them refocused. When they did refocus, she praised them (e.g., "James, thanks for watching me"). As she offered a mini-lesson on the run, Chris always was aware whether students were paying attention and let them know when she sensed they were less than raptly attentive (e.g., "Hello. I'm losing your eye contact. Look up here").

Chris communicated to her students that she was asking them to do challenging things, but she also consistently sent the message to students in her class that they were very capable:

> "This is not easy. I've had adults have trouble with this."
>
> "I learned this as an adult, not in third grade."
>
> "Now, I have something awesome—something you might not learn until fourth or fifth grade, but I'll teach you now."
>
> "Here's something Ms. W teaches in middle school. When you get to middle school, you'll be bored."
>
> "This is hard stuff, and you're doing great."

In short, Chris taught at the edge of her students' competence, letting them know they were meeting challenges, supporting the students as much as needed so that they could succeed. Chris accomplished this through hints and mini-lessons for students who needed assistance. When many of the students were getting good enough at a task to do it on their own with some effort, Chris often announced that she would be giving no more hints, providing no more help. She followed through on that promise with the stronger students. With weaker students, however, Chris quietly continued to give them support. Her students received the help they needed to make progress, but not more. As they did succeed, Chris flooded them with many comments about how impressive their efforts and achievements were!

Challenging Tasks

Virtually every theory of educational motivation includes the tenet that tasks that are a little bit challenging are more motivating than tasks which are too easy or very difficult. Coming up with tasks that are challenging enough for students to do with support is easier said than done. That is, the teacher has to come up with tasks that are neither too easy nor too difficult for every student in the class. Chris Nemeth did it every day we observed. One example was the academic games she used, which always seemed challenging. None was so hard that the students could not do it, and none was so hard that any student did not have a chance to experience some success in the game. The games all had some stretch so that the difficulty could be adjusted. Thus, if the students were getting all the questions right in science-review Jeopardy, Chris simply asked harder questions. Also, the hands-on science tasks always required reflective cooperation among the cooperative teams of four students at each table.

Chris revealed during an interview that she skipped many of the projects in the published science curriculum because her students would have found the activities too easy. She told us that one of her students' greatest strengths when they leave third grade was being "ready to take the challenges." When Chris realized that a homework assignment was too easy, she changed it. Thus, having written one assignment on the board, she announced at the end of a math lesson, "I'm going to change your homework. You guys are so intelligent. That page would be too cinchy." On the day when the class successfully reviewed the multiples of four aloud in class, Chris further challenged them, "Now you did so well, you get to do fives today!" The students' response was one of complete enthusiasm as they looked forward to the challenge.

Praise and Reinforcement

In general, Chris praised her students lavishly. Thus, after the class made a hand cream as part of a science demonstration, Chris pointed out to classroom visitors this accomplishment: "You'll have to try the hand cream we made in science." The day was filled with comments like "I love the way Nick is waiting patiently for me," "Good independent thinking. You're doing a great job," "Hey, your prediction was right on the money," "I think we have the routine of investigations down," "Good idea—getting books out and reading while you're waiting," and "Imagine that. Good for you." The walls were also filled with student work, sending the message to visitors that the students in this classroom did much that should be displayed. Student accomplishments in math were summarized in one set of charts in the room; music accomplishments were recorded on other charts; perfect spelling papers were framed and labeled "A+." Every student's achievement was displayed somewhere in the room!

In addition to the praise, Chris also used concrete reinforcement. She explained to us that she motivated students with a point system: "If the students are caught being good or doing what the expectations are, they earn 5 or 10 points. When they reach 100 points, they get a reward. For instance, now they've earned 100 points and get to watch *Hercules, The Movie*. If they decide to save up for another 100, I promised them ice cream or cupcakes. We also have a chart hanging on my desk. When students are caught individually following expectations, they can earn a line, and when they have earned 4 lines and made a box, they get a boxseat, which means they get to move their desk to anywhere in the classroom that they want to."

If the class was attentive and worked hard, Chris would play an academic game with them as a reward. A favorite was "around the world," which was a quiz game that provided review of math material that would be on an upcoming test. When the students did well on their math facts, Chris turned drilling the facts into a speed game (i.e., two students competing with one another to provide the correct answer more quickly than the other). After a round of "around the world," all students received stickers for their efforts, while the student who did exceptionally well also received a heart-shaped hand stamp. Each day students brought in their homework, they received an "X" on a card, with a week of Xs earning a lottery ticket in a prize drawing held every Friday.

It could not be missed that the tone in this class was consistently positive. Even when Chris had to deal with a behavior problem, she did it in a nonconfrontational way that was effective. Thus, one child's talkativeness ended after Chris remarked, "Whoever is whispering, I wish you would stop." When the class as a whole was noisy during a lesson, Chris simply reminded the students that they would not be allowed to come to the board to work a problem if they were talking. The class immediately became quiet, for going to the board was an opportunity valued by the students. Often Chris managed her students by using positive messages such as, "It's going to be a fun day, but we have to work together. We have a lot to accomplish."

Accountability and High Expectations

That Chris diligently checked homework was consistent with the generally high accountability in her classroom. Chris assigned nightly homework in math and reading. On Monday, she assigned spelling homework for the week. Once a week, students worked on a faith journal, with the intent to link religion learned in the classroom to home. Chris checked and graded seatwork, with the grades recorded. There were tests in all subjects, with many reminders of upcoming tests. Moreover, after tests were graded, parents signed them. In addition to daily assignments, the students also completed periodic book reports to complement the Book-It reading program. Every month students were required to read four books and write one book report. For example, in January students focused on biographies and made a puppet as part of the book report. In February, students did poetry for Valentine's Day. In March, the students made cereal box book reports, placing their written book report in a diorama displayed on a stage created from the cereal box.

Chris frequently let her students know that they were responsible for learning what was taught in class, making clear to students what was to be learned. Thus, when she introduced the multiplication facts for four, she told the class, "I don't expect you to have these math facts memorized today, but tomorrow I do." The magic math multiplier went home with each student that night so that everyone could practice multiplying by four. Chris also announced that there would be a test on the multiples of 4 later in the week.

For every class activity that we observed, Chris made certain students knew exactly what they were to do. Thus, students knew precisely what they were to look for when doing the plant protection exercise. During writing, the directions and expectations were similarly clear. For example, it was typical to hear comments from Chris like "Make certain you have complete sentences, and make sure each sentence makes sense."

Curricular Connections

Chris constantly was making connections across the curriculum and across the school year (i.e., relating content encountered today with ideas covered previously in the class or ideas that would be covered in the future). For example, when she did a science lesson on mass, the students were required to make estimations about various masses. As part of the lesson on mass, Chris reviewed the process of estimation, which had been covered earlier in the year. When the students had to calculate the differences between various masses, Chris reminded students that the word *difference* meant that subtraction would be used, connecting the operations in the math lesson to the science lesson. When students had to use decimals in science, Chris reminded them about how decimals had been used when they studied money. Venn diagramming occurred in some science lessons, which was a skill first introduced in mathematics. The classroom post office was connected to lessons in social studies (e.g., coverage of how a letter moves from deposit in a mailbox to delivery, learning about postage and designing of stamps) and writing (i.e., composing many letters for many different purposes). When the students studied trial procedures as part of social studies, they held a mock trial of Foxy Loxy, connecting the social studies activity to language arts. Academic content learning and service learning were connected in this classroom, with the students doing a math-a-thon to raise money to help elderly, sick people. When spelling words were related to concepts covered previously, Chris reminded students of those connections. While studying the novel *Sadako and the Thousand Paper Cranes*, connections were made to ethics and values by discussing the devastation caused by the atomic bombing of Hiroshima in World War II and the students' future mission to bring about world peace. Additionally, book reports connected to art (e.g., the cereal box book reports, which entailed using a cereal box to build a stage for a book report). In short, students were constantly reminded about how the tasks they were doing today connected to their learning in the past, with science, mathematics, social studies, and language arts often related to one another. In addition, Chris often let the students know that the skills and ideas encountered in her third-grade class would be useful in fourth grade and beyond (e.g., "This is something usually taught in fourth grade").

Building Excitement

Chris was always creating anticipation in the students about upcoming content. Thus, the day before she began teaching percentages in math, Chris told the class that they would be learning about how she calculated the percentages put on their tests as grades, which was clearly an interesting process for the students. In fact, there was a short exchange between Chris and several students about how cool this would be. Chris used the word "cool" often to get her students charged up about what would be occurring later in the day or week (e.g., "If we have time, I have a cool video I want to show you"). Chris introduced *Sadako and the Thousand Paper Cranes* as a beautiful story, reading a few pages of the book to the students on the first day of its coverage. When she stopped, Chris teased the class, "Now, I'll make you wait." Building anticipation was one way in which Chris made learning fun for her students. Chris knew what tasks and activities her students enjoyed and used their enjoyment of these activities to motivate students to learn new material (e.g., "We're getting close to the part where we get to use calculators," which elicited lots of "oohs" and aahs" from students).

Effort Emphasized

Chris often reminded students that they could do what was being asked of them. She also explicitly connected their achievements to their efforts. Thus, when a student knew all the math facts that had been assigned as homework, Chris remarked, "Did you practice last night? See what happens!"

Encouraging Autonomy

Chris encouraged her students to take control over their learning, expressing confidence that her students were capable of being independent learners. During her interview, Chris told us that one primary goal for third grade was to teach the students responsibility. She consistently encouraged her students to be in charge of their learning and try to work independently before asking for help (e.g., "Keep going. You've got to do a little thinking on your own"). In instances when Chris recognized that her students needed some help, she continued to encourage autonomy but provided small hints to help them as they worked (e.g., "I want to see how much you can do on your own. Be careful on number 2"). Chris remarked to us that at the beginning of the year her students come into class wanting her "to do everything for them," but her goal was to make them "mature" and "responsible" learners by the time they left. This goal was consistently reflected in her encouragement of autonomy and independent thinking.

Critical Thinking

Chris consistently required her students to think critically and use skills and strategies they had learned in class (e.g., "Now think of the strategies I had on the board"). There were many science and math lessons requiring students to hypothesize, investigate, analyze, and conclude—such as the plant protection investigation or the lesson about mass. Chris told us that, at first, her students had trouble hypothesizing, because it was a difficult concept for them to grasp. With encouragement and practice, the students learned the concept and could do it on their own.

Risk Taking

Chris supported her students as they took reasonable academic risks. Consequently, her students did not avoid challenges because they were afraid of making mistakes. During whole-group instruction, Chris explicitly asked for a "risk taker" to answer her questions, signaling to students that it was good to take risks, even if they were unsure of answers. During the lesson about mass, Chris had students communicate with each other about their hypotheses for the mass of each object and the order in which they placed each object. In one group, two students did not agree about the mass of a particular object, and Chris said to them, "If you disagree with someone at your table, that's OK. That's good independent thinking." Chris expressed much support for her students, so that they were comfortable advancing a variety of hypotheses. They never seemed paralyzed by uncertainty.

Recognizing Individual Differences

Chris knew that, as a teacher, she needed to recognize and understand her students' individual differences. In the interview, she told us that her general teaching philosophy was "to look at the gifts of the whole child and develop them academically and emotionally." She also said that it was important for her not to compare each student to another student or to compare this year's class to another year. Rather, she "adjusted her teaching to that year to make sure they were getting what they needed." Most importantly, Chris often communicated the importance of respecting individual differences to her students (e.g., "Different people learn different ways. Some by . . . and others by. . . ."). Chris's students understood that it was important to recognize and respect individual differences.

Community of Learners

Chris worked hard to build a sense of community among her students, often using pronouns such as "we" and "our class." Teamwork was an important aspect to building community in Chris's class. During science lessons, students often were grouped in teams and urged to communicate with each other as they worked on assignments. During writing exercises, Chris encouraged her students to share their work with a partner. Before introducing a new activity, Chris told the class, "We have a lot to do. We have to work together." In addition to the teamwork, Chris used a reward system to motivate her class as a whole to respect each other and maintain good behavior. The class goal was 100 points each week, which Chris kept track of on the front board. If the class reached 100 points by Friday, they earned a special reward.

Chris also built community by emphasizing kindness and respect among her students (e.g., "I want this to be fun. We need to be polite to each other"). Consistently, Chris modeled cooperative behaviors, saying, "Thank you" and "You're welcome" to her students. In turn, her students interacted constructively with each other.

Teacher Enthusiasm/Playfulness

Chris consistently created a positive tone, showing enthusiasm for learning and interacting playfully with her students. For example, during the math lessons on multiples of four, Chris allowed her students to dance and sing along to a musical tape while they learned their multiplication. She used fun words like "cool" and "awesome" to get the students excited about learning. She joked often with her students as a way to encourage their efforts (e.g., "Sometimes the answers are as plain as the nose on your face. Sometimes you need to use what's between your ears"). Even her behavior management sent a positive message to the students by couching warnings in humorous terms (e.g., "Put some glue in your seat").

Chris expressed the same enthusiasm to encourage reading among her students. As a way for her students to learn oral reading, Chris had her students take an imaginary trip in their minds, letting them know that "it magically happens when you read." She had the students close their eyes and imagine riding a bus to a big theater, describing the theater in every detail down to the plushy, velvet seats. Then, Chris had the students pretend they were actors and actresses reading aloud in front of an audience. During oral reading, Chris reminded her students, "Remember when we went on a field trip in our minds to my reading theater. We are actresses and actors on the stage when we read." The message was sent often and convincingly that reading, writing, and learning are transformative experiences that can magically affect children if they exert the efforts and take the risks.

A DAY IN CHRIS'S THIRD GRADE

You could not spend a day in Chris Nemeth's classroom without observing one or more hands-on activities. What students did was carefully planned. Chris explained step-by-step what students should do as they carried out the activities in the class. Consequently, students were always busy, knowing what they should do and doing it.

A typical morning began with a language arts lesson. Chris reviewed the previous day's lesson, connecting what they had learned previously to today's new material. For example, the reading lessons from their anthology books were based on the following routine: On Monday, the story was introduced; on Tuesday, the class listened to a tape of the story; on Wednesday, the class read the story; on Thursday, the class did a comprehension check over the story (i.e., answered questions about the story posed by Chris). Thus, the students were aware of what was expected and what the task was for the day. However, if Chris decided to alter her routine, she informed her class so that they were prepared for the change. For example, one morning, instead of working on an anthology story, the class began reading from a novel, which they would continue working on for the following 2 weeks. Thus, when *Sadako and the Thousand Paper Cranes* was the novel, the class read a few pages together aloud, reflecting on the book as a fictional account set in World War II. This introduction was followed by listening to a CD describing the bombing of Hiroshima that brought an end to the war. Chris took the opportunity to connect the destructiveness of war to the students' own values and the goal of world peace, for example, asking the students why August 6 is Peace Day. She made another social studies connection by asking the students, "What is Memorial Day?"

After introducing the lesson, Chris had the students complete a vocabulary worksheet. The students worked cooperatively in pairs, which was common in Chris's class. Before the assignment, she carefully introduced the lesson and explained her expectations. She told the students that before they could begin the fun activities associated with the novel, like making the paper cranes, they had to learn the vocabulary. She proceeded by writing the phrase "context clues" on the board. She told the students to be detectives and try to find out what a new vocabulary word meant from the context clues, and then she guided them through an example. As the students attempted to figure out the meanings of vocabulary words from context clues, Chris monitored them for their progress and helped them when they needed assistance.

A short recess followed language arts. However, the recess activities in Chris's class were not typical of most third grades. Recess was when the class worked on their post office jobs. Each student was responsible for a particular job in the school-wide post office operated by Chris's class. Students applied for particular jobs at the beginning of the year, ranging from postmaster to mail sorter to mail carrier. During recess, each student who had a job assignment for the week performed his or her responsibilities, whether it was picking up mail around the school, making express deliveries, or passing mail through the station. The students had prepared to run the post office by taking a field trip to the city's post office and by watching a video that showed the process of getting a letter to its destination. These multiple experiences motivated the students to run their own post office at their school, an activity that permitted language arts, social studies, and service learning connections. Chris had developed the post office not only to motivate her own students but also other students in the school. As she related during an interview, "It's really a great way to motivate letter writing throughout the entire school and to work on those writing skills." Chris did not close her classroom door and focus on only the students in her charge, but, rather, was concerned about all of the students in the school.

After recess, the students returned for math. Chris often used a hands-on approach to develop mathematical understandings in her students. On this day, Chris first reviewed the previous day's lesson and connected it to what students would be focusing on today: "Yesterday we introduced what? We started a brand new chapter. What was it on?" The students responded, "Fractions." Chris continued to review: "And yesterday, we learned a fraction has two parts. The top part has a name and the bottom has a name." She continued by asking what the names of those parts were, and the students enthusiastically raised their hands to answer *numerator* and *denominator*. Chris then injected some humor by having the students "pump up" their arms and practice saying the word denominator by "being a bunch of Arnold's" (referring to Arnold Schwarzenegger). All the students and Chris proceeded to lift up their arms and pronounce *denominator* using an "Arnold-like" voice. She reminded them, however, not to get silly. This activity did make memorable that the denominator was on the bottom of the fraction and held up the numerator. Whenever Chris had fun like this, the students were in on the joke, but the humor never prevailed to the point that learning was undermined.

Chris then explained that the class was going to make fractional people. She carefully explained each step and made sure the students understood, asking for "thumbs up if you're with me." Making fractional people required each student to construct a picture of him- or herself using whole squares of different colors. After creating his or her person, each student listed the colors on the side of the paper and wrote the fraction of the person that the color represented. For example, one student may have been $\frac{12}{53}$ brown, $\frac{9}{53}$ peach, $\frac{8}{53}$ green, $\frac{1}{53}$ red, $\frac{1}{53}$ yellow, and $\frac{10}{53}$ blue. Then the students added the numerators to demonstrate that the total of the numerators was equal to the denominator, $\frac{53}{53}$, thus adding up to one whole person. Chris explained each step and reinforced the importance of equaling one whole person at the end. During the lesson, Chris monitored the students by walking around, offering suggestions, but also praising students for creative ideas and for sharing their ideas with classmates. She also told them that she would display their fractional people in the hallway, ending the lesson by saying, "You have worked very hard on these, and they look really, really good. . . . They truly do look like you. . . . It really shows how each part of you is a. . . ." The class in unison finished her sentence with the word "Fraction!"

A day in Chris's third grade was filled with lessons that motivated the students. Chris always reinforced the students with praise and consistently monitored their understanding. Expectations were made clear as she explained the directions step-by-step. Each day's lessons built on one another. The students were clearly learning the material and were engaged and enthusiastically participating all of the time. The students were responding to the very motivating lessons being provided to them by their teacher, who was constantly doing things to motivate them.

SUMMARY

With every visit to Chris Nemeth's class, there was something new happening with the post office. With every visit, the researchers observed a new hands-on activity. The researchers were delighted when they learned that she would be moving to a larger classroom in the new wing, because every bit of storage space in her current class was already filled with materials for lessons. So, too, the days in Chris's classroom were filled to overflowing with engaging lessons. As was the case with Nancy and Angel, Chris did everything summarized in Table 2.4 and nothing that is included in Table 2.5. From the moment of arrival to the moment of departure, Chris motivated her students. None of the students ever appeared discouraged, for none of them ever were discouraged by Chris Nemeth.

CHAPTER 6

Reflections on the Research

In this chapter, we first reflect about what will come to mind in the future when we recall this 3-year research effort. What will we remember about the classrooms and teachers? We do so to set the stage to persuade readers who are primary-grade teachers to try to teach as engaging teachers do. Hence, the next and final chapter is about what teachers can do concretely to motivate their students.

MEMORIES OF A QUEST

We will never forget how difficult it was to find the really effective teachers highlighted here. Readers should keep in mind that effectively motivating teaching is rare, even with the selection biases that drove our sampling. Recall that we asked principals to nominate teachers they felt were effective, ones they felt represented their schools well. We were clear that we did not want to see weak teachers. Still, only about 20% of the teachers we observed had classrooms where students were engaged, were certainly "into" academic work, and were definitely making easy-to-spot progress with respect to academic development.

That engaging teachers were so difficult to find impresses us that those who are concerned about the quality of teaching in schools have a point. We visited many classrooms where engagement could have been much, much greater. That there were some exceptional classrooms, however, makes clear that there are no easy generalizations about the quality of teaching and learning in primary-level classrooms in the United States. We left this study having no doubt some children get much more out of a year of primary schooling than others largely because of the quality of teaching they experience in an effective teacher's classroom relative to agemates who are taught by less effective teachers. We also left this study with the sense that most children are losers in the primary-grade teacher lottery. In both the second- and third-grade studies, our first observations of a really engaging and effective teacher came after watching seven or eight less effective teachers. At the third-grade level, we completed the study feeling that only one of the teachers we observed was so exceptionally strong as to warrant detailed coverage in this book. And, of course, there were only two effective teachers at both the first- and second-grade levels.

The low proportion of effectively engaging teachers in the investigations summarized in this volume is consistent with a low proportion of such teachers found in our past work (e.g., Pressley, Allington, Wharton-McDonald, Block, & Morrow, 2001; Wharton-McDonald, Pressley, & Hampston, 1998). The type of primary-grade teaching highlighted in this volume and our previous work is relatively rare. It is compelling and even beautiful when it occurs, however, which motivates our hope that this volume will stimulate many primary-grade teachers to attempt to make their instruction much more motivating.

ENGAGED STUDENTS

We were struck by the complete academic engagement of students in the most effective classrooms observed, the ones that were the focus of this volume. When we entered such classrooms, the students did not seem to notice, for they had other things on their minds! This was quite in contrast to our arrivals in most classrooms. In the typical classrooms visited in the investigations reported here, we were distracting to students from the moment we tried to sneak in the door until we departed. In such classrooms, students often found us to be much more interesting than the lessons.

That we were so unnoticeable in the effective classrooms was consistent with the general ethos in these places that work goes on no matter what else happens, whether the teacher is in the room watching over the students or dashing in and out of the room to gather materials for the next bit of instruction. Classroom visitors are just no big deal in effective classrooms, except that most visitors are put to productive work, with effective teachers making good use of whatever resources are available. Visiting parents tutor children a great deal and participate extensively in special projects in the most effective classrooms we observed. In general, people in these classrooms—students and visitors—know what they are supposed to be doing, and they do it. Effective teachers expect the folks in their classrooms to be self-regulated in the sense that they keep themselves on the tasks that the teacher expects them to be accomplishing. The most effective classrooms we observed were attractively engaged places. They were classroom worlds filled with students who clearly loved learning and adults who helped students as needed.

We will never forget just how good the lessons were in the engaging classrooms and the products that resulted from such engaging teaching. We have great memories of impressive stories composed in the classrooms showcased in this book. There were bulletin boards covered with student-written stories: Often, every single student in these classes was composing long, coherent, well-spelled, and capably punctuated compositions by the end of the school year. The same classrooms tended to have many big books that the class had written and published, which were a point of pride for the students and their teachers. If you are in a primary-grade classroom in May when the children are out of the room, the best tip-off that the classroom is exceptionally effective is the quality of the writing artifacts (see Wharton-McDonald et al., 1998). If there are many of them, and they are good, that is a telling, positive sign.

In such classrooms, it was also apparent that children read a lot. We saw them doing it, heard the children talking about books they read, and noted the piles of books on their desks, always close at hand when students had a free moment. Reading was becoming a habit of life and mind for children in such classrooms, not a forced habit but one driven by the pleasures of reading that the students were experiencing. A tip-off that you are in a classroom that reads is that books move around in the room. In effective classrooms, the library books on display are picked up and read, sometimes shared with others, sometimes taken home to be read to and with parents. We witnessed many ineffective classrooms where books on display did not move the entire year!

The engaging teacher does much to encourage student motivation to read, for example, by reading great stories and books to the students regularly. As such teachers read to their students, we always witnessed rapt attention and much reaction by the students to the stories, even to tales that often were quite complex. There was little doubt in these classrooms that children loved good stories well told. Furthermore, the stories and informational books read in effective classrooms were very, very good readings, often ones that the teachers had been using for years because they worked well every year and stimulated worthwhile knowledge and understanding in children. We knew the students looked forward to story reading, for they showed so many signs of anticipation of it (e.g., asking, "When will you read some more of . . . ?"). The students talked amongst themselves about the stories and books read by the teacher. The stories read in class were often discussed at home with parents. Such home reading accounts, in part, for the great awareness in the school communities about the books and stories read in the most engaging classrooms. For example, we encountered one parent in the community who wanted to know how she could assure that her child would have Nancy Masters as a teacher, because she wanted her child to be exposed as a first grader to books like *A Tale of Two Cities* and *The Call of the Wild*, two of the many titles read by Nancy to her students.

Teacher read-alouds often were part of larger units; we have many memories of primary students in effective classrooms completely captivated by social studies and science units they experienced. Thus, we will never forget the jungle canopy in one first-grade classroom that was part of a jungle unit, which included literature experiences connecting strongly to science and social studies. The students participated in lively discussions about the jungle. They also read and wrote much about the topic, as did students in another engaging classroom, when the unit was the life cycle of insects. Then, there was the third-grade classroom that did a full year of activities related to the post office. Engaging classrooms are filled with great themes covered in ways that make concepts very clear and ideas very memorable for the children experiencing them.

Students in the most effective classrooms we studied loved learning, but why not? These classrooms were loaded with practices that would be expected to increase student motivation (Stipek, 1998, 2002): The students' teachers were consistent models of the love of learning. They did everything possible to increase the students' confidence that they could learn, everything possible to encourage reasonable risk taking by students. The engaging teachers encouraged their students to take pride in their accomplishments. Indeed, in giving these students challenging tasks that always were accomplished, these teachers probably very much increased their students' feelings of competence. Doing such tasks undoubtedly increased students' understanding of material, which increases mastery orientation more than a competitive mindset (e.g., Knapp, Marder, Adelman, & Needels, 1995), as do many messages that everyone can and will learn in the class, that learning is the goal (Ames, 1992; Anderman,

Maehr, & Midgley, 1999; Dweck, 1986; Meece, Blumenfeld, & Puro, 1989; Roeser, Midgley, & Urdan, 1996). We witnessed mostly positive emotions in these classrooms, including much student satisfaction about work being well done. Such feelings encouraged student interest and enjoyment (Deci, 1975; Deci & Ryan, 1985; White, 1959). These teachers made certain that their students felt up to the challenges they were facing in their classrooms (Csikszentmihalyi, 1988; Turner et al., 1998). These teachers let the students participate actively, which is motivating (Brophy, 1987, 1988). The active learning included the students being in control to a great extent, from choosing the books they read to the approaches they took to solve problems. Such choices encourage feelings of autonomy, which motivates high engagement and great interest (Deci, Schwartz, Sheinman, & Ryan, 1981; Stipek, 1998). But, of course, interest often was high from the very first moment of instruction, because the effective teachers consistently filled lessons with content that was really interesting to the students (Krapp, 1999; Renninger, Hidi, & Krapp, 1992; Schiefele & Krapp, 1996). The summary point, however, is that there were so many efforts made in the effective classrooms to make them more motivating. Our memories of the effective classrooms often seem like memories of classrooms too good to be true, certainly in contrast to less effective classrooms, which were populated with not-so-engaged students.

NOT-SO-ENGAGED STUDENTS

Sadly, we leave this study with far too many more memories of not-so-engaged students than memories of students absorbed in work they enjoyed. In less engaging classrooms, we saw countless work sheets assigned, ones that were completed by most students quickly, who often, then, had little or nothing to do. Indeed, the most common tasks in many primary classes are easy tasks—ones covering material mastered long ago, ones far below the level where the student could perform. We often saw students off-task with their teachers completely unaware. Typically, the same students would be off-task later in the visit. Our memories of free reading in less engaging classrooms were of students leafing through the pages of picture books without reading a single word. Similarly, we have memories of 45 minutes of composing in less engaging classrooms, which resulted in many students producing only a word or two of text.

That is not to say there was nothing happening in the less effective classrooms. In fact, there was a great deal of squirreling around in these classrooms. As a result, there were many disciplinary interactions, ones that often made us feel uncomfortable as observers. We could not miss that the disciplinary actions typically were not very effective. As soon as the teacher's attention was elsewhere, the just-punished student often was off-task again. Why not? It could be a few days before the teacher would notice again that the child was goofing off! Students in these classrooms were anything but self-controlled, often with order only when the teacher demanded it by yelling at the class. When someone came to the door, it was common to see everything come unwound as the teacher talked with the visitor. It was easy to understand why reading and writing were not as advanced in these classrooms as in the more engaging classrooms: The students' distraction and misbehavior translated into much less time involved in academic tasks. Writing long compositions and reading demanding books requires a great deal of focused attention. Long periods of focused attention are only possible in primary classrooms when the teacher has developed his or her students into self-regulating students, and when the instruction is compelling—that is, interesting and appropriately challenging. That, however, is a tall order. The love of learning was not nearly as obvious in most classrooms as it was in the classrooms highlighted in the case studies reported in this book.

But then, why should there have been much engagement in most of the classrooms we visited? The teachers in these classrooms generally used few of the mechanisms expected to increase motivation. Indeed, we saw many practices that would be expected to undermine student motivation (Stipek, 1998, 2002). The teachers often were unenthusiastic about what they were teaching. We saw much encouragement of task completion (e.g., worksheets, small art projects) but little encouragement of learning, especially the making of connections across content or days of instruction. There were infrequent opportunities to do things that students could really be proud of, few tasks that were challenging or resulted in products that were memorable and meaningful to students (e.g., Who is proud of completing a day's worksheets?). If we had been trying to design teaching that would turn students off, it would have been hard to have been more complete and effective than some of the primary teachers we observed in the 3 years of this study.

Just as the effective teachers achieved engagement through the use of multiple motivations, so, too, the ineffective teachers seemed to undermine engagement through multiple mechanisms (e.g., boring unit themes, conveyed through stories that were dull, followed by very easy tasks that did not obviously connect to the theme of the unit). As they did so, they also failed to include in their teaching most of the positive motivational procedures so prominent in the most engaging classrooms we encountered. There was just nothing subtle about most of the class-rooms we studied. They were either massively motivating or they were not, flooded with a variety of instructional practices that should positively impact engagement or overflowing with instructional practices certain to kill engagement.

THE COMPLEXITY OF MOTIVATING INSTRUCTION

As we were doing this project, we had the feeling that psychologists inter-ested in educational motivation were shifting their emphases. During the last quarter of the 20th century, there were many investigations targeting the individual motivational mechanisms—for example, positive and neg-ative effects of reinforcement, the impacts of different types of attribu-tions, and the motivating power of choice. (See Chapter 1 for a review of the many single mechanisms that been proposed by researchers as espe-cially potent, lone determinants of achievement.)

As the new century began, there emerged calls from the educational motivational researchers for much more integrative perspectives. For ex-ample, Stipek and Seal (2001) offered a book intended to inform parents about how they could instill the love of learning in their children. When we reflect back on this project, we will remember encountering the Stipek and Seal (2001) book and sensing that we were not alone in advocating the use of many mechanisms to motivate children rather than arguing for reliance on single mechanisms.

What did Stipek and Seal (2001) recommend that parents do in or-der to raise children who would want to learn? They advocated a multi-faceted approach to the problem:

• Connect learning to the real world. Today's weather and this eve-ning's sunset provide opportunities for science mini-lessons. Current events can be discussed in ways that increase knowledge of social studies. Good literature can be read and discussed. Parents can let their children know how they use math in everyday life.

• Expand learning beyond the home and school, in particular, taking advantage of community resources (e.g., museums, libraries).

• Encourage a child's interests and passions. Use these interests to stimulate broader learning (e.g., much science can be connected to a visit to the zoo).

• Model enthusiasm for learning. Not only can parents read, they can let children know how much they enjoy reading and how much they learn from it that is worthwhile.

• Make learning playful! Thus, the fun of going to the zoo should be in the forefront no matter how much learning occurs during a day at the zoo.

• Let kids take control of experiences. So, when a child plays restaurant, let him or her take the lead. Maybe the attentive parent slips in a little math lesson, perhaps when paying the bill (e.g., counting the play money out carefully and making certain it adds up to the total of the bill).

• Promote healthy play that encourages learning (e.g., prosocial behaviors like playing store or watching good movies); discourage unhealthy play that has the potential to undermine academic motivation (e.g., watching television with antischool themes, playing violent videogames that can encourage aggression).

• Promote a child's competence by encouraging appropriately challenging activities, ones that are neither too easy nor too hard.

• Fill the child's world with intelligent conversation that requires the child to talk about worthwhile ideas.

• Encourage reading and math activities.

• Especially encourage girls with respect to math and science, for there are many messages in the larger world that girls experience difficulties with math and science.

• Teach children study skills that permit them to get academic tasks done efficiently and well. Teach them about accomplishing big tasks by doing a little bit each day; encourage them to use helpful references (dictionaries, thesauri); let them know about the advantages of practice (e.g., how famous athletes practiced for years).

• Promote children's competence by providing positive feedback, letting them know they can do academic things.

• Provide constructive criticism—that is, information about how a child can do better.

• Set realistic goals for children.

• Acknowledge when tasks are difficult; break the tasks into doable components. Alternatively, change the task so that it is at a more appropriate level or reset the goal (e.g., to complete 2 problems today rather than 20).

• Do not provide pity when a child experiences difficulty, for it sends the message that the child cannot do anything to improve his or her situation.

• Do not compare the child unfavorably to a sibling (e.g., "Your older brother always did well in reading").

• Provide the child choices of interesting and academically stimulating things to do.

• Encourage the child's autonomy, sending the message that it is expected that the child be self-regulated. Resist taking over when a child experiences difficulties, in favor of providing just enough support so the child can carry on (i.e., scaffolding).

• Ask questions to find out if the student has homework or an upcoming exam or project due date.

• Set up a framework (e.g., a schedule, a place to study) for homework.

• Send the message to the child that he or she is responsible for the academic work; provide consequences when the child does not meet academic responsibilities (e.g., no TV until all grades are B or higher).

• Show your children that you care by accepting them, connecting with them, and supporting them. Take an interest in your children, spending time with them, and accept your children.

• Live your values visibly and communicate them to the child, including how much you value learning and achievement.

• Send the message that success depends on effort more than any other factor.

• Encourage the child to have learning goals (i.e., to want to learn or do something) rather than performance goals (i.e., to do better than other students at school). In general, downplay academic competition with others.

• Encourage academic cooperation with others.

• Provide rewards for academic activities the child will not do on his or her own; avoid providing explicit rewards for those academic activities that are intrinsically motivating to the child.

• Use praise rather than tangible rewards.

• Finally, look for a school for your child that tries to motivate in all these ways.

In short, Stipek and Seal (2001) recommend that parents use all of the motivational mechanisms that we observed being used by engaging primary teachers. What was missing from their book, however, was evidence that there are parents anywhere who do all these things and that such parents have more academically motivated kids. In contrast, a strength of the work reported here is that we provided an existence proof of teachers who are massively motivating, who saturate children's school worlds with motivation, and, in doing so, succeed in engaging students. This is a much-needed existence proof, one that motivates us to encourage more teachers to do much more to motivate their students.

As we were preparing this book, we were pleased to learn about another program of qualitative research that also is generating existence proofs similar to the ones summarized in this volume. Perry, VandeKamp, Mercer, and Nordby (2002; also Perry, 1998, and Perry & Vandekamp, 2000) identified two teachers who were very successful in promoting self-regulated reading in primary-level readers: They were very good at teaching students to be strategic as they read and wrote—to plan, monitor, problem-solve, and evaluate as they performed challenging reading and writing tasks. Just as was the case in the classrooms covered in this volume, there was a lot of teaching of reading and writing in the classrooms Perry et al. (2002) documented. Moreover, the teachers did much to motivate literacy in their students and self-regulated use of literacy skills. Thus, the students were given choices about what they read, although encouraged to choose stories that were appropriately challenging. There was also a great deal of teacher scaffolding to assure student success during reading. Evaluations were not threatening; in fact, they were mastery oriented, providing evidence to the students that they had accomplished what they were supposed to accomplish. Students discussed what they read with others, with many cooperative learning opportunities. Indeed, there was a general ethic in these classrooms for students to help one another, and they did so. Many connections to content learning occurred during in-class discussions. Students also were given choices with respect to writing, in particular, to what they wrote about. In short, just as we observed high student engagement and competence when primary-level teachers did much to motivate their students' reading and writing, so, too, have Perry and her colleagues observed that literacy engagement and competence occur in classrooms that are saturated with motivating and excellent literacy instruction.

As we close this section, of course, we remind readers that despite the focus of many motivational researchers on individual mechanisms and validation of single approaches as affecting classroom motivation, there have been calls in the past for educators to use many mechanisms to promote classroom engagement, with Brophy (1987, 1988; see Chapter 1 of this volume) especially notable in this regard. We provided evidence in this volume that there are teachers doing as Brophy urged. In addition, we fleshed out many specific ways that engaging primary-grade teachers can be motivating, especially with respect to literacy.

When we reflect on Brophy's historically important proposals, our work, and Stipek's writings aimed at parents, we find ourselves asking how much difference it would make if a child encountered consistently, massively motivating worlds—parents who saturated the child with motivation and year-in, year-out teaching that resembled the types of instruction we observed in the most impressive classrooms we visited as part of this study. All we can offer at this juncture is the hypothesis that such consistent encouragement of things academic would result in children who are more academically engaged, who habitually self-regulate themselves and their minds into activities that result in academic growth.

We hope that this book goes far in stimulating changes in the world of school—and that Stipek's work impacts parents similarly—so that before much more time passes, it will be possible to assess just how much difference is made when children encounter worlds that are consistently encouraging their intellectual efforts.

OVERCOMING DECLINES IN MOTIVATION WITH ADVANCING AGE

As we did this work, we could never forget that student motivation to read and attitudes about reading decline dramatically during the elementary school years (e.g., Anderman & Maehr, 1994; Eccles & Midgley, 1990a; McKenna, Ellsworth, & Kear, 1995), with the decline starting in the primary years for many students who experience difficulties with beginning reading (Gambrell, Mazzoni, & Korkeamaki, 1996; Lepola, Salonen, & Vauras, 2000; Mazzoni, Gambrell, & Korkeamaki, 1999; Sperling & Head, 2002). We believe, based on the research summarized in this volume, that we do have something to say about how such decline might be averted. Our perspective also is informed by an important research-based, theoretical analysis of the factors causing the decline provided by Mark Lepper and his colleagues (Lepper & Henderlong, 2000). Why does motivation decline with advancing grades during school? Lepper & Henderlong suggest the following factors:

• School is often boring, something that has been noted again and again by observers of education in the United States.

- Being controlled is not motivating, and, in fact, as children mature, they desire greater autonomy (Eccles & Midgley, 1990a, 1990b). To the extent that schooling is controlling, and it often is, student motivation should be undermined, with motivation progressively declining as students desire greater and greater freedom with advancing age. Indeed, rather than responding with greater freedom as students advance in age, schools often increase the emphasis on discipline with advancing age and reduce student choices (Eccles et al., 1993).

- Learning in context with lots of concrete supports and references is motivating (e.g., Bruner, 1962, 1966), for example, discovery learning lessons in science (Bruner, 1961). With increasing grade, however, learning and instruction often become increasingly more abstract and divorced from context, for example, with much that is to be learned read about in textbooks rather than tangibly experienced.

- Learning goals promote academic achievement and intrinsic motivation to do things academic more than do performance goals (i.e., desiring to earn high marks and do better than other students). That performance goals become increasingly important with advancing grade level (Midgley, Anderman, & Hicks, 1995) probably contributes to declining academic motivation with advancing grade levels.

- One of the best-established principles in motivation research is that motivation increases when tasks are appropriately challenging, neither too easy nor too difficult for students. There are increasing suspicions that academic tasks get progressively less challenging relative to student capabilities with increasing grade level (Eccles et al., 1993), which could contribute to declines in academic motivation.

In short, the research on academic motivation provides some clear guidance about what might be wrong with schooling that makes it less motivating for the oldest children in an elementary school compared to the youngest. This same literature also provides clear implications about potential remedies for the decline (Lepper & Henderlong, 2000; Renninger, 2000):

1. Do all possible to make learning interesting—both by selecting specific tasks and activities that are interesting to children in general but also by appealing to the interests of particular students (e.g., encouraging students who are interested in science fiction to read terrific science fiction and those who are interested in nature to read wonderful books about natural science).

2. Encourage teachers to provide more choices for students to increase student perceptions of autonomy and control.

3. Decrease the use of salient external rewards which are clearly contingent on doing academic work and performing at high levels in school. Such rewards can seem controlling (i.e., students feeling that they are doing academic work only to earn rewards, such as grades). Do everything possible to send the message to students that they are in control of their own learning, that they can succeed through their own controllable efforts.

4. Make academic work more meaningful by increasing contextualization, for example, teaching with the project method (e.g., doing an ecology unit that provides students with opportunities to explore the local environment, including environmental hazards in it).

5. In general, emphasize learning goals rather than performance goals, making clear that learning for its own sake is a terrific reward.

6. Provide appropriately challenging tasks for all students, which typically will mean personalized instructions and assignments. A challenging classroom is very individualized, for some students are capable of much more difficult tasks than others.

Of course, the exemplary teaching documented in this book looks terrific in light of Lepper and Henderlong's (2000) analysis: The primary-grade teachers featured in this book did all they could to make instruction interesting, encouraged their students to be autonomous, and downplayed extrinsic rewards in favor of an emphasis on learning as rewarding, provided experiences that were clearly learning by doing, and consistently varied the level of challenge for their students. The teachers highlighted in this book are an existence proof that instruction consistent with the best motivational theorizing is possible, at least at the primary grades. Whether it is possible for such instruction to occur in upper elementary, middle school, and high school settings deserves intense attention. We hope the analyses provided in this book stimulate researchers and educators alike to determine just how such theoretically compelling instruction might be fostered in all of education, for, if the outcomes reported in this book are any indicator, such instruction saturated with theoretically sensible practices might go far to improving the engagement and achievement of students. We do not believe that developmental declines in academic motivation are inevitable, but rather believe that they reflect the environments that have been created in schools to date. School can be done differently, and if modified in ways suggested by contemporary educational motivation research, school might be more effective as well as more attractive to many students.

PRAISING WELL

In the first chapter, we highlighted Brophy's (1981) classic advice on praise. Our awareness of Brophy's perspective probably heightened our awareness of much praise in the most engaging classrooms in this study, praise consistent with Brophy's recommendations. In the very recent past, doubts about whether praise has positive effects on children's long-term motivation have been raised (Deci, Koestner, & Ryan, 1999; Ryan & Deci, 2000).

Henderlong and Lepper (2002) provided a reflective analysis of the available literature related to this issue, basically coming to Brophy's (1981) point of view: Whether praise is effective in motivating children depends on it being sincere, specific, and informative about what the child did well and why the child did well (e.g., What process or strategy did the student use that was effective?), and minimizing perceptions that the praise is intended to control the child's behavior. The teacher who praises effectively does not praise the child for accomplishing easy tasks, for that can send the message that the child has little competence. The teacher who praises well does not send the message that only accomplishing very difficult tasks is worthy of praise, for such a message does nothing to motivate the child to attempt tasks that are appropriately challenging. The teacher who praises well provides realistic expectations about what the child can accomplish with appropriate effort, sending the clear message that such effort is expected, as is accomplishing tasks that are just a bit beyond what the child can accomplish without being challenged. The teacher who praises effectively does so without making comparisons between students (e.g., Johnny, you've gotten so many more problems done than Jimmy!), but, rather, praises each child for mastering tasks that challenge him or her. Praise is not the only form of reward in the best classrooms we observed. Rather, the children there were rewarded often by achieving in ways that meant something very positive to them—for example, taking pride in big books constructed by the class and little books that they wrote individually; making scientific discoveries that are interesting to them which make obvious that they have learned something important; and reading progressively more challenging books, ones they want to read because there is an excitement about good books in the classroom.

As you read the case studies, we hope you noted that praise was well done, as Brophy (1981) suggested and Henderlong and Lepper (2002) have reaffirmed. Henderlong and Lepper noted that, in research, often praise was not well separated from other motivational elements of instruction. From a scientific perspective, this makes it difficult to be absolutely certain that many effects attributed to praise were, in fact, due to praise. Those authors concluded, however—and we agree—that there has been enough sufficiently analytical experimentation to have confidence that praise can be used effectively and that the approaches recommended in the last paragraph are sound.

That confounding of praise and other motivational interventions has occurred often in research, however, mirrors well what happens in the classrooms of engaging primary teachers. Praise is never used alone, but rather is one of a variety of motivational interventions. Praise is given often, however. In contrast, in less engaging classrooms, there is less praise and/or praise used poorly. For example, in less engaging classrooms, the praise we heard was often very general ("You're genius children!") or provided for accomplishing unchallenging tasks ("Excellent" for completing a worksheet in a matter of seconds, one that was so easy because it tapped material the child had mastered long ago).

Thus, praise is a form of reinforcement that is cheap in that there is no tangible cost to it—no pizzas need to be bought when praise is the reinforcer! The cost of praise for the teacher is learning when to do it and how to do it well and then making the effort to praise as part of a larger program to enhance motivation in the classroom. As we watched the engaging teachers documented in this book, they had learned how to do it so well that it was part of their being. They were now teachers who praise habitually and do it well. So, in this concluding chapter, we flag prominently that motivating teachers praise their students a lot, with praise probably the most frequent motivational mechanism we observed. It occurred all the time in the motivating classrooms, often as a remark in passing ("Oh, you're doing that so well," or "I'm so proud of how much you are reading with your mom"). We could not miss that when we interacted outside the classroom with the teachers highlighted in this volume, their positiveness overflowed into their entire world of interactions and transactions. Small wonder that these very motivating teachers were viewed by the principals and fellow teachers as unambiguously positive forces in their schools, teachers who often were praised by colleagues, parents, and others. A huge message is that engaging teachers are over-the-top positive people, with their students and everyone else in their school worlds.

IMPRESSIVE TEACHERS WHO ARE HUMBLE
AND LESS IMPRESSIVE TEACHERS WHO ARE NOT

We will never forget that the most impressive teachers in our studies definitely attributed their successes to their efforts rather than believing they were naturally good teachers. Moreover, to a person, all of the really motivating teachers documented in this volume believed they could become better teachers. One especially fond memory we have of our first meeting with Nancy Masters was that she exacted a condition from us: She would be in the study only if we promised feedback to her about what she could do to improve as a teacher. Chris Nemeth was similarly demanding throughout her participation. The most effective teachers we have met are certain that there remains room for improvement in their teaching. Of course, the irony is that these teachers had the least room for improvement, because they were already very good.

In contrast, during final interviews with much less effective teachers, we were often shocked about how confident they were about their teaching. Many projected the belief that they had learned to be teachers at some point (e.g., in their first teaching job) and their learning was completed. They expected to continue to teach as they now taught, believing their current teaching to be excellent. When we were doing the research reported in this book, the authors were associated with a teacher education program that employs master teachers as support personnel for students in the program: The only teachers in the studies reported in this book who have contacted us about potential employment in the program have been less engaging teachers! Indeed, the one who was most emphatic in her efforts to be a master teacher in the program (claiming repeatedly she was well qualified for the post) was one of the least motivating, least engaging teachers we observed over the 3 years of the research. (We did not hire her as a master teacher.)

The ineffective, nonengaging teachers we observed seem not to monitor how well they were teaching either in an absolute sense or relative to other teachers. They consistently seemed confident in their teaching. In contrast, the most effective grade 2 teacher almost withdrew from the study because she was so concerned that her teaching was problematic. She was not aware that even on a bad day for her, she was much more engaging, doing much more to motivate students than many of the teachers we have seen in this research effort.

That teachers lack awareness of whether they are motivating presents some challenges with respect to changing teacher behavior. If a teacher does not sense that he or she needs to improve, there is no incentive to try to improve or to go looking for ways that one could improve. To the extent that teachers are left to themselves to decide whether they need professional development, we are not optimistic they will seek out professional development aimed at improving their skills in motivating students—unless they are already good at motivating students! Clearly, we should not be leaving it up to the teachers to decide whether they need to work on motivating students, although in the next chapter we suggest that teachers try to self-appraise whether they need to motivate their students more.

Principals and other administrators reading this book might be appropriate decision makers for deciding which teachers need professional development in motivating students. Principals who want to increase engagement in their school should first size up their classrooms with respect to the engagement in them. The classrooms featured in this book are ones where children are always busy . . . seemingly on their own. That is, walk into the classroom. If the children are all working productively on reading and writing, that is a good sign. If over the course of an hour of observation, they all continue to remain active, that is another very good sign, especially if the students more or less move themselves along to appropriate new tasks as they complete what they are doing (e.g., after reading an assigned book, they begin to write about it). When children in a class are not so engaged, that is a sign that the teacher might profit from input about how to motivate students.

Identifying who would benefit from instruction about how to motivate students is but one problem, however. Educating teachers about how to increase the academic engagement of their students is very, very complex and only part of what needs to be accomplished for instruction to be effective. Moreover, those who want to carry the message to teachers that they need to do more to motivate their students should not assume that the message they are bearing necessarily will be well received.

RESISTANCE TO SATURATING CLASSROOMS WITH MOTIVATION

We have had a number of opportunities to present the findings reported in this book to teachers and teachers in training. The obvious question for these groups is what these results should mean for teachers. We believe the implication is that most primary-grade teachers need to think hard about increasing what they do to motivate students and about decreasing their teaching behaviors that potentially undermine student motivation.

Many teachers who hear our message resist because they seem to believe that we are talking about superstar teachers who have some ability that most teachers do not have. This is akin to the idea that good teachers are born rather than made. Teachers who so believe have no motivation to try hard, consistent with Weiner's (1979) observation that ability attributions undermine motivation to try! In general, we have encountered a number of teachers who make strong ability attributions about teachers (e.g., there are "natural" teachers) and who make frequent reference to ability differences to explain differences in achievement among their students as well. Just as such ability attributions have the potential to undermine students' motivation to learn, they also have the potential to undermine teachers' motivations to teach better than they are now teaching. Such teachers just do not accept the possibility that encouraging greater student efforts will do much to promote the achievement of some students, whom they perceive to be inherently weak students. In general, when a teacher is stongly committed to the position that human (i.e., teacher and student) performances are determined by ability, it is difficult to persuade them to change their teaching behaviors to encourage student motivation and engagement.

We have heard the claim that students should not need to be motivated, that they are intrinsically motivated to learn so long as adults do not mess it up! Of course, that academic motivation goes down with each advancing year in school confirms that adults are messing it up somehow. Our hypothesis is that if more teachers were like the ones detailed here, there would be less decline in academic motivation as students make their way through school. At the very least this seems like a hypothesis worth testing, in our view. There is no compelling case that continuing schooling as is will reduce the proportions of unmotivated students. Pointing to the fact that many children begin their schooling with high academic motivation as part of the rationale for not attempting to increase their motivation seems completely misguided to us, although we have certainly encountered that line of argument from educators who try to make the case that they are acting responsibly by not attempting to motivate their students. They have interpreted arguments made in the popular education literature that some approaches to motivation can undermine intrinsic motivation (e.g., Kohn, 1993) to mean that any efforts to motivate students have the potential to undermine student motivation. Nothing could be farther from the truth!

More generally, many teachers perceive that what is described here flies in the face of what they have been taught is the right way to teach. Thus, a variety of approaches to behavior management emphasize consequences for misbehavior (e.g., Canter & Canter, 2002) more than the positive approach taken by the motivating teachers documented in this volume. Not punishing students is viewed as not motivating correct behaviors, from this perspective. Of course, our counterargument is that when we are in engaging classrooms the teacher is not punishing because there are no behaviors that need to be punished! The motivational mechanisms used by the teachers described in this book go far in creating classroom environments where students constructively participate most of the time. We are struck that months went by in engaged classrooms before we saw any disciplinary events or need for discipline. In contrast, in most of the classrooms we visited, rarely did a single observation occur when there was not one or more disciplinary events.

Other teachers resist specific elements of the recommendations made here. Many seem to believe that competition is as American as apple pie, and for that reason alone should be preserved. For example, when schools make proposals to change traditional A–F grading approaches, we have observed inevitable resistance. On those occasions when we know of schools succeeding in changing grading from the traditional approach, there was an immediate, steady stream of pressure to return to the traditional approach. Thus, the first author's son was in a private school without grades until parental pressure (not from author Pressley, however) required that grades be recorded that are comparable to the grades that would have been earned at the local public school. Anything but traditional grading is very difficult for many people to accept.

Cooperation and cooperative learning often meet with resistance from teachers. One reason is that teachers who try cooperative approaches face parents of high-achieving students who complain that their students are being held back by having to work with weaker students. Another frequent concern is that cooperative learning means that students will be talking, and if the principal has the perspective that high-achieving classrooms are quiet classrooms (and, apparently, many principals do hold such a perspective), there can be problems for a teacher who encourages the productive noise that accompanies cooperation and collaboration. Teacher reluctance to attempt cooperative practices are understandable in light of such parental and administrative pressures.

Emphasizing interesting problems and topics is often seen as challenging to many teachers, given the coverage demands they face in many schools. Topics just have to be covered if they are going to appear on the end-of-the-year standardized test! Our counterargument is that achievement as documented by standardized tests seems to be higher in classrooms like those featured here than in more conventional classrooms, especially for students at risk for educational difficulties (Pressley et al., 2001). An additional observation we have made over the past decade is that effective teachers somehow find ways to make required topics that are dull in other classrooms come alive in their classrooms. So, as we reflect on Chris Nemeth's teaching about characteristics of plants, which involved extensive active exploration of plants, we recall exciting lessons. We can also recall lessons on the same topic in another, more typical classroom that boiled down to boring discussions that did not include touching a single plant. Effective teachers transform the passive and rote into the active and conceptual, setting up situations that permit discovery and prompting students to think about ideas deeply rather than superficially. Whether a topic is dull or exciting depends much on the teacher and what the teacher does to motivate the instruction pertaining to the topic. Such effective teaching requires very hard work and extensive preparation. We suspect that some of the reluctance to commit to the motivational perspectives favored in this book is that they represent a call for much more teacher effort than many teachers are willing to expend.

In summary, the message to teach to motivate children is not one that is universally appealing to teachers. Many object to it, with a variety of objections offered. Most of the objections are to changing the way teaching is now being done, typically in the direction of requiring more effort by the teacher. We try to persuade teachers to exert this effort by emphasizing that student achievement in their classrooms will improve, but, there is also something in it for the teacher. The effective classrooms we have observed are happy, peaceful places. The students like being there and so do the teachers. Engaged students are well behaved students, so that aversive encounters with students are few and far between in effective classrooms. A hypothesis worth considering is that being a teacher who showers his or her students with motivation is being a teacher who has a happier, more fulfilling, and more peaceful existence. This idea deserves to be tested as motivating instruction is evaluated additionally— and it should be so evaluated, for we do not know how much of a difference supermotivating instruction might make in promoting the achievement of students in the nation. We have begun working on the issue.

THE BIG HYPOTHESIS AND INITIAL TESTS OF IT

The major conclusion to emerge from Pressley, Allington, et al. (2001) was that effective primary-grade instruction is very complex. It involves a balancing of diverse curriculum and instruction, classroom management, and motivational components. Moreover, all three of the major elements in the balance are composed of many smaller elements.

Thus, curriculum and instruction in such classrooms is complex, highlighting interesting content presented in engaging ways and through engaging activities. For example, students do not just read about the annual dog sled races in Alaska (the Iditerod), but rather they follow the race on the Web and communicate with other classes around the world via the Internet about the race and issues surrounding it. (Is it cruel to have teams of dogs driven to the extremes required in the race?) The curriculum and instruction in effective classrooms is also intense, with content encountered all day as instruction occurs in whole groups, small groups, and individually. There is much reading and writing, punctuated by mini-lessons on an as-needed basis. The many mini-lessons permit the work to be appropriately challenging, with the teacher scaffolding students as they require assistance, providing just enough help to move them along rather than doing the task for them. Because scaffolded mini-lessons require much teacher monitoring to know what students need and when they need it, the engaging teacher knows much about his or her students, including whether the lessons being provided are clear and helpful to students. The cross-curricular connections in engaging classrooms are extensive and intensive. Hence, the dog sled race can be connected to science and social studies, although the students focus on reading and writing about the race. The research on the Internet communications via e-mail permit the students many opportunities to use technology just the way adults do when they need to access information. The curriculum and instruction in effective classrooms is aimed at expanding student thinking processes, that is, at increasing students' understanding of how texts are constructed in order for them to get the most out of reading and be able to construct new texts that are filled with the messages that they want to convey. The students receive many lessons about how to read like excellent readers do, write like excellent writers write, and reason like excellent thinkers reason.

Classroom management in effective classrooms is also multidimensional. Rather than emphasizing the teacher as in control, the effective teacher permits the student to take control of his or her own behavior—

that is, emphasizes that students should self-regulate and teaches them how to do so (e.g., teaching classroom routines; inculcating the expectation that the natural next move when completing one task is to move on to another task). The classroom expectations make sense to students because the teacher goes to great lengths to explains to students the reasons for what he or she is doing and how the lessons connect to the students' futures. The excellent teacher does not do it alone, but, rather, works with other adults (e.g., parent volunteers in the classroom, special education teachers) to make certain that resources are aligned to accomplish educational goals (i.e., parent volunteers provide lessons on skills that are required in the child's curriculum; special educators work on skills making sense given the demands the children face in the classroom). In short, the effective teacher manages the many human resources in his or her classroom well, from the students, to other professionals who interact with the classroom, to parents.

Finally, as detailed in this volume, effective primary teachers flood their classrooms with motivating instruction. Both the physical and psychological environments of these classrooms are designed to increase student commitment to learning and academic engagement. By this point, it should be obvious that effective classrooms are democratic, interesting places, with teachers having high expectations that students can learn. The result is a classroom in which academic efforts abound.

Now that we know what effective primary-grade classrooms are like, an important question is whether more such classrooms can be developed (Pressley et al., 2003). Can teachers-in-training be taught to be like the most effective teachers? Can veteran teachers who are not yet effective teachers be provided professional development that moves them closer to the ideals documented in this volume and in Pressley, Allington, et al. (2001)? Recently, members of Michael Pressley's research group (especially Alysia Roehrig) have worked on these questions. During the past 2 years, intensive professional development has been provided to young teachers who are not yet fully effective teachers. The professional development has included extensive mentoring of the young teachers by effective teachers, classroom coaching by Roehrig and the mentor teachers, and review and reflection sessions, where videotapes of teaching are reviewed. Over the course of a year, the young teachers in the program receive a great deal of input about the nature of effective teaching and feedback about how their teaching can improve to approach the ideal. Has this professional development worked? So far, the answer is no. More positively, we have observed that one third of the teachers make great progress toward becoming much better teachers during their first year of teaching (i.e., with or without intensive mentoring), progress toward becoming like the best teachers in our work of the past decade. About a third of the teachers make little progress during the year. Sadly, a third actually get worse over the course of the first year.

Based on this work and other research we have conducted (Roehrig, Pressley, & Talotta, 2002), we are coming to realize that even a great deal of support during the first year of teaching is probably not going to produce great teachers quickly. In fact, something that is apparent when we reflect on the excellent teachers we have studied over the past decade—reported in this volume and elsewhere (e.g., Pressley, Allington, et al., 2001; Wharton-McDonald et al., 1998)—is that it takes a while to become really good at primary-grade teaching, to be really motivating and effective. We have never encountered an engaging primary-grade teacher who had not been in a primary-grade classroom for at least a few years. Those familiar with the teacher expertise literature will recognize that this specific conclusion about the development of expert teaching is consistent with Berliner's conclusion that teacher expertise takes a few years of teaching to develop, when it develops at all (Berliner, 1986; Carter, Cushing, Sabers, Stein, & Berliner, 1988; Carter, Sabers, Cushing, Pinnegar, & Berliner, 1987; Sabers, Cushing, & Berliner, 1991).

The implication of this is that if you want to make your primary-grade classroom more motivating, what is going to be required is a long-term plan. There is no quick fix but, rather, much that can be done to be more motivating as a teacher. It probably takes a while to learn how to do all that is required to be a terrific teacher. Even so, the positive classroom worlds that we have observed when teachers are over-the-top engaging encourages us to encourage you to do all possible to be more motivating with your students. The big hypothesis that effective primary-grade teaching articulates multiple forms of effective instruction, excellent classroom management, and motivational flooding of the classroom has a corollary hypothesis now: Such complicated teaching takes a while to develop. To get there requires instructional efforts and innovations for many Monday mornings to come. The next chapter focuses on what we hope many of you will be doing on those Monday mornings ahead.

CHAPTER 7

What to Do Monday Morning and Many Mornings to Come

Our purpose in writing this book was to do more than inform about academic motivation. It was to encourage many more teachers to be more motivating in their classrooms. So, if you are a primary-grade teacher, what can you do to make your classroom more motivating? Admittedly, all we can offer at this point are hypotheses, for we have not attempted to put the professional development model detailed in this section to a test. On the other hand, we are not certain it ever could be put to a test, for an understanding that we have developed from conducting research on effective primary-grade teachers is that mostly these are teachers who developed themselves as teachers, doing so over years. At the center of their being is a set of attitudes that propel them to become better teachers, and, thus, the first focus of anyone wanting to become a more engaging primary-grade teacher is to confront one's own attitudes.

THE ATTITUDES AND BELIEFS OF EFFECTIVE TEACHERS

We have really gotten to know many primary-grade teachers well during the past decade, excellent teachers, weak teachers, and in-between teachers. Although the emphasis in this volume was on observed teaching, there is no doubt in our minds that the beliefs and attitudes of the best teachers are very different from the beliefs and attitudes of other teachers.

First, the best teachers deeply care about their students, with that care translating into determination that all of their students will learn.

The best teachers make it clear that learning will happen for their kids, no matter how much teaching effort is required. If it means working with difficult parents, excellent teachers get as much as they can out of the parents. If it means squeezing scarce resources out of the school, they'll do what they have to do to get the resources they need. There is just no doubt in these teachers' minds that they can help the kids in their charge.

Second, the best teachers are just certain they can get better as teachers. They are the teachers who ask the most questions of us as outside observers about what they could be doing better. They are the ones who are always talking about innovations they are trying and workshops they are attending. They seem on a constant quest to find better stories for their students to read, better thematic units, and better pedagogy. As they try new approaches, they also are keenly aware of whether the approaches are working with their students and which ones. If an approach works, it stays. If it does not, it goes. These teachers not only innovate and try innovations, they reflect on their teaching and act on those reflections. These are very reflective practitioners, ones with classrooms that are dynamic in that they are always changing for the better.

So, you can start your journey to better teaching by asking yourself some questions: Do you believe every student can learn . . . and demand they do so in your class? Or do you accept that some students cannot learn in your class? (For example, do you sometimes explain a child's failure to learn to read as "not being ready to learn to read"?) Do you work hard to find ways to increase the achievement of even the hard-to-reach students? Are you always looking for ways to improve, or is one year pretty much the same as the next in your classroom? As you try innovations, do you monitor carefully whether the innovations are working, expanding use of approaches that work and eliminating approaches that do not work? If you want to be a more motivating and effective teacher, changing your attitudes and beliefs is very important, for the positive attitudes and beliefs of effective teachers clearly go far in motivating the motivating teaching they do. We suspect that it helps to come to believe, with all your heart, the following:

- All of your students can learn.
- You can do much to help every one of your students to learn more and better.
- You can learn to teach better. There are lots of interesting stories out there that you can find for your students to read, lots of inter-

esting and worthwhile activities that you can adapt to your classroom.

- You should be learning to teach better every year. The professional
  teacher is always improving. Teaching is not a skill learned in one's
  youth (i.e., during college or the first few years of teaching) but
  rather a complex competency that requires continuous honing and
  improvement.
- An important part of becoming a better teacher is reflecting constantly on one'e teaching—reflecting on the progress of every student and every instructional tactic attempted with every student.
  This means asking whether your teaching is impacting students: If
  it is not, try something else; if it is, reflect on why the approach is
  working and how the approach can be used most profitably in your
  setting.

Without exception, every motivating and effective primary-grade
teacher we have encountered has the attitudes summarized in this subsec-
tion. They are exceptionally positive people, positive about the children
they teach, certain they can make an enormous, positive difference in
their students' lives. It is not a Pollyanna certainty, but, rather, a positiveness rooted in confidence that they can find a way to reach and advance
every student, that they will find the energy and time to exert the necessary efforts and that these will pay off. We believe that such attitudes are
essential if a teacher is to become an engaging primary-grade teacher. Developing such attitudes and beliefs should be a high priority if you want to
change for the better as a primary-grade teacher.

ASSESSING THE NEED IN YOUR CLASSROOM

You need to assess candidly how much you need to improve. As researchers, we came to realize that we knew whether a teacher was motivating within a few minutes of arriving in the classroom. Basically, motivating teachers are motivating all the time. So, this morning, take a
look around. Are most of your students working away most of the time
without you having to be on top of them? If so, there's a good chance
you are already doing much to motivate your students. What we found
was that about 20% of the primary-grade teachers we watched were very
motivating.

Alternatively, if many of your students are off-task much of the time, fooling around or not knowing what they should be doing, that is a strong signal that there is room for improvement. The more students who are off-task and the more often they are off-task, the stronger the signal that something is amiss. Based on our research, we conclude that there is room for improvement in the majority of primary-level classrooms. We also estimate there is *great* need for improvement in at least one third of primary-level classrooms.

We hope that if you detect that less than 90% of your students are doing worthwhile reading and writing (or other worthwhile academic activities) less than 90% of the time, that will motivate you to do something about it. If it does, resolve to start doing business differently immediately. As you do so, however, you should keep in mind that the excellent teachers we observed became excellent over time. Between 2 and 5 years probably is required to become good at primary-grade teaching, good in that teaching is consistent with the big hypothesis reviewed earlier in this chapter. So, start today, or start with the new school year, but we urge you to get started soon if your students are not now highly engaged most of the time. Then work away at improving and be patient as your teaching is transformed, becoming more engaging as you learn more and more about how to motivate your students.

STARTING THE SCHOOL YEAR

A quarter of a century ago, a group at the University of Texas carried out a classic study, documenting that excellent primary-grade teachers start the school year differently than other teachers. Emmer, Evertson, and Anderson (1980) and Evertson and Emmer (1982) established that teachers with classrooms that were well managed at mid year began the year by emphasizing classroom management, establishing the important classroom routines and expectations the very first days of school, and making certain students knew what was expected of them (with high behavioral expectations the norm).

More recently, Day, Woodside-Jiron, and Johnston (1999) observed the first few days of school of grade 1 and grade 4 teachers who were known from previous observations to produce high engagement and high achievement in their classrooms. A particularly important finding was that the effective teachers emphasized that their students should be self-regulated. The teachers not only introduced classroom routines during the first few days of school but emphasized that students should be self-regulated. The excellent teachers also emphasized that it was important that students respect one another, including disagreeing respectfully. In fact, there was a strong emphasis on collaborative interaction during the first few days of school, with the effective teachers making clear that students would be working together throughout the year. In addition, the effective teachers emphasized that the year would be filled with exciting academic tasks—the reading of terrific literature and the opportunity to do exciting writing. The excellent teachers made very clear that the work ahead was to be anticipated with excitement, for it was worthwhile and interesting.

Bohn, Roehrig, and Pressley (2002) also evaluated the first few days of school in excellent primary-grade classrooms, explicitly comparing the first few days in such classrooms with the first few days in more typical primary-grade classrooms. What they observed was that the first few days of school were very different in the classrooms of the more effective teachers, as follows:

• The effective teachers did much to establish a positive atmosphere, with well-planned and fun activities, ones that were carried out efficiently by the class. Part of the positiveness was that the effective teachers knew the names of their students from the moments they entered the door. The more effective teachers listened carefully to their students' thoughts, needs, and concerns and responded compassionately. They emphasized with their students that the classroom was a community, one where good manners were expected as a sign of respect for one another. There was over-the-top emphasis on cooperation and meeting responsibilities as part of being a good community member.

• The teachers introduced the curriculum with enthusiasm. They let the students know that they loved to read and write and that reading and writing was going to be great in this classroom, filled with interesting and exciting texts.

• The effective teachers projected high and positive expectations to their students, letting them know that they expected them to behave well and achieve academically. The message was very, very clear: "I know you can do it."

• The effective teachers made certain that the students really understood the classroom procedures, although making certain as well that the students knew the procedures were not the real focus of school—reading, writing, math, and other exciting content learning is what school is really about! Thus, the effective teachers had their students practice the procedures being taught. Because the effective teachers taught procedures that were very efficient, the students experienced the efficiency firsthand. Thus, in the effective classrooms, getting ready to leave school at the end of the day was done very quickly, in contrast to some classrooms of ineffective teachers, where students had no idea where to look for the materials they were to take home.

• The effective teachers emphasized self-regulation in students. They made clear that they expected students to carry out routines and do work without teacher oversight. The message was that students were to take charge of themselves. This contrasted with a clear message in some of the less effective classrooms that students were to behave on cue from the teacher, who was in charge at all times. Thus, in the more effective classrooms the teachers made clear that students were to clean up after themselves, attempt to answer questions for themselves before asking the teacher, attempt all tasks by themselves before seeking help (e.g., opening snacks at morning break), and autonomously use strategies they were taught during reading and writing (e.g., to use the word wall on their own to spell words in their writing).

• The effective teachers modeled extensively for students, letting them know how to do many things expected of primary-grade students (from how to use scissors to how to find information in a book). They also modeled enthusiasm and kindness to other people. In addition, when effective teachers saw students doing something well, they pointed out to other children that their classmate was doing well—how the classmate was a good model. In contrast to less effective teachers, the more effective teachers never pointed out when a student was misbehaving or doing something poorly, handling such situations quietly so that other students would not notice.

In summary, the first few days of school are very different in engaging compared to less engaging classrooms. Encourage your students especially to believe that they can self-regulate, that they can behave well and achieve at high levels. Do everything you can do to transform your first few days of school to be like the first few days witnessed by Day et al. (1999) and Bohn et al. (2002). If you do, it is a good start on a better year than if you do not emphasize student self-regulation and engagement. Even so, it is important to keep it up, for school years are 180 days, not just a few days in the early autumn.

CHANGING YOUR TEACHING FOR THE BETTER
EVERY MINUTE OF EVERY DAY OF THE SCHOOL YEAR

A teaching goal we urge that you adopt is to motivate every student for every minute of every day, while simultaneously not doing anything that might undermine motivation. That, of course, is an ambitious goal, but, fortunately, this goal can be reduced to a list of more concrete suggestions, which include the following:

• Flood the classroom with books and fill each day and the curriculum with great reading experiences. Model reading for students (e.g., by reading aloud to students, dramatically and expressively to make clear your interest in what is being read) and encourage students to read extensively themselves. Complement book reading with other media experiences (e.g., books on tape, computer software, etc.), as many worthwhile books now available in a variety of formats. The listening center is often popular in engaging classrooms. Students in engaging classrooms can often be heard making comparisons between the Harry Potter books and the movies. Good books are a big deal in engaging classrooms, as are media connections to good books.

• Fill the classroom with inviting and attractive decorations, including displays that celebrate student accomplishments (e.g., final drafts of stories written by students).

• Let the students know that you believe they can do well in school and expect them to try hard to do so, for what is being learned in school is important. Communicate high expectations with respect to all aspects of classroom life, from doing assignments to adhering to classroom rules and procedures to keeping the room clean and orderly.

• Let every student know that you expect them to improve, no matter how well or poorly they have done in the past. Set as your goal the improvement of individual students relative to where they are right now. If a student is writing stories that are already a page long, urge the student to try writing longer and more complex stories (e.g., perhaps a two-page story with a surprise ending). If the student is having trouble writing even one complete sentence, teach the child how to write a one-sentence story and applaud the achievement. Develop an attitude in yourself that improvement is what matters, steady improvement by each and every student. Develop as well the commitment to interact positively with every child, applauding every child's advancements.

• Provide consistently upbeat communications, such as letting students know about exciting new content that will be covered ("We're starting the unit on ecology tomorrow, which will mean thinking about animals in lots of interesting, new ways"). Sometimes it also makes sense to provide tangible rewards, especially for activities that are important but that students might not do on their own (e.g., pizza incentives for students who are not avid readers). Tangible rewards should be downplayed, however. The most important and frequent reinforcer should be praise for very specific accomplishments. Engaging teachers praise many children for specific achievements every hour of every school day. They are on the lookout for behaviors, intentions, and achievements that legitimately can be complimented. Your students are doing much that deserves positive notice. Give it to them.

• Procedures for moving from one task to another are important. Make certain students know the signals for transition and provide clear procedures for making transitions rapidly and in an orderly fashion.

• Let students know why classroom life is the way it is. In particular, let them know the rationales for classroom rules. Make certain students know the reasons for all that happens in school.

• Foster cooperation between you and the students and between the students. This can be part of a general prosocial attitude in the class, that the world is better when people help one another. Downplay (or better yet, eliminate) competition. With a little thought, you will be able to identify many opportunities for student cooperation across the school day, from buddy reading and writing to science experiment collaboration (e.g., groups of fours) to division of labors for cleanup. Part of cooperation for students is assuring that everyone is doing their part, so that cooperative self-regulation by students should be the goal (e.g., when seatwork assignments are completed, students know to find a buddy who will read with them; when reading a story is completed, students know to begin writing and to seek a writing buddy to listen to their drafted story).

• In fostering cooperation in the classroom, it is also essential to require individual achievement and accountability. Thus, it is essential to monitor carefully to assure that all children in cooperative groups are working on the task, rather than allowing one child to do all the work. The individual progress of every child is essential, with cooperative learning experiences only a means to the end of individual accomplishment and growth.

• When discipline is necessary, make it a natural consequence of the misbehavior (e.g., staying in to complete work when students fail to do so

because of inattention). Keep disciplinary events as private as possible, resolved as quickly as possible. The less disciplinary events are even noticed
by other students in the room, the better. The more that disciplinary firm-
ness is accompanied by kindness and positiveness, the better.

• Do all possible to find interesting ways to cover material and load
the curriculum with as interesting content as possible. Concept-oriented
instruction can cover a lot of academic territory and be very exciting, providing concrete learning and hands-on experiences. Use games and playful activities some of the time, especially to review content. Monitor
carefully whether stories, writing activities, thematic units "grab" the students, and, in future years, use and expand coverage of the grabbers and
reduce (or eliminate) use of materials and activities that are not so compelling. Our years of observations have convinced us that for virtually every topic covered in the primary grades, there are more and less compelling and motivating ways to cover the topic. Your job is consistently to be
finding the most compelling way to cover content your students need to
learn.

• Make certain that what you are teaching is valuable to know and
that your students know why it is valuable. Definitely ask yourself
whether a unit is worthwhile science or social studies before spending a
month on the topic! When teaching vocabulary, teach the words that students really need to know, ones they have not acquired through their everyday conversations. If you do teach content that is worthwhile, it will
be easy to make the case to students that what they are learning is valuable, for they will be able to see how it does help them to understand the
world. Thus, an ecology unit about wildlife in the city can be a grabber for
urban children, because they will then notice and understand much more
about the ecology in which they live, recognizing how the animals they
encounter daily survive and enrich the lives of cities. Such a unit con-
nects with urban students, helping them to understand better their world,
and thus, making the relevance of science obvious in ways that coverage
of a more abstract topic might not be (e.g., an ecology unit focusing on
the lives of Arctic animals).

• Do make connections between what students already know and
what is being covered in school. This can be done in a number of ways,
including discussions in advance of a topic: "What do you know about the
wild animals that live in this neighborhood?" "Does anyone know why
these wild animals live so close to humans . . . any ideas?" "How are our
lives better by having wild animals in the neighborhood?" Connections
can happen during field trips, for example, walks in the neighborhood as

the unit on wildlife in the city proceeds, talking about observations during the walk that can be related to the ideas covered in the unit. Think hard about how every topic and idea covered in your classroom can be connected to students' lives. There often are strong connections to children's lives that can be made during lessons. In engaging classrooms, connections are being made all the time.

• Give students tasks that are challenging, rather than easy, but not so challenging that the tasks cannot be accomplished with some effort and appropriate support from you or by students working together cooperatively. When students need assistance, give them enough to let them carry on—that is, enough to help without doing the task for them. This should be part of showing that you care about students and their progress, part of a positive classroom atmosphere.

In addition, let the students know that they are tackling challenging tasks, reminding them that they are now doing tasks that are more difficult than the ones they could do a month ago, a week ago, or yesterday. Let them know that through their own efforts, trying hard every day, they are becoming more competent. Let them know that you are giving them tasks that require impressive efforts, ones they are capable of expending. Let them know you are giving them tasks that encourage and permit them to grow, that school is about getting more competent with every passing day, week, and month. Your classroom is a place where minds continuously change for the better.

Engaged classrooms are ones where there is hard-earned success everywhere. Every student is making progress with effort, with no one obviously frustrated to the point of defeat. This requires a great deal of tailoring of materials, tasks, and activities as well as much student-specific support. Nonetheless, it can happen. Thus, if the assignment is to be reading a particular story, some children can be reading the story independently and urged to read another book related to the story after finishing the assigned story. Other children can be asked to read with peers, providing mutual support. Still others might do best with a teacher helping them. With such adjustments, everyone can read the story and get something out of the class time spent. Everyone can feel successful.

• Be available to your students, especially providing help when they are struggling (i.e., scaffolding instruction when students need it). To know when they need help requires teacher monitoring as students work: Monitor constantly to be aware of who needs help and then provide the coaching required for students who are not making progress. In engaging classrooms, the teacher does much coaching, with part of coaching being to move students on to more demanding tasks when they are ready.

• One of the most important resources in the motivating classroom is the books! Fill your teaching and your classroom with books that students want to read, worthwhile literature and informational books that cover the topics your students want to know about. Then arrange your classroom and schedule so that the books are read, rather than sitting on the shelves. For example, establish buddy reading as an activity that can be done when other work is completed. Encourage students to take books home and read them to their parents, perhaps having parents sign off on a form to indicate they listened to their child read. Provide students with opportunities to share worthwhile books with the class, perhaps through a "reader's chair" or an opportunity to read a favorite book to a small group of classmates or to younger students in the school. Have students keep a pile of books at their desk that they can read if there is nothing else for them to do, sending the clear expectation that students can and should read.

• Listen often to students reading, especially books that are a bit challenging. This gives you an opportunity to provide individualized help both as the child is reading (i.e., scaffolding) and in the selection of additional books that the child could read, ones topically related to a current selection or perhaps a bit more challenging (e.g., if the child can read the current selection with ease). One especially attractive option we have seen is students reading to younger children. The first grade loves to visit the kindergarten to read to the younger students!

• Students also like encountering a second version of a story they have read, for example, reading an electronic version of a book previously read in conventional format. Having students read electronic books is a good use of the classroom computer.

• Computers can be dreaded if they are just used for skill-drilling programs. They can be distracting if simply loaded with arcade-type games. Alternatively, they can be filled with software that engages real reading, writing, and problem solving and can be gateways to the Internet, with its plethora of connections to all the most important primary-level social studies and science topics. We remember vividly the excitement students experienced in the classroom where the students consulted the Internet daily for progress about the annual Iditarod dog race. The interaction on the computer related to reading, writing, and map problem-solving tasks that were ongoing in the classroom, all as part of a unit on Alaska. There was no doubt that the computer was being used to engage students in a mind-expanding adventure. Computers used well can really spice up a classroom and do good things for children's minds.

• After doing a reading or covering some content in class, review the big ideas with the students, to make certain that they did not just pick up on seductive, tangential details, but rather understood and will remember the major points that were intended. Doing so assures that students leave lessons better informed and that they know what is going on.

• In general, review important ideas often, especially when it is obvious that students need the review. Do not spend time, however, going over material that students already know, which bores students. What is critical is to review the ideas that may only partially be understood at this point, keeping at it until it is certain that students know what they are supposed to know, but without overdrilling points.

• Encourage students to communicate with others about what they have read and how they feel about it. This can be through class discussions, sharing of book reports, or comments during buddy reading. Alternatively, students can be encouraged to write e-mails to students in other classes about books they have read, or they can be asked to talk with or even write to their parents or other adults about books they have read. There is always a great deal of communications about what has been read in engaged classrooms. Great stories and books are hot topics of conversation in such classrooms.

• Emphasize that successes and failures are due to effort (or lack of it), that trying hard pays off. Send the message that the responsible, mature approach to tasks is to try. Avoid making ability attributions of any kind. Even some well-intended ability attributions have the potential to undermine motivation, for example, comments like "You're getting these right because you are so smart, such intelligent children."

• When possible, give students some choice—about which books to read, what they are writing, which part of a large group project they will do, where they work in the room, and so on. Let them also feel some ownership of their work, celebrating their choices in books, their writing, and their unique contributions to class projects.

• Plan lessons and units well, including thinking about the directions given to students so that task demands are clear and the materials needed for activities are assembled. Make your plans for the week, day, and unit apparent to the students, so that they know why they are doing what they are doing. Make plans so that the pace is neither too slow nor rapid, monitoring whether the original planned time is sufficient, adjusting the plan to schedule more or less time as needed.

• Encourage students to see that there can be more than one way to think about issues. Encourage discussion and reflection about ideas, stories, and projects, which works especially well if these are ones that are of obvious importance to kids (e.g., whether Harry Potter is worthwhile literature, how knowing about local birds provides important information about the local ecology). Listen to student questions, and permit students time to reflect before answering your questions. In short, encourage students to think about ideas being covered and to participate in the intellectual life of the classroom.

• Involve families in the classroom, at a minimum letting them know what is occurring in class and encouraging them to work with students on homework. Invite parents to contribute as they can to classroom life, for example, perhaps providing input to class projects (e.g., a parent who is a police officer making a presentation during a conceptual unit on responsible citizenship) or serving as a parent volunteer in the classroom or a tutor.

• Vary teaching across the day, using whole groups, small groups, and one-on-one teaching, mixing and matching groups of students to provide the teaching specific students need.

• Teach students strategies that permit them to comprehend, write, and problem solve well. (Teachers who do not yet know such strategies should make it a priority to learn them and then teach them to their students.) As part of teaching strategies, be a model of strategy use yourself, modeling for students how to comprehend text (especially challenging text), write, and problem solve. An important part of being a strategy user is knowing when strategies are required: For example, they are helpful when reading is challenging. Therefore, teach students to be aware of when they are experiencing difficulties reading, with such difficulties not a signal to give up, but, rather, a signal to try a reading strategy such as sounding out words when unfamiliar new words are encountered or going back and rereading when confused.

In summary, there really is a flood of possibilities for making primary-level classrooms more engaging and inviting. The case studies in this book make clear that there are real teachers who can and do flood their classrooms with the type of motivating instruction considered in this section. You can, too, although it may take a while to try the many possibilities just reviewed and to develop your teaching to the point that something motivating is happening every minute of every day. However, that should be the goal, for we have seen classrooms where that happens, and they are classrooms that really work well for students. The students are learning all the time in such classrooms, doing the worthwhile stuff that is real reading, demanding writing, and important social studies, math, and science.

NOT DOING BAD TEACHING EVERY MINUTE OF EVERY SCHOOL DAY

As you take these proactive measures to increase student motivation, keep in mind that engaging teachers also do not do anything to undermine their students' motivation. Remember all the ways that teachers can undermine student motivation:

- Ability, task, and luck attributions have potential to discourage student effort.
- Emphasis on high grades and competition discourages many more kids than it encourages.
- Standardized tests do not motivate kids.
- Punishment and criticism are rare in engaging classrooms.
- Negative people turn kids (and everyone else) off.
- Criticism definitely does not inspire students to do better.
- Aloof teachers turn off kids in contrast to teachers who interact with students, who are aware of what and how students are doing.
- Anti-intellectual teachers do not inspire kids to do things intellectual (e.g., teachers who do not read do not inspire their students to read).
- Both easy tasks and overly difficult tasks discourage students from trying hard.
- Both too little time to do academic tasks and too much time discourage academic efforts.
- Boring work turns kids off.
- Confusing communications (e.g., poor directions) do not result in engaged students.
- Poorly planned instruction rarely is engaging instruction.
- When the teacher is always looking for "right" answers, that does not inspire students to be reflective or to take intellectual risks.
- Disconnected tasks often do not make sense to students.
- When students are spending much time on art relative to more academic pursuits, they are not learning much.
- Both ignoring families (i.e., by never corresponding with them) and paying too much attention to them (e.g., talking more with

parent volunteers than with students) can undermine student motivation.
- Rewarding students for what they would do anyway sometimes re-
duces the likelihood they will continue to do it (e.g., giving pizza
incentives for reading to avid readers).

In summary, there are some bad habits that we have observed in
classrooms that do not engage students. An important step in becoming
an engaging teacher is to confront your teaching habits that might undermine your effectiveness and eliminate those habits. To do so requires becoming very self-conscious of just what you are doing. What we are calling on you to do is to be positively motivating every minute of every
school day and to refrain from doing anything that can undermine the
positiveness of the classroom. This is a very tall order, one that will require hard work on your part and great attention to your own behavior.
We anticipate that if you are successful, you will find your students much
more engaged in their learning, with much less reason for you even to
consider being negative. Classroom life will be more positive, which ultimately will make it easy for you to be consistently positive.

BUT WHAT ABOUT THE REST
OF THE BIG HYPOTHESIS?

As you will recall, the big hypothesis is that excellent teachers use diverse
teaching and learning techniques, are excellent at classroom management, and flood their classrooms with motivation. Yet the focus in this
book has been motivation more than anything else.

An insight we have had as we have completed this work is that by focusing on motivation, everything else follows. Consider teaching and
learning in the classrooms described here: There is a great deal of scaffolding, which motivates because the students are being challenged but also
supported. There is a great deal of real reading and writing and teaching
of real reading and writing. Teachers make efforts to identify compelling
materials for students to read and great topics for them to write about.
Teaching comprehension and writing strategies has motivational implications, because such strategies make tasks more doable, more rewarding,
and more fun. Diverse, excellent instruction and motivation go hand and
hand. By focusing on motivation, great instruction will follow, because so
many motivational techniques are also instructional techniques.

What about classroom management? Classroom management in

classrooms consistent with the big hypothesis boils down to students managing themselves. The teacher teaches students that they are to be in control of themselves. The students are praised often when they are so self-controlled, and there are natural consequences: The classroom is neat and orderly, things get done without the teacher ever reprimanding, and there are many and wonderful cooperative interactions between students, who are respectful to one another. Thus, part of motivating instruction is an approach to classroom management that emphasizes student self-regulation—students being expected to behave well and learn much, with substantial praise and positive outcomes associated with self-management. Motivating instruction as described here folds in excellent classroom management, which can be so good that it is hard to discern the teacher's approach to discipline because disciplining students is so rarely required.

At this point in time, our hypothesis is that the route to becoming an engaging and effective teacher is to be a motivating teacher, to flood the classroom with motivation using the many tactics employed by engaging, effective teachers, as covered repeatedly in this book. Although we suspect it will take a while to try all that needs to be tried, reflect on it, and build a repertoire of motivating techniques, we are certain it can be done by at least some teachers, for we have seen ones who have done it, the ones featured in this book.

If you do decide to test our hypothesis that your teaching can be much more engaging and effective if you attempt to flood the classroom with motivation as described in this volume, let us know how it goes for you. (See the Appendix for a concise summary of how to increase the motivation in your classroom.) We are very interested in testing our hypothesis that primary-grade teachers can transform themselves into engaging teachers. The only way we will ever know is by teachers, such as many of the readers of this book, actually trying very hard to become like the engaging teachers summarized in this volume. Start this Monday or in the new school year, but start now. We think there is a good chance that your classroom will be a lot better for your efforts. The engaging teachers we have studied loved their jobs. Every student in their classrooms loved school. The parents were thrilled with the education their children received in such environments. The only concern principals had about such teachers was that some other school might steal them away! Imagine a whole school year when there is not one salient disciplinary event. Imagine a whole week when there are no disciplinary events at all. Imagine that every day every student is interested, excited, and obviously making progress. It happens in some classrooms. Maybe it can happen in yours.

QUESTIONS WE HEAR OFTEN FROM EDUCATORS

In presenting the results summarized in this book, there have been frequent questions. One is "Would the results presented here generalize above the primary grades?" The answer is that we do not know. As we have offered that answer, we have often heard replies from audience members that they believe the situation we describe here probably does apply beyond the primary grades. The case has definitely been made to us that there are relatively few extremely motivating teachers. Those who exist are effective in engaging their students, teaching them better than other teachers. Moreover, those who exist use many of the same tactics that we observed in the most engaging primary-grade classrooms that we studied. Our response at this point is that it makes sense to consider these ideas as hypotheses. That we cannot find anything in the existing literature that permits a response to the questions about motivation in the upper grades makes obvious that there is a need to know here.

A second question posed to us has been "Why did the National Reading Panel (2000) not take up the issue of motivation in literacy instruction?" We do not have an answer, except that the panel restricted their coverage of the relevant instructional literature from the outset of their efforts. They obviously did not feel that the motivational variables that we focused on here were as relevant to their mission as evaluation of alphabetics instruction, development of fluency, comprehension instruction, teacher education, and computer technology. Although all of the engaging teachers we have studied were concerned with the development of alphabetic competencies, fluency, and comprehension, their instruction was much fuller than the narrow skills instruction that concerned the panel. Our hypothesis is that really effective literacy instruction includes all of the components cited as critical by the panel—now referenced as five factors in many discussions (i.e., development of phonemic awareness, phonics, vocabulary instruction, development of fluency, comprehension instruction)—but it is much, much more. In particular, the instruction is delivered in a variety of ways with diverse materials; it occurs in well-managed classrooms; and the instruction is massively motivating, as we have detailed in this volume.

One objection we have heard as we have described our work as science is that we did not follow the preferred methodology of the National Reading Panel, which is experimentation. That is absolutely true, although the work summarized here is unambiguously scientific. Consistent with the thinking of many excellent educational scientists, we believe that qualitative and quantative approaches intermix as part of a complete science (Shavelson & Towne, 2002). In particular, qualitative approaches are very helpful in trying to understand complex situations that are not yet much understood. We felt that was the case with respect to the nature of excellent primary-grade instruction when we began our study of the problem in the middle 1990s (see also Pressley, Allington, et al., 2001; Pressley, Wharton-McDonald, et al., 2001; Wharton-McDonald, Pressley, & Hampston, 1998). As that work proceeded, we came to understand that there was also not much understood about motivating instruction per se in effective classrooms, and, hence, we responded with our recent qualitative work, including the research summarized in this book (Bogner, Raphael, & Pressley, 2002; Dolezal, Welsh, Pressley, & Vincent, 2003). Consistent with all of the research accepted by the National Reading Panel, most of our work has appeared in very selective peer-reviewed journals. We believe that anyone interested in evidence-based, excellent primary-grade reading instruction should be reflecting on the program of research that we have conducted, including the recent work presented in some detail in this volume.

A third question that we have encountered is "But what can teachers do if they are required by their school to use a particular program?" Quite frankly, we think that most of the motivational mechanisms used by the engaging teachers we studied could be used even in the context of a fairly structured program. One possible problem is that the basal readers control the literature that children read. Even so, in examining the contemporary comprehensive programs on the market, most of the selections in the basals are good children's literature, and there is much encouragement for children to read beyond the basal. In fact, one way of reading the basal anthologies is that they provide constant pressure on teachers to be presenting literature to children and point teachers in the directions of authors that are ones children should know about and do find appealing. In examining the list of approaches for enhancing classroom motivation that are summarized in the Appendix and discussed throughout this volume, most are ones that could be used with a variety of curriculum materials. In fact, one audience we hope to reach with this work is the authors of basal programs, for we think that they could do much in their programs to encourage teachers to use the motivational mechanisms highlighted here. Our reading of the basal manuals is that basal program authors are like many others concerned with beginning reading instruction: They have not thought much about how their programs can be more motivating. Given that a very high proportion of schools still use comprehensive, published programs, it is important to attempt to impact the development of such materials so that teachers using the programs are encouraged to do much motivating for and with their students.

Another question that comes up is "Is the type of excellent teaching you have observed possible in schools serving disadvantaged children?" The answer to this question is easy: Many of the teachers we have showcased across the years of our investigations have been serving disadvantaged students. In addition, we also point out that being from an advantaged population does not guarantee good teaching, for we have seen a number of classrooms populated with upper-middle-class children where engagement has been very low. Our view is that the teaching is what makes the difference in classroom engagement, much more than the socioeconomic status of the children being served.

Finally, a commentary, posed as a question, that often comes our way is something like the following: "There is no quick fix, is there?" That's right, but there is a fix for individual teachers. We know a great deal about individual practices that teachers can adopt in their classrooms to increase literacy achievement by their students. Based on our work and that of our colleagues (e.g., Pressley, Allington, et al., 2001; Pressley, Wharton-McDonald, et al., 2001; Wharton-McDonald et al., 1998), we also know that excellent teachers orchestrate the use of many of the well-validated procedures. What was highlighted in this book was how excellent teachers also go to great lengths to provide motivating instruction to their students, with such instruction both complementing and accentuating other best practices (e.g., scaffolding is at the heart of motivation, but is just as much an instructional strategy as a motivational tactic). Although not a quick fix, what we have seen and documented is a great fix, one that results in primary-grade classrooms that are more exciting and engaging than most primary-grade classrooms, ones filled with writing that students and their teachers can be proud of, ones where students are always moving on to more advanced books, and ones where classroom life is a joy to watch (something we as observers are certain of). If you are a primary-grade teacher, we urge you to begin the journey to the motivated classroom described here. Your life and the lives of your students will be better for it.

Summary of What Primary-Grade Teachers Can Do to Flood Their Classrooms with Motivating Instruction

ATTITUDE SHIFTS

1. Care about each of your students and all of your students. Be there for them, interacting with them extensively in class and outside of class.
2. Convince yourself that all of your students can learn and will improve in your classroom. Be determined that you will find a way for all of your students to learn.
3. Be determined to become a better teacher, every day, every week, every month, and every year. Seek out information about how to teach better, and try new methods, approaches, and materials that might make sense in your classroom.
4. Set a goal that 90% of your students will be engaged in worthwhile academic activities 90% of the time.
5. Resolve to do something every minute of every school day to motivate your students.
6. Be positive with your students, all the time. Emphasize what students do well. Punish rarely.

TEACHING PRACTICES

1. Get off to a good start the first few days of school: Go over classroom routines, making certain students understand them, especially procedures for transitions from one activity to another. Send the message that students are responsible for carrying out the routines, doing their work, and interacting

respectfully and cooperatively with one another. That is, from day 1, emphasize student self-regulation rather than the teacher being in control.

2. Have lots of cooperative learning experiences for students, but accountability should always be at the individual level (i.e., each of the buddies who are reading need to read well; all of the students in a cooperative science team need to learn the content).

3. Let students know that you are excited about the reading, writing, and content coverage, that what will be happening in the class is important and interesting.

4. Plan well and extensively. Be ready for every lesson. As part of the planning, make certain that directions given to your students are clear.

5. Have high expectations of all your students and let them know it. Let them know that you expect them to behave well in class and achieve.

6. Try new approaches. As you do, reflect on whether the approach is working. If it does not work, and there is no apparent way to improve it, then do not continue to use the approach.

7. Model extensively for your students, not only showing them how to do academic tasks but also how to interact respectfully with people (i.e., by interacting respectfully with students). In general, model positiveness by being positive; model caring by caring for your students. Model that you love reading and writing and find the content being covered to be interesting and worthwhile.

8. Make certain that the content you are teaching is, in fact, interesting and worthwhile. Find ways to make every lesson interesting. Monitor whether the students are finding the lesson interesting. If they are bored, do what you can to find ways to spice the lesson up. Every topic can be presented in ways that are more or less interesting to students.

9. Monitor how each and every student is doing—what they are doing and accomplishing, whether they need help. Praise specific accomplishments of students often; provide scaffolding as needed (i.e., just enough support, in the form of instructions or hints, to get students started on tasks that initially are a bit beyond them).

10. Give students tasks that are moderately challenging, ones that require student effort to accomplish but that can be accomplished with such effort and perhaps some teacher scaffolding.

11. Do not get in the habit of using concrete rewards extensively. Rather, reserve such rewards for when students will not do something important for them to do unless they are provided powerful incentives.

12. If a student misbehaves, handle the situation as quickly and unobtrusively as possible. Make consequences as natural as possible (e.g., for not getting work done because of inattention, staying in at recess to complete work).

13. Flood the classroom with good literature and informational books that are appealing to students. Flood your classroom with literate experiences, includ-

ing teacher read-alouds, students reading individually and with others, and students writing on their own and together. Encourage students to communicate with one another and with their parents about what they are reading and learning.

14. Include computers and other media in the classroom, making certain that technology is used to present interesting and worthwhile materials and activities.

15. Demand a little more of every student every day. For example, demand that they read progressively more challenging texts and write progressively more complex and complete texts. Require that they get deeper into the content with every passing day.

16. Consider using thematic instruction, which provides reading and writing connections across the curriculum. Themes are often social studies or science themes or ones that have both social studies and science implications, such as ecology or climate or business.

17. Make connections between what the students know, their worlds, and material being covered in lessons.

18. Make certain students know what the big ideas are in lessons and that they remember them.

19. Emphasize that effort produces success. Downplay the effects of natural ability on achievement.

20. Give students choices about what they read, write, and study.

21. Have discussions about what is read and the content being covered. Encourage multiple perspectives during these discussions, allowing students to express and defend their viewpoints.

22. Vary teaching across the day and days, using whole group, small group, and one-on-one approaches.

23. Teach the students powerful strategies for learning—comprehension and memory strategies, writing and communications strategies. If you do not know what strategies to teach, seek out information about powerful academic strategies that can be taught to your students.

24. Do not emphasize competition between students or getting higher grades than other students.

25. Do not emphasize standardized tests.

26. Allow students enough time to complete tasks but not too much time. Make certain there are other things for students to do when they are finished, sending the consistent message that finishing one tasks is a signal to get busy on some other work than needs to be completed.

27. Decorate the room in ways that invite and celebrate academic behaviors—displays of books that could be read, word walls, charts summarizing strategies that students can use, and so on.

28. Let families know what is going on in school and how they can academically support their children.

References

Allington, R. L. (1984). Oral reading. In P. D. Pearson (Ed.), *Handbook of reading research*. New York: Longman.

Ames, C. (1984). Competitive, cooperative, and individualistic goal structures: A motivational analysis. In R. Ames & C. Ames (Eds.), *Research on motivation in education* (Vol. 1, pp. 117–207). New York: Academic Press.

Ames, C. (1992). Classrooms: Goals, structures, and student motivation. *Journal of Educational Psychology, 84*, 261–271.

Ames, C., & Ames, R. (1981). Competitive versus individualistic goal structures: The salience of past performance information for causal attributions and affect. *Journal of Educational Psychology, 73*, 411–418.

Ames, C., & Felker, D. W. (1979). Effects of self-concept on children's causal attributions and self-reinforcement. *Journal of Educational Psychology, 71*, 613–619.

Anderman, E. M., & Maehr, M. L. (1994). Motivation and schooling in the middle grades. *Review of Educational Research, 64*, 287–309.

Anderman, E. M., Maehr, M. L., & Midgley, C. (1999). Declining motivation after the transition to middle school: Schools can make a difference. *Journal of Research and Development in Education, 32*, 131–147.

Anderson, L. W. (1989). *The effective teacher: Study guide and readings*. New York: McGraw-Hill.

Anderson, R. C., & Pearson, P. D. (1984). A schema-theoretic view of basic processes in reading. In P. D. Pearson (Ed.), *Handbook of reading research* (pp. 255–291). New York: Longman.

Anderson, R. C., Shirey, L. L., Wilson, P. T., & Fielding, L. G. (1987). Interestingness of children's reading material. In R. E. Snow & M. J. Farr (Eds.), *Aptitude, learning, and instruction: Vol. 3. Conative and affective process analyses* (pp. 287–299). Hillsdale, NJ: Erlbaum.

Au, K. (2001). What we know about multicultural education and students of diverse backgrounds. In R. F. Flippo (Ed.), *Reading researchers in search of common ground* (pp. 101–117). Newark, DE: International Reading Association.

Bandura, A. (1977). Self-efficacy: Toward a unifying theory of behavioral change. *Psychological Review, 84,* 191–215.

Bandura, A. (1986). *Social foundations of thought and action: A social cognitive theory.* Englewood Cliffs, NJ: Prentice-Hall.

Bandura, A., & Schunk, D. H. (1981). Cultivating competence, self-efficacy, and intrinsic interest through proximal self-instruction. *Journal of Personality and Social Psychology, 41,* 586–598.

Barnett, M., & Andrews, J. (1977). Sex differences in children's reward allocation under competitive and cooperative instructional sets. *Developmental Psychology, 13,* 85–86.

Barton, D. (2001). Literacy in everyday contexts. In L. Verhoeven & C. E. Snow (Eds.), *Literacy and motivation: Reading engagement in individuals and groups* (pp. 23–37). Mahwah, NJ: Erlbaum.

Berliner, D. (1986). In pursuit of the expert pedagogue. *Educational Researcher, 15*(7), 5–13.

Berndt, T. J., & Miller, K. E. (1990). Expectancies, values, and achievement in junior high school. *Journal of Educational Psychology, 82,* 319–326.

Block, C., & Mangieri, J. (1994). *Creating powerful thinking in teachers and students.* Fort Worth, TX: Harcourt Brace.

Boekaerts, M., Pintrich, P. R., & Zeidner, M. (Eds.). (2001). *Handbook of self-regulation.* San Diego: Academic Press.

Bogner, K., Raphael, L. M., & Pressley, M. (2002). How grade-1 teachers motivate literate activity by their students. *Scientific Studies of Reading, 6,* 135–165.

Bohn, K., Roehrig, A., & Pressley, M. (2002, December). *The first days of school in effective and less effective primary-grade classrooms.* Paper presented at the annual meeting of the National Reading Conference, Miami, FL.

Borkowski, J. G., Carr, M., Rellinger, E. A., & Pressley, M. (1990). Self-regulated strategy use: Interdependence of metacognition, attributions, and self-esteem. In B. F. Jones (Ed.), *Dimensions of thinking: Review of research* (pp. 53–92). Hillsdale, NJ: Erlbaum.

Bromley, K. D., Winters, D., & Schlimmer, K. (1994). Book buddies: Creating enthusiasm for literacy learning. *Reading Teacher, 47,* 392–400.

Brophy, J. (1981). Teacher praise: A functional analysis. *Review of Educational Research, 51,* 5–32.

Brophy, J. (1985). Teacher–student interaction. In J. B. Dusek (Ed.), *Teacher expectancies* (pp. 303–328). Hillsdale, NJ: Erlbaum.

Brophy, J. (1986, October). *On motivating students* (Occasional Paper No. 101). East Lansing, MI: Michigan State University, Institute for Research on Teaching.

Brophy, J. (1987). Socializing students' motivation to learning. In M. L. Maehr & D. A. Kleiber (Eds.), *Advances in motivation and achievement: Enhancing motivation* (Vol. 5, pp. 181–210). Greenwich, CT: JAI Press.

Brophy, J. (1988). Research linking teacher behavior to student achievement: Potential implications for instruction of Chapter 1 students. *Educational Psychologist, 23*, 235–286.

Brophy, J., & Good, T. (1970). Teachers' communication of differential expectations for children's classroom performance: Some behavioral data. *Journal of Educational Psychology, 61*, 365–374.

Brophy, J., & Good, T. (1974). *Teacher–student relationships: Causes and consequences.* New York: Holt, Rinehart & Winston.

Brophy, J., & Good, T. (1986). Teacher behavior and student achievement. In M. Wittrock (Ed.), *Handbook of research on teaching* (pp. 340–370). New York: Macmillan.

Bruner, J. S. (1961). The act of discovery. *Harvard Educational Review, 31*, 21–32.

Bruner, J. S. (1962). *On knowing: Essays for the left hand.* Cambridge, MA: Harvard University Press.

Bruner, J. S. (1966). *Toward a theory of instruction.* Cambridge, MA: Harvard University Press.

Burbules, N. C., & Callister, T. A., Jr. (2000). Universities in transition: The promise and the challenge of new technologies. *Teachers College Record, 102*, 273–295.

Calkins, L. M. (2001). *The art of teaching reading.* New York: Addison-Wesley Longman.

Cameron, J. (2001). Negative effects of reward on intrinsic motivation— A limited phenomenon: Comment on Deci, Koestner, and Ryan (2001). *Review of Educational Research, 71*, 29–42.

Cameron, J., & Pierce, W. D. (1994). Reinforcement, reward, and intrinsic motivation: A meta-analysis. *Review of Educational Research, 64*, 363–423.

Cameron, J., & Pierce, W. D. (1996). The debate about rewards and intrinsic motivation: Protests and accusations do not alter the results. *Review of Educational Research, 66*, 39–52.

Canter, L., & Canter, M. (2002). *Assertive discipline: Positive behavior management for today's classroom.* Santa Monica, CA: Lee Canter.

Cantor, N., Markus, H., Niedenthal, P., & Nurius, P. (1986). On motivation and self-concept. In R. M. Sorrentino & E. T. Higgins (Eds.), *Handbook of motivation and cognition: Foundations of social behavior* (pp. 99–127). New York: Guilford Press.

Carr, M., & Borkowski, J. G. (1989). Attributional training and the generalization of reading strategies with underachieving children. *Learning and Individual Differences, 1*, 327–341.

Carr, M., Borkowski, J. G., & Maxwell, S. E. (1991). Motivational components of underachievement. *Developmental Psychology, 27*, 108–118.

Carter, K., Cushing, K., Sabers, D., Stein, P., & Berliner, D. (1988). Expert–novice differences in perceiving and processing visual classroom information. *Journal of Teacher Education, 39*, 25–31.

Carter, K., Sabers, D., Cushing, K., Pinnegar, S., & Berliner, D. C. (1987). Processing and using information about students: A study of expert, novice, and postulant teachers. *Teaching and Teacher Education, 3,* 147–157.

Chambliss, M. J., & McKillop, M. (2000). Creating a print- and technology-rich classroom library to entice children to read. In L. Baker, M. J. Dreher, & J. T. Guthrie (Eds.), *Engaging young readers: Promoting achievement and motivation* (pp. 94–118). New York: Guilford Press.

Charles, R. E., & Runco, M. A. (2001). Developmental trends in the evaluative and divergent thinking of children. *Creativity Resource Journal, 13,* 417–437.

Cheng, Y. C. (1994). Classroom environment and students affective performance: An effective profile. *Journal of Experimental Education, 62,* 221–239.

Cheyne, J. A., & Tarulli, D. (1999). Dialogue, difference, and the "third voice" in the zone of proximal development. *Theory and Psychology, 9,* 5–28.

Chien, M. F. (1984). The effect of teacher leadership style on adjustment of elementary school children. *Bulletin of Educational Psychology, 17,* 99–120.

Chinn, C. A., & Malhotra, B. A. (2002). Children's responses to anomalous scientific data: How is conceptual change impeded? *Journal of Educational Psychology, 94,* 327–343.

Clifford, M. M. (1975). Validity of expectation: A developmental function. *Alberta Journal of Educational Research, 21,* 11–17.

Clifford, M. M. (1978). The effects of quantitative feedback on children's expectations of success. *Journal of Educational Psychology, 48,* 220–226.

Clifford, M. M. (1991). Risk taking: Theoretical, empirical, and educational considerations. *Educational Psychologist, 26,* 263–297.

Coerr, E. (1999). *Sadako and the thousand paper cranes.* New York: Puffin.

Collins, A., Brown, J. S., & Newman, S. E. (1989). Cognitive apprenticeship: Teaching the crafts of reading, writing, and mathematics. In L. B. Resnick (Ed.), *Knowing, learning, and instruction: Essays in honor of Robert Glaser* (pp. 453–494). Hillsdale, NJ: Erlbaum.

Cooper, H., & Valentine, J. C. (2001). Using research to answer practical questions about homework. *Educational Psychologist, 36,* 143–154.

Coopersmith, S. (1967). *The antecedents of self-esteem.* San Francisco: Freeman.

Covington, M. V. (1987). Achievement motivation, self-attributions, and the exceptional learner. In J. D. Day & J. G. Borkowski (Eds.), *Intelligence and exceptionality* (pp. 355–389). Norwood, NJ: Ablex.

Covington, M. V. (1992). *Making the grade: A self-worth perspective on motivation and school reform.* New York: Cambridge University Press.

Covington, M. V. (1998). *The will to learn: A guide to motivating young people.* New York: Cambridge University Press.

Covington, M. V., & Omelich, C. L. (1979a). Effort: The double-edged sword in school achievement. *Journal of Educational Psychology, 71,* 169–182.

Covington, M. V., & Omelich, C. L. (1979b). It's best to be able and virtuous too:

Student and teacher evaluative responses to successful effort. *Journal of Educational Psychology, 71,* 688–700.

Covington, M. V., & Omelich, C. L. (1981). As failures mount: Affective and cognitive consequences of ability demotion in the classroom. *Journal of Educational Psychology, 73,* 796–808.

Covington, M. V., & Omelich, C. L. (1984). Task-oriented versus competitive learning structures: Motivational and performance consequences. *Journal of Educational Psychology, 6,* 1038–1050.

Csikszentmihalyi, M. (1988). The flow experience and its significance for human psychology. In M. Csikszentmihalyi & I. Csikszentmihalyi, *Optimal experience* (pp. 15–35). Cambridge, UK: Cambridge University Press.

Csikszentmihalyi, M. (1990). *Flow: The psychology of optimal experience.* New York: Harper & Row.

Csikszentmihalyi, M. (1997). *Finding flow: The psychology of engagement with everyday life.* New York: Basic Books.

Cunningham, P. M., & Hall, D. P. (1994). *Making words: Multilevel, hands-on developmentally appropriate spelling and phonics activities.* Torrance, CA: Good Apple.

Day, J. D., Borkowski, J. G., Dietmeyer, D. L., Howsepian, B. A., & Saenz, D. S. (1992). Possible selves and academic achievement. In L. Winegar & J. Valsiner (Eds.), *Children's development within social contexts* (pp. 181–201). Hillsdale, NJ: Erlbaum.

Day, J., Woodside-Jiron, H., & Johnston, P. (1999). *Principles of practice—the common and unique.* Paper presented at the annual conference of the National Reading Conference, Austin, TX.

deCharms, R. (1968). *Personal causation.* New York: Academic Press.

Deci, E. L. (1975). *Intrinsic motivation.* New York: Plenum.

Deci, E. L., Koestner, R., & Ryan, R. M. (1999). A meta-analytic review of experiments examining the effects of extrinsic rewards on intrinsic motivation. *Psychological Bulletin, 125,* 627–668.

Deci, E. L., Koestner, R., & Ryan, R. M. (2001a). Extrinsic rewards and intrinsic motivation in education: Reconsidered once again. *Review of Educational Research, 71,* 1–27.

Deci, E. L., Koestner, R., & Ryan, R. M. (2001b). The pervasive negative effects of rewards on intrinsic motivation: Response to Cameron (2001). *Review of Educational Research, 71,* 43–51.

Deci, E. L., & Ryan, R. M. (1985). *Intrinsic motivation and self-determination in human behavior.* New York: Plenum.

Deci, E. L., Schwartz, A., Sheinman, L., & Ryan, R. (1981). An instrument to assess adults' orientation toward control versus autonomy with children: Reflections on intrinsic motivation and perceived competence. *Journal of Educational Psychology, 73,* 642–650.

Deshler, D. D., & Schumaker, J. B. (1988). An instructional model for teaching students how to learn. In J. L. Graden, J. E. Zins, & M. J. Curtis (Eds.), *Alternative educational delivery systems: Enhancing instructional options for all students* (pp. 391–411). Washington, DC: National Association of School Psychologists.

Dewey, J. (1913). *Interest and effort in education.* Boston: Riverside.

DiPerna, J. C., Volpe, R. J., & Elliott, S. N. (2002). A model of academic enablers and elementary reading/language arts achievement. *School Psychology Review, 31,* 298–312.

Dolezal, S. E., Welsh, L. M., Pressley, M., & Vincent, M. (2003). How do grade 3 teachers motivate their students? *Elementary School Journal, 103,* 239–267.

Doyle, W. (1986). Classroom organization and management. In M. C. Wittrock (Ed.), *Handbook of research on teaching* (3rd ed., pp. 392–431). New York: MacMillan.

Dweck, C. S. (1986). Motivational processes affecting learning. *American Psychologist, 41,* 1040–1048.

Dweck, C. S., & Bempechat, J. (1983). Children's theories of intelligence: Consequences for learning. In S. G. Paris, G. M. Olson, & H. W. Stevenson (Eds.), *Learning and motivation in the classroom* (pp. 239–256). Hillsdale, NJ: Erlbaum.

Dweck, C. S., & Leggett, E. L. (1988). A social-cognitive approach to motivation and personality. *Psychological Review, 95,* 256–273.

Dweck, C. S., & Licht, B. G. (1980). Learned helplessness and intellectual achievement. In J. Garber & M. E. P. Seligman (Eds.), *Human helplessness: Theory and applications* (pp. 197–221). New York: Academic Press.

Eccles, J. S., & Midgley, C. (1990a). Changes in academic motivation and self-perceptions during early adolescence. In R. Montemayor, G. R. Adams, & T. P. Giolotta (Eds.), *Advances in adolescent development: From childhood to adolescence* (Vol. 2, pp. 134–155). Newbury Park, CA: Sage.

Eccles, J. S., & Midgley, C. (1990b). Stage/environment fit: Developmentally appropriate classrooms for early adolescents. In R. E. Ames & C. Ames (Eds.), *Research on motivation in education* (Vol. 3, pp. 139–186). San Diego: Academic Press.

Eccles, J. S., Midgley, C., Wigfield, A., Buchanan, C. M., Reuman, D., Flanagan, C., & MacIver, D. (1993). Development during adolescence: The impact of stage–environment fit on young adolescents' experiences in school and in families. *American Psychologist, 48,* 90–101.

Eisner, E. W. (1998). Does experience in the arts boost academic achievement? *Art Education, 5,* 7–15.

Elley, W. B. (1992). *How in the world do students read?* Hamburg, Germany: International Association for the Evaluation of Educational Achievement.

Elley, W. B. (Ed.). (1994). *The IEA study of reading literacy: Achievement and instruction in 32 school systems.* Oxford, UK: Pergamon.

Elley, W. B. (2001). Literacy in the present world: Realities and possibilities. In L. Verhoeven & C. E. Snow (Eds.), *Literacy and motivation: Reading engagement in individuals and groups* (pp. 225– 242). Mahwah, NJ: Erlbaum.

Elliott, E. S., & Dweck, C. S. (1988). Goals: An approach to motivation and achievement. *Journal of Personality and Social Psychology, 54,* 5–12.

Emmer, E., Evertson, C., & Anderson, L. (1980). Effective classroom management at the beginning of the school year. *Elementary School Journal, 80,* 219–231.

Entwisle, D., & Hayduk, L. (1978). *Too great expectations: The academic outlook of young children.* Baltimore, MD: Johns Hopkins University Press.

Evertson, C., & Emmer, E. (1982). Effective classroom management at the beginning of the year in junior high classes. *Journal of Educational Psychology, 74,* 485–498.

Evertson, E. M., Emmer, E. T., & Worsham, M. E. (2002). *Classroom management for elementary teachers* (6th ed.). Boston: Allyn & Bacon.

Fantuzzo, J., King, J., & Heller, L. R. (1992). Effects of reciprocal peer tutoring on mathematics and school adjustment: A component analysis. *Journal of Educational Psychology, 84,* 331–339.

Fawson, P. C., & Moore, S. A. (1999). Reading incentive programs: Beliefs and practices. *Reading Psychology, 20,* 325–340.

Fincham, F. D., Hokoda, A., & Sanders, R., Jr. (1989). Learned helplessness, text anxiety, and academic achievement: A longitudinal analysis. *Child Development, 60,* 138–145.

Fink, R. P. (1995). Successful dyslexics: A constructivist study of passionate interest reading. *Journal of Adolescent and Adult Literacy, 394,* 268–80.

Finn, J. D., Fulton, B. D., Zaharias, J. B., & Nye, B. A. (1989). Carry-over effects of small classes. *The Peabody Journal, 67,* 1–23.

Flavell, J. H., Friedrichs, A. G., & Hoyt, J. D. (1970). Developmental changes in memorization processes. *Cognitive Psychology, 1,* 324–340.

Flippo, R. F. (1998). Points of agreement: A display of professional unity in our field. *Reading Teacher, 52,* 30–40.

Fractor, J., Woodruff, M. C., Martinez, M. G., & Teale, W. H. (1993). Let's not miss opportunities to promote voluntary reading: Classroom libraries in the elementary school. *Reading Teacher, 46,* 476–485.

Gambrell, L. B. (1996). Creating classroom cultures that foster reading motivation. *Reading Teacher, 50,* 14–25.

Gambrell, L. B., Codling, R. M., & Palmer, B. M. (1996). *Elementary students' motivation to read.* [Research report]. College Park, MD, and Athens, GA: National Reading Research Center, Universities of Maryland and Georgia.

Gambrell, L. B., Mazzoni, S. A., & Almasi, J. F. (2000). Promoting collaboration, social interaction, and engagement with text. In L. Baker, M. J. Dreher, & J. T. Guthrie (Eds.), *Engaging young readers: Promoting achievement and motivation* (pp. 119–139). New York: Guilford Press.

Gambrell, L. B., Mazzoni, S., & Korkeamaki, R. L. (1996, April). *Cross-cultural models of home–school early literacy practices.* Paper presented at the annual meeting of the American Educational Research Association, New York.

Gambrell, L. B., & Morrow, L. M. (1995). Creating motivating contexts for literacy learning. In L. Baker, P. Afflerbach, & D. Reinking (Eds.), *Developing engaged readers in home and school communities* (pp. 115–136). Mahwah, NJ: Erlbaum.

Garner, R. (1992). Learning from school texts. *Educational Psychologist, 27,* 53–63.

Garner, R., Alexander, P. A., Gillingham, M. G., Kulikowich, J. M., & Brown, R. (1991). Interest and learning from text. *American Educational Research Journal, 28,* 643–660.

Ginsberg, M. B., & Wlodkowski, R. J. (2000). *Creating highly motivating classrooms for all students.* San Francisco: Jossey-Bass.

Glaser, B., & Strauss, A. (1967). *The discovery of grounded theory.* Chicago: Aldine.

Goldenberg, C. (1992). The limits of expectations: A case for case knowledge about teacher expectancy effects. *American Educational Research Journal, 29,* 517–544.

Good, T. L., & Brophy, J. E. (2002). *Looking in classrooms* (9th ed.). Boston: Allyn & Bacon.

Goss, A. M. (1968). Estimated versus actual physical strength in three ethnic groups. *Child Development, 39,* 283–290.

Graham, S., & Harris, K. (1996). Addressing problems in attention, memory, and executive functioning: An example of self-regulated strategy development. In G. R. Lyon & N. A. Krasnegor (Eds.), *Attention, memory and executive function* (pp. 349–365). Baltimore: Brookes.

Gump, P. V. (1982). School settings and their keeping. In D. L. Duke (Ed.), *Helping teachers manage classrooms* (pp. 98–114). Alexandria, VA: Association for Supervision and Curriculum Development.

Guthrie, J. T. (1996). Educational contexts for engagement in literacy. *Reading Teacher, 49,* 432–445.

Guthrie, J. T. (2002). Engagement and motivation in reading instruction. In M. L. Kamil, J. B. Manning, & H. J. Walberg (Eds.), *Successful reading instruction* (pp. 137–154). Greenwich, CT: Information Age.

Guthrie, J. T., Anderson, E., Alao, S., & Rinehart, J. (1999). Influences of concept-oriented reading instruction on strategy use and conceptual learning from text. *Elementary School Journal, 99,* 343–366.

Guthrie, J. T., & Knowles, K. T. (2001). Promoting reading motivation. In L. Verhoeven & K. E. Snow (Eds.), *Literacy and motivation: Reading engagement in individuals and groups* (pp. 159–176). Mahwah, NJ: Erlbaum.

Guthrie, J. T., Van Meter, P., Hancock, G. R., McCann, A., Anderson, E., & Alao, S. (1998). Does concept-oriented reading instruction increase strategy-use and conceptual learning from text? *Journal of Educational Psychology, 90,* 261–278.

Guthrie, J. T., Van Meter, P., McCann, A. D., Wigfield, A., Bennett, L., Poundstone, C. C., Rice, M. E., Faibisch, F. M., Hunt, B., & Mitchell, A. M. (1996). Growth of literacy engagement: Changes in motivations and strategies during concept-oriented reading instruction. *Reading Research Quarterly, 31,* 306–332.

Guthrie, J. T., & Wigfield, A. (2000). Engagement and motivation in reading. In M. Kamil, R. Barr, P. Mosenthal, & P. D. Pearson (Eds.), *Handbook of reading research* (Vol. 3, pp. 403–425). Mahwah, NJ: Erlbaum.

Guthrie, J. T., Wigfield, A., & VonSecker, C. (2000). Effects of integrated instruction on motivation and strategy use in reading. *Journal of Educational Psychology, 92,* 331–341.

Guzzetti, B. J. (1990). Enhancing comprehension through trade books in high school English classes. *Journal of Reading, 33,* 411–413.

Harter, S. (1978a). Effectance motivation reconsidered: Toward a developmental model. *Human Development, 21,* 34–64.

Harter, S. (1978b). Pleasure derived from challenge and the effects of receiving grades on children's difficulty level choices. *Child Development, 49,* 788–799.

Harter, S. (1981). A new self-report scale of intrinsic versus extrinsic orientation in the classroom: Motivational and informational components. *Developmental Psychology, 17,* 300–312.

Hebb, D. O. (1955). Drives and the C.N.S. (central nervous system). *Scientific American, 62,* 243–254.

Henderlong, J. H., & Lepper, M. R. (2002). The effects of praise on children's intrinsic motivation: A review and synthesis. *Psychological Bulletin, 128,* 774–795.

Henderson, V. L., & Dweck, C. S. (1990). Motivation and achievement. In S. S. Feldman & G. R. Elliott (Eds.), *At the threshold: The developing adolescent* (pp. 308–329). Cambridge, MA: Harvard University Press.

Herrold, W. G., Jr., Stanchfield, J., & Serabian, A. J. (1989). Comparison of the effect of a middle school, literature-based listening program on male and female attitudes toward reading. *Educational Research Quarterly, 13*(4), 43–46.

Hidi, S. (1990). Interest and its contribution as a mental resource for learning. *Review of Educational Research, 60,* 549–571.

Hoffman, M. L. (1970). Moral development. In P. H. Mussen (Ed.), *Carmichael's manual of child psychology* (3rd ed., Vol. 2, pp. 261–360). New York: Wiley.

Jacobsen, B., Lowery, B., & DuCette, J. (1986). Attributions of learning disabled children. *Journal of Educational Psychology, 78,* 59–64.

Jagacinski, C., & Nicholls, J. (1987). Confidence and affect in task involvement: The impact of social comparison information. *Journal of Educational Psychology, 79,* 107–114.

Johnson, D. W., & Johnson, R. (1974). Instructional goal structure: Cooperative versus competitive or individualistic. *Review of Educational Research, 44,* 213–40.

Johnson, D. W., & Johnson, R. (1975). *Learning together and alone: Cooperation, competition, and individualization.* Englewood Cliffs, NJ: Prentice-Hall.

Johnson, D. W., & Johnson, R. (1979). Conflict in the classroom: Controversy and learning. *Review of Educational Research, 49,* 51–70.

Johnson, D. W., & Johnson, R. (1985). Classroom conflict: Controversy over debate in learning groups. *American Educational Research Journal, 22,* 237–256.

Jussim, L., Smith, A., Madon, S., & Palumbo, P. (1998). Teacher expectations. In J. Brophy (Ed.), *Advances in research on teaching: Expectations in the classroom* (pp. 1–48). Greenwich, CT: JAI Press.

Juvonen, J. (1988). Outcome and attributional disagreements between students and their teachers. *Journal of Educational Psychology, 80,* 330–336.

Karchmer, R. A. (2001). The journey ahead: Thirteen teachers report how the Internet influences literacy and literacy instruction in their K–12 classrooms. *Reading Research Quarterly, 36,* 442–466.

Kistner, J. A., Osborne, M., & LeVerrier, L. (1988). Causal attributions of learning-disabled children: Developmental patterns and relation to academic progress. *Journal of Educational Psychology, 80,* 82–89.

Kloosterman, P. (1988). Self-confidence and motivation in mathematics. *Journal of Educational Psychology, 80,* 345–351.

Knapp, M. S., Marder, C., Adelman, N. E., & Needels, M. C. (1995). The outcomes for meaning in high-poverty classrooms. In M. S. Knapp & Associates, *Teaching for meaning in high-poverty classrooms* (pp. 124–144). New York: Teachers College Press.

Kohn, A. (1993). *Punished by rewards: The trouble with gold stars, incentive plans, A's, praise, and other bribes.* New York: Houghton-Mifflin.

Koskinen, P. S., Blum, I. H., Bisson, S. A., Phillips, S. A., Creamer, T. S., & Baker, T. A. (2000). Book access, shared reading, and audio models: The effects of supporting the literacy learning of linguistically diverse students in school and at home. *Journal of Educational Psychology, 92,* 23–36.

Krajcik, J. S. (1991). Developing students' understanding of chemical concepts. In S. M. Glynn, R. H. Yeany, & B. K. Britton (Eds.), *The psychology of learning science* (pp. 117–147). Hillsdale, NJ: Erlbaum.

Krapp, A. (1999). Interest, motivation, and learning: An educational psychological perspective. *European Journal of Psychology of Education, 14,* 23–40.

Kulik, J. A., & Kulik, C. C. (1984). Effects of accelerated instruction on students. *Review of Education Research, 54,* 409–425.

Langer, J. A. (1995). *Envisioning literature: Literary understanding and literature instruction.* New York: Teachers College Press.

Langer, J. A. (2001). Literature as an environment for engaged readers. In L. Verhoeven & C. E. Snow (Eds.), *Literacy and motivation: Reading engagement in individuals and groups (pp. 177–194)*. Mahwah, NJ: Erlbaum.

Lantieri, L., & Patti, J. (1996). *Waging peace in our schools*. Boston: Beacon.

Laseman, P. P. M., & de Jong, P. F. (2001). How important is home literacy for acquiring literacy in school? In L. Verhoeven & C. Snow (Eds.), *Literacy and motivation: Reading engagement in individuals and groups* (pp. 71–93). Mahwah, NJ: Erlbaum.

Leal, D. J. (1993). The power of literacy peer group discussions: How children collaboratively negotiate meaning. *Reading Teacher, 47,* 114–120.

Leland, C., & Fitzpatrick, R. (1993/1994). Cross-age interaction builds enthusiasm for reading and writing. *Reading Teacher, 47,* 292–301.

Lepola, J., Salonen, P., & Vauras, M. (2000). The development of motivational orientations as a function of divergent reading careers from pre-school to the second grade. *Learning and Instruction, 10,* 153–177.

Lepola, J., Vaurus, M., & Maeki, H. (2000). Gender differences in the development of academic self-concept of attainment from the 2nd to the 6th grade: Relations with achievement and perceived motivational orientation. *Psychology: The Journal of the Hellenic Psychological Society, 7,* 290–308.

Lepper, M. R. (1988). Motivational considerations in the study of instruction. *Cognition and Instruction, 5,* 289–309.

Lepper, M. R., Greene, D., & Nisbett, R. E. (1973). Undermining children's intrinsic interest with extrinsic rewards: A test of the "over-justification" hypothesis. *Journal of Personality and Social Psychology, 28,* 129–137.

Lepper, M. R., & Henderlong, J. (2000). Turning "play" into "work" and "work" into "play": 25 years of research on intrinsic versus extrinsic motivation. In C. Sansone & J. M. Harackiewicz (Eds.), *Intrinsic and extrinsic motivation: The search for optimal motivation and performance* (pp. 257–307). San Diego: Academic Press.

Lepper, M. R., & Hodell, M. (1989). Intrinsic motivation in the classroom. In C. Ames & R. Ames (Eds.), *Research on motivation in education: Vol. 3. Goals and cognitions* (pp. 73–105). San Diego: Academic Press.

Lepper, M. R., & Malone, T. W. (1987). Intrinsic motivation and instructional effectiveness in computer-based education. In R. E. Snow & M. J. Farr (Eds.), *Aptitude, learning, and instruction: Vol. 3. Conative and affective process analyses* (pp. 255–286). Hillsdale, NJ: Erlbaum.

Levin, J. R., Yussen, S. R., DeRose, T. M., & Pressley, M. (1977). Developmental changes in assessing recall and recognition memory. *Developmental Psychology, 13,* 608–615.

Levine, J. M. (1983). Social comparison and education. In J. M. Levine & M. C. Wang (Eds.), *Teacher and student perceptions: Implications for learning* (pp. 29–55). Hillsdale, NJ: Erlbaum.

Lewis, C. S. (1997). *The lion, the witch, and the wardrobe.* New York: Harper-Collins.

Lewis, R. (2001). Classroom discipline and student responsibility: The students' view. *Teaching and Teacher Education, 17,* 307–319.

Lickona, T. (1991). *Educating for character: How our schools can teach respect and responsibility.* New York: Bantam Books.

Llatov, Z. Z., Shamai, S., Hertz-Lazarovitz, R., & Mayer-Young, S. (1998). Teacher–student classroom interactions: The influence of gender, academic dominance, and teacher communication style. *Adolescence, 33,* 269–277.

Loveland, K. K., & Olley, J. G. (1979). The effect of external reward on interest and quality of task performance in children of high and low intrinsic motivation. *Child Development, 50,* 1207–1210.

Malone, T. W., & Lepper, M. R. (1987). Making learning fun: A taxonomy of intrinsic motivation for learning. In R. E. Snow & M. J. Farr (Eds.), *Aptitude, learning, and instruction: Vol. 3. Conative and affective process analyses* (pp. 223–253). Hillsdale, NJ: Erlbaum.

Markus, H., & Nurius, P. (1986). Possible selves. *American Psychologist, 41,* 954–969.

Marsh, H. W. (1990). Causal ordering of academic self-concept and academic achievement: A multiwave, longitudinal panel analysis. *Journal of Educational Psychology, 82,* 646–656.

Martin, J., & Martin, W. (1983). *Personal development: Self-instruction for personal agency.* Calgary, Alberta, Canada: Detselig Enterprises.

Martinez, M. G., & McGee, L. M. (2000). Children's literature and reading instruction: Past, present, and future. *Reading Research Quarterly, 35,* 154–169.

Mazzoni, S. A., Gambrell, L. B., & Korkeamaki, R. L. (1999). A cross-cultural perspective of early literacy motivation. *Reading Psychology, 20,* 237–253.

McGill-Franzen, A., Allington, R., Yokoi, L., & Brooks, G. (1999). Putting books in the room seems necessary but not sufficient. *Journal of Educational Research, 93,* 67–74.

McKenna, M. C. (1994). Toward a model of reading attitude acquisition. In E. H. Cramer & M. Castle (Eds.), *Fostering the life-long love of reading: The affective domain in reading education* (pp. 18–40). Newark, DE: International Reading Association.

McKenna, M. C. (2001). Development of reading attitudes. In L. Verhoeven & C. E. Snow (Eds.), *Literacy and motivation: Reading engagement in individuals and groups* (pp. 135–158). Mahwah, NJ: Erlbaum.

McKenna, M. C., Ellsworth, R. A., & Kear, D. J. (1995). Children's attitudes toward reading: A national survey. *Reading Research Quarterly, 30,* 934–956.

McKenna, M. C., & Watkins, J. H. (1995, November). *Effects of computer-*

mediated books on the development of beginning readers. Paper presented at the meeting of the National Reading Conference, New Orleans, LA.

McLoyd, V. C. (1979). The effects of extrinsic rewards of differential value on high and low intrinsic interest. *Child Development, 50,* 1010–1019.

McQuillan, J. (1997). The effects of incentives on reading. *Reading Research and Instruction, 36,* 111–125.

McVey, G. (1971). *Sensory factors in the school learning environment: What research says to the teacher* (National Education Association Report, Series No. 35). Washington, DC: National Education Association.

Meece, J. L., Blumenfeld, P. C., & Hoyle, R. H. (1988). Students' goal orientations and cognitive engagement in classroom activities. *Journal of Educational Psychology, 80,* 514–523.

Meece, J. L., Blumenfeld, P., & Puro, P. (1989). A motivational analysis of elementary science learning environments. In M. Matyas, K. Tobin, & B. Fraser (Eds.), *Looking into windows: Qualitative research in science education* (pp. 13–23). Washington, DC: American Association for the Advancement of Science.

Meece, J. L., & Miller, S. D. (1999). Changes in elementary school children's achievement goals for reading and writing: Results of a longitudinal and an intervention study. *Scientific Studies of Reading, 3,* 207–229.

Mehan, H. (1979). *Social organization in the classroom.* Cambridge, MA: Harvard University Press.

Meyerson, M. J, & Kulesza, D. L. (2001). *Strategies for struggling readers: Step by step.* Englewood Cliffs, NJ: Prentice-Hall.

Midgley, C., Anderman, E. M., & Hicks, L. (1995). Differences between elementary and middle school teachers and students: A goal theory approach. *Journal of Early Adolescence, 15,* 90–113.

Miller, G. E. (1987). School interventions for dishonest behavior. *Special Services in the Schools, 3,* 21–36.

Miller, S. D., & Meece, J. L. (1999). Third graders' motivational preferences for reading and writing tasks. *Elementary School Journal, 100,* 19–35.

Mondale, S., & Patton, S. B. (Eds.). (2001). *School: The story of American public education.* Boston: Beacon Press.

Morrow, L. M. (1983). Home and school correlates of early interest in literature. *Journal of Educational Research, 76,* 221–230.

Morrow, L. M. (1992). The impact of a literature-based program on literacy achievement, use of literature, and attitudes of children from minority backgrounds. *Reading Research Quarterly, 27,* 250–275.

Morrow, L. M. (2002). *The literacy center: Contexts for reading and writing* (2nd ed.). Portsmouth, NH: Stenhouse.

Morrow, L. M., & Sharkey, E. A. (1993). Motivating independent reading and writing in the primary grades through social cooperative literacy experiences. *Reading Teacher, 47,* 162–164.

Murphy, S., Shannon, P., Johnston, P., & Hansen, J. (1998). *Fragile evidence: A critique of reading assessment.* Mahwah, NJ: Erlbaum.

National Reading Panel. (2000). *Teaching children to read: An evidence-based assessment of the scientific research literature on reading and its implications for reading instruction: Reports of the subgroups.* Washington, DC: National Institute of Child Health and Development.

Neuman, S. B., & Roskos, K. (1993). Access to print for children of poverty: Differential effects of adult mediation and literacy-enriched play settings on environments and functional print tasks. *American Educational Research Journal, 30,* 95–122.

Nicholls, J. G. (1989). *The competitive ethos and democratic education.* Cambridge, MA: Harvard University Press.

Nickerson, R. S., Perkins, D. N., & Smith, E. E. (1985). *The teaching of thinking.* Hillsdale, NJ: Erlbaum.

Noddings, N. (1984). *Caring: A feminine approach to ethics and moral education.* Berkeley: University of California Press.

O'Flahavan, J., Gambrell, L. B., Guthrie, J., Stahl, S., Baumann, J., & Alvermann, D. (1992). Poll results guide activities of research center. *Reading Today, 10,* 12.

Oldfather, P. (1991). Students' perceptions of their own reasons/purposes for being or not being involved in learning activities: A qualitative study of student motivation. *Dissertation Abstracts International, 52,* 853A.

Oldfather, P., & Dahl, K. (1994). Toward a social constructivist reconceptualization of intrinsic motivation for literacy learning. *Journal of Reading Behavior, 26,* 139–158.

Palmer, B. M., Codling, R. M., & Gambrell, L. B. (1994). In their own words: What elementary students have to say about motivation to read. *Reading Teacher, 48,* 176–178.

Parsons, J., & Ruble, D. (1977). The development of achievement-related expectancies. *Child Development, 48,* 1075–1079.

Payne, B. D., & Manning, B. H. (1992). Basal reader instruction: Effects of comprehension monitoring training on reading comprehension, strategy use and attitude. *Reading Research and Instruction, 32*(1), 29–38.

Pearl, R. (1982). LD children's attributions for success and failure: A replication with a labeled LD sample. *Learning Disability Quarterly, 5,* 173–176.

Perry, N. E. (1998). Young children's self-regulated learning and contexts that support it. *Journal of Educational Psychology, 90,* 715–729.

Perry, N. E., & VandeKamp, K. O. (2000). Creating classroom contexts that support young children's development of self-regulated learning. *International Journal of Educational Research, 33,* 821–843.

Perry, N. E., VandeKamp, K. O., Mercer, L. K., & Nordby, C. J. (2002). Investigating teacher–student interactions that foster self-regulated learning. *Educational Psychologist, 37,* 5–15.

Pierson, J. M. (1999). Transforming engagement in literacy instruction: the role of student genuine interest and ability. *Annals of Dyslexia, 49,* 307–329.

Pressley, M., Allington, R. L., Wharton-McDonald, R., Block, C. C., & Morrow, L. M. (2001). *Learning to read: Lessons from exemplary first grade classrooms.* New York: Guilford Press.

Pressley, M., El-Dinary, P. B., Gaskins, I., Schuder, T., Bergman, J. L., Almasi, J., & Brown, R. (1992). Beyond direct explanation: Transactional instruction of reading comprehension strategies. *Elementary School Journal, 92,* 511–554.

Pressley, M., Roehrig, A., Raphael, L., Dolezal, S., Bohn, K., Mohan, L., Wharton-McDonald, R., & Bogner, K. (2003). Teaching processes in elementary and secondary education. In W. M. Reynolds & G. E. Miller (Eds.), *Comprehensive handbook of psychology: Vol. 7. Educational psychology.* New York: Wiley.

Pressley, M., Wharton-McDonald, R., Allington, R., Block, C. C., Morrow, L., Tracey, D., Baker, K., Brooks, G., Cronin, J., Nelson, E., & Woo, D. (2001). A study of effective grade-1 literacy instruction. *Scientific Studies of Reading, 5,* 35–58.

Pressley, M., Woloshyn, V. E., & Associates. (1995). *Cognitive strategy instruction that really works with children* (2nd ed.). Cambridge, MA: Brookline Books.

Purcell-Gates, V., McIntyre, E., & Freppon, P. A. (1995). Learning written storybook language in school: A comparison of low-SES children in skills-based and whole language classrooms. *American Educational Research Journal, 32,* 659–685.

Raffini, J. (1993). *Winners without losers: Structures and strategies for increasing student motivation to learn.* Boston: Allyn & Bacon.

Renick, M. J., & Harter, S. (1989). Impact of social comparisons on the developing self-perceptions of learning disabled students. *Journal of Educational Psychology, 81,* 631–638.

Renninger, K. A. (1990). Children's play interests, representation, and activity. In R. Fivush & J. Hudson (Eds.), *Knowing and remembering in young children* (pp. 127–165). Cambridge, MA: Cambridge University Press.

Renninger, K. A. (2000). Individual interest and its implications for understanding intrinsic motivation. In C. Sansone & J. M. Harackiewicz (Eds.), *Intrinsic and extrinsic motivation: The search for optimal motivation and performance* (pp. 373–404). San Diego: Academic Press.

Renninger, K. A., Hidi, S., & Krapp, A. (Eds.). (1992). *The role of interest in learning and development.* Hillsdale, NJ: Erlbaum.

Renninger, K. A., & Wozniak, R. H. (1985). Effect of interest on attentional shift, recognition, and recall in young children. *Developmental Psychology, 21,* 624–632.

Rist, R. (1970). Student social class and teacher expectations: The self-fulfilling prophecy in ghetto education. *Harvard Educational Review, 40*(3) 411–451.

Roehrig, A. D., Pressley, M., & Talotta, D. A. (2002). *Stories of beginning Teachers:*

First-year challenges and beyond. Notre Dame, IN: University of Notre Dame Press.

Roeser, R. W., Midgley, C., & Urdan, T. C. (1996). Perceptions of the school psychological environment and early adolescents' psychological and behavioral functioning in school: The mediating role of goals and belonging. *Journal of Educational Psychology, 88,* 408–422.

Rosenthal, R. (1985). From unconscious experimenter bias to teacher expectancy effects. In J. B. Dusek (Ed.), *Teacher expectancies* (pp. 37–65). Hillsdale, NJ: Erlbaum.

Rosenthal, R., & Jacobson, L. (1968). *Pygmalion in the classroom: Teacher expectation and pupils' intellectual development.* New York: Holt, Rinehart & Winston.

Ryan, R. M., & Deci, E. L. (2000). When rewards compete with nature: The undermining of intrinsic motivation and self-regulation. In C. Sansone & J. M. Harackiewicz (Eds.), *Intrinsic and extrinsic motivation: The search for optimal motivation and performance* (pp. 13–54). San Diego: Academic Press.

Sabers, D. S., Cushing, K. S., & Berliner, D. C. (1991). Differences among teachers in a task characterized by simultaneity, multidimensionality, and immediacy. *American Educational Research Journal, 28,* 63–88.

Sacks, C. H., & Mergendoller, J. R. (1997). The relationship between teachers' theoretical orientation toward reading and student outcomes in kindergarten children with different initial reading abilities. *American Educational Research Journal, 34,* 721–740.

Scardamalia, M., & Bereiter, C. (1992a). An architecture for collaborative knowledge building. In E. DeCorte, M. Linn, H. Mandl, & L. Verschaffel (Eds.), *Computer-based learning environments and problem solving* (pp. 41–66). Berlin: Springer-Verlag.

Scardamalia, M., & Bereiter, C. (1992b). Two models of classroom learning using a communal database. In S. Dijkstra, M. Krammer, & J. Merrienboer (Eds.), *Instructional models in computer based learning environments* (pp. 229–241). Berlin: Springer-Verlag.

Schiefele, U., & Krapp, A. (1996). Topic interest and free recall of expository text. *Learning and Individual Differences, 8,* 141–160.

Schunk, D. H. (1990). Goal setting and self-efficacy during self-regulated learning. *Educational Psychologist, 25,* 71–86.

Schunk, D. H. (1991). Self-efficacy and academic motivation. *Educational Psychologist, 26,* 207–232.

Schunk, D. H., & Zimmerman, B. J. (Eds.). (1998). *Self-regulated learning: From teaching to self-reflective practice.* New York: Guilford Press.

Segal, J. W., Chipman, S. F., & Glaser, R. (1985). *Thinking and learning skills: Vol. 1. Relating instruction to research.* Hillsdale, NJ: Erlbaum.

Shavelson, R. J. (1983). Review of research on teachers' pedagogical judgments, plans, and decisions. *Elementary School Journal, 83,* 392–413.

Shavelson, R. J., & Towne, L. (Eds.). (2002). *Scientific research in education*. Washington, DC: National Academy Press.

Shiefele, V. (1991). Interest, learning and motivation: expanding the theoretical framework. *Educational Psychologist, 26*(3, 4), 299–323.

Skinner, B. F. (1953a). *Science and human behavior*. New York: Free Press.

Skinner, B. F. (1953b). Some contributions of an experimental analysis of behavior to psychology as a whole. *American Psychologist, 8*, 69–78.

Slavin, R. (1985a). An introduction to cooperative learning research. In R. Slavin, S. Sharan, S. Kagan, R. H. Lazarowitz, C. Webb, & R. Schmuck (Eds.), *Learning to cooperate, cooperating to learn* (pp. 5–15). New York: Plenum.

Slavin, R. (1985b). Team-assisted individualization: Combining cooperative learning and individualized instruction in mathematics. In R. Slavin, S. Sharan, S. Kagan, R. H. Lazarowitz, C. Webb, & R. Schmuck (Eds.), *Learning to cooperate, cooperating to learn* (pp. 177–209). New York: Plenum.

Smith, S. E., Jr., & Backman, C. A. (1975). *Games and puzzles for elementary and middle school mathematics*. Reston, VA: National Council of Teachers of Mathematics.

Southern, W. T., & Jones, E. D. (Eds.). (1991). *The academic acceleration of gifted children*. New York: Teachers College Press.

Sowell, E. J. (1989). Effects of manipulative materials in mathematics instruction. *Journal for Research in Mathematics Education, 20*, 498–505.

Sperling, R. A., & Head, D. M. (2002). Reading attitudes and literacy skills in prekindergarten and kindergarten children. *Early Childhood Education Quarterly, 29*, 233–236.

Spiro, R. J., Feltovich, P. J., Jacobson, M. J., & Coulson, R. L. (1992). Cognitive flexibility, constructivism and hypertext: Random access instruction for advanced knowledge acquisition in ill-structured domains. In T. Duffy & D. Jonassen (Eds.), *Constructivism and the technology of instruction* (pp. 57–75). Hillsdale, NJ: Erlbaum.

Stipek, D. (1998). *Motivation to learn: From theory to practice* (3rd ed.). Needham Heights, MA: Allyn & Bacon.

Stipek, D. (2002). Good instruction is motivating. In A. Wigfield & J. S. Eccles (Eds.), *Development of achievement motivation: A volume in the educational psychology series* (pp. 309–332). San Diego: Academic Press.

Stipek, D. J., & Hoffman, J. M. (1980). Children's achievement-related expectancies as a function of academic performance histories and sex. *Journal of Educational Psychology, 72*, 861–865.

Stipek, D., & Seal, K. (2001). *Motivated minds: Raising children to love learning*. New York: Henry Holt.

Tang, S., & Hall V. C. (1995). A meta-analytic review of the overjustification effect. *Applied Cognitive Psychology, 9*, 365–404.

Tobin, K. (1987). The role of wait time in higher cognitive level learning. *Review of Educational Research, 57,* 69–95.

Trelease, J. (1995). *The read-aloud handbook* (4th ed.). New York: Penguin.

Turner, H. S., & Watson, T. S. (1999). Consultant's guide for the use of time-out in the preschool and elementary classroom. *Psychology in the Schools, 36,* 135–148.

Turner, J. C. (1995). The influence of classroom contexts on young children's motivation for literacy. *Reading Research Quarterly, 30,* 410–441.

Turner, J. C., Meyer, D., Cox, K., Logan, C., DiCintio, M., & Thomas, C. (1998). Creating contexts for involvement in mathematics. *Journal of Educational Psychology, 90,* 730–745.

Ugwoglu, M. E., & Walberg, H. J. (1986). Predicting achievement and motivation. *Journal of Research and Development in Education, 19,* 1–12.

Verhoeven, L., & Snow, C. (2001). *Literacy and motivation: Reading engagement in individuals and groups.* Mahwah, NJ: Erlbaum.

Wade, S. E., & Adams, R. B. (1990). Effects of importance and interest on recall of biographic text. *Journal of Reading Behavior, 22,* 331–353.

Wade, S. E., Schraw, G., Buxton, W. M., & Hayes, M. T. (1993). Seduction of the strategic reader: Effects of interest on strategies and recall. *Reading Research Quarterly, 28,* 93–114.

Walker, B. J., & Scherry, R. J. (2001). America reads tutoring: Communities working together. In L. M. Morrow & D. G. Woo (Eds.), *Tutoring programs for struggling readers: The America Reads challenge* (pp. 15–30). New York: Guilford Press.

Wallbrown, F. H., Brown, D. H., & Engin, A. W. (1978). A factor analysis of reading attitudes along with measures of reading achievement and scholastic aptitude. *Psychology in the Schools, 15,* 160–165.

Webb, M. (1990). *Multicultural education in elementary and secondary schools.* (ERIC Document Reproduction Services, Digest Number 67, ED327613)

Weiner, B. (1979). A theory of motivation for some classroom experiences. *Journal of Educational Psychology, 71,* 3–25.

Weinstein, C., & Mignano, A. (1997). *Elementary classroom management: Lessons from research and practice.* New York: McGraw-Hill.

Wharton-McDonald, R., Pressley, M., & Hampston, J. M. (1998). Outstanding literacy instruction in first grade: Teacher practices and student achievement. *Elementary School Journal, 99,* 101–128.

White, R. W. (1959). Motivation reconsidered: The concept of competence. *Psychological Review, 66,* 297–333.

Wigfield, A. (2000). Facilitating children's reading motivation. In L. Baker, M. J. Dreher, & J. T. Guthrie (Eds.), *Engaging young readers: Promoting achievement and motivation* (pp. 140–158). New York: Guilford Press.

Wigfield, A., Eccles, J. S., MacIver, D., Reuman, D. A., & Midgley, C. (1991). Transitions during early adolescence: Changes in children's domain-specific self-perceptions and general self-esteem across the transition to junior high school. *Developmental Psychology, 27*, 552–565.

Wlodkowski, R. J., & Jaynes, J. H. (1991). *Eager to learn: Helping children become motivated and love learning.* San Francisco: Jossey-Bass.

Wood, R., & Bandura, A. (1989). Impact of conceptions of ability on self-regulatory mechanisms and complex decision-making. *Journal of Personality and Social Psychology, 56*, 407–415.

Wood, S. S., Bruner, J. S., & Ross, G. (1976). The role of tutoring in problem solving. *Journal of Child Psychology and Psychiatry, 17*, 89–100.

Yopp, R. H., & Yopp, H. K. (2000). *Literature-based reading activities.* Boston: Allyn & Bacon.

Zimmerman, B. J. (1989a). Models of self-regulated learning and academic achievement. In B. J. Zimmerman & D. H. Schunk (Eds.), *Self-regulated learning and academic achievement* (pp. 1–25). New York: Springer-Verlag.

Zimmerman, B. J. (1989b). A social cognitive view of self-regulated academic learning. *Journal of Educational Psychology, 81*, 329–339.

Zimmerman, B. J. (1990a). Self-regulated learning and academic achievement: An overview. *Educational Psychologist, 25*, 3–18.

Zimmerman, B. J. (1990b). Self-regulating academic learning and achievement: The emergence of a social-cognitive perspective. *Educational Psychology Review, 2*, 173–201.

Zimmerman, B. J. (1998). Developing self-fulfilling cycles of academic regulation: An analysis of exemplary instructional models. In D. H. Schunk & B. J. Zimmerman (Eds.), *Self-regulated learning: From teaching to self-reflective practice* (pp. 1–19). New York: Guilford Press.

Zimmerman, B. J., Bandura, A., & Martinez-Pons, M. (1992). Self-motivation for academic attainment: The role of self-efficacy beliefs and personal goal setting. *American Educational Research Journal, 29*, 663–676.

Zimmerman, B. J., & Schunk, D. H. (Eds.). (2001). *Self-regulated learning and academic achievement: Theoretical perspectives.* Mahwah, NJ: Erlbaum.

Index